D0627135

REDISCOVERING
the soul of
LEADERSHIP

EUGENE B. HABECKER
30th President of Taylor University

TAYLOR UNIVERSITY PRESS
UPLAND, INDIANA

Unless otherwise noted, all scripture references are from the
Holy Bible, New International Version®. Copyright © 1973, 1978, 1984
by the International Bible Society. Used by permission of
Zondervan Publishing House. All rights reserved;
other references are from *The Amplified New Testament* (AMP),
© 1954, 1958, The Lockman Foundation; *The Living Bible* (TLB),
© 1971, Tyndale House Publishers, Wheaton, IL 60189.
Used by permission; *The Contemporary English Version* (CEV),
copyright © 1995, American Bible Society; *Today's English Version* (TEV),
© American Bible Society 1966, 1971, 1976, 1992;
and the *Authorized (King James) Version* (KJV).

Editor: Barbara Williams
Cover Design: Steven Christensen

Copyright © 1996 by Eugene B. Habecker
Third Printing 2006
First published 1996 by Zondervan Publishing House

No part of this book may be reproduced in any form without written permission,
except for brief quotations in books and critical reviews.

ISBN 0-9740758-4-1

Adapted from *The Other Side of Leadership* © 1987 and
Leading with a Follower's Heart © 1990, both by SP Publications, Inc.

Published by Taylor University Press
236 West Reade Avenue, Upland, Indiana 46989-1001

REDISCOVERING
the soul of
LEADERSHIP

Commemorative Edition

in honor of

The Inauguration of the 30th President

of

Taylor University

EUGENE B. HABECKER

April 28, 2006

TAYLOR UNIVERSITY

UPLAND, INDIANA

On the occasion of the Inauguration of Eugene B. Habecker, 30th President of Taylor University, and in honor of one who lives out the "soul of leadership":

"Dr. Habecker has put his finger on the real issue with his title, *Rediscovering the Soul of Leadership*. Being a Christian in a position of leadership does not ensure that the leadership is Christian. Dr. Habecker rightly helps us understand that Christ must be Lord of both the leader as a person and the process of leadership itself. In short, to be a Christian leader implies followership of Christ and His example. This, indeed, is 'the soul of leadership.'"

Jay Kesler, President Emeritus
Taylor University

"Gene's personality and vision for the future are so full of enthusiasm and energy that the Taylor campus was transformed within days of his arrival in Upland."

LaRita R. Boren, Executive Vice President
Avis Industrial Corporation

"These principles of leadership do not come from a theorist who spends his life simply telling others how to lead. These principles come from a man who first, through discipline and study, prepared himself to lead, then spent the rest of his life leading. Twice a successful college president, leader in an important association of colleges, president of the oldest and largest world-wide Bible distribution organization, and guiding force in shaping young leaders all along his path, Gene Habecker is truly a leader with a passion for excellence and integrity in leadership.

If there ever was a time when leaders of intelligence and integrity are desperately needed, it is now. If there ever was a collection of life-tested principles bright potential leaders must master, *Rediscovering the Soul of Leadership* is it."

> Gloria Gaither
> Author and Lyricist

"Here are fresh insights from the mind and heart of a man whose life models the gift and grace of leadership. The Lordship of Jesus Christ is seen as foundational in developing Christian leaders who will want to become more like Him in order to do His work effectively."

> David C. Le Shana, President Emeritus
> George Fox University and Seattle Pacific University

"Gene Habecker's leadership is one that is characterized by faithfulness, vulnerability, a dependence upon prayer and his love for those he leads. His model of Christ-centered, biblically-based servant leadership is refreshing and inspiring."

> Vonette Z. Bright, Co-Founder
> Campus Crusade for Christ, International

Contents

Preface

There are nearly as many books on the subject of leadership as there are definitions of it. The "leadership" industry is a substantial one--speakers, authors, and consultants abound and all have something useful to say on the subject.

Leaders, however, all lead within a given context and are influenced by the values of their cultural experiences. As a result, leaders need boundaries, baselines, benchmarks, and rock-solid foundations that guide how they "do" leadership. Without it, leaders often lose their way. Examples abound in business, politics, and even the church.

This book is based on the assumption that biblical texts provide unshakable and unassailable boundaries, standards, and principles for leaders. And those who ignore these biblical texts in their leadership do so at their own peril. As a result, biblical examples and references appear throughout the book.

Unfortunately, there are critics who assail biblical principles in leadership given the personal or professional leadership failings of those who depend on them. Fortunately, ineffective implementation of a biblically informed leadership principle says more about a leader than it does about a biblical principle's validity.

This book reprint offers itself as a contribution for continuing the discussion so necessary for preparing the next generation of leaders.

Eugene B. Habecker

Foreword

Books on leadership abound today. One reason for this is the need for authentic leadership has never been greater. The question, however, is what does real leadership look like. What is its character, and how does it operate.

In this wonderful, well-documented, yet easy-to-read work by Dr. Eugene Habecker these questions and their application for Christians are clearly and precisely presented. Dr. Habecker truly does help us in *Rediscovering the Soul of Leadership*. He shows us that the person who would lead others must first of all become a follower of Christ. Only to the degree that one expresses the servant spirit of Christ in relation to others will he be able to properly lead others. By maintaining this perspective, Dr. Habecker sets forth and develops the key distinctive nature of Christian leadership. It always moves in concert with the goals and purposes of God.

The beauty of this work is that the principles can be applied to leaders on any and every level, whether a husband leading his family, an executive businessman or businesswoman leading an organization, or a pastor leading his congregation. The tension between leadership and servanthood is addressed in such a way as to affirm both without compromising either. After reading this work it becomes quite clear that it is possible to be a follower without giving up one's leadership role. In such a scenario everyone wins.

The fundamental reason this book works is because it is strongly rooted in a Christian perspective of leadership. It defines leadership in terms of God's perspective. It illustrates leadership from the life and words of Christ and it directs leadership toward biblical ends. This bibliocentric perspective is maintained while addressing the many pragmatic issues that must be addressed in any serious discussion of leadership.

Dr. Habecker has done the Christian community a service by putting the subject of leadership on a low enough self for all of us to reach while simultaneously giving us the help we need to ascend to the high calling to which the role of leadership bids us.

Rediscovering the Soul of Leadership is must reading for any existing or would-be leader who wishes to execute this high calling from a distinctly Christian perspective.

Tony Evans
Senior Pastor
Oak Cliff Bible Fellowship

Introduction

In Brazil, the dream of a Christian leader was to build a magnificent new bindery which would make it possible to provide every person in Brazil with the good news of the Gospel of Christ in their own Bible. That bindery is now in operation and is an impressive tool of the church for outreach.

In China, more than 2 million Bibles are printed and distributed every year with the approval of the government. Again, the result of a dream and prayer.

In Argentina, a maximum security prison has become one of the primary centers for Christian evangelism and discipleship, while in Puerto Rico, one person's dream to create a Bible center which all churches, regardless of denomination, could use to pursue the message of the Gospel, is now in place.

In Russia, the dream of providing Bibles and New Testaments for distribution, produced totally inside Russia, is now a reality. And millions of people have come to faith in Christ as a result. In Ghana, a person dreamed of and has succeeded in providing Scriptures to those who can't read, using their own language. And there are countless similar examples in the United States and around the world. I know, because I have seen the people behind these dreams in action. They model and practice what you are about to read in this book.

Too often, presentations and discussions about leadership have a distinctly Western perspective. The biases of the West tend to filter our thinking. The world of leadership, however, is precisely that, global. Regardless of country and culture, denomination and tradition, there are thousands and hundreds of thousands of Christian leaders who are in the process of pursuing their God-given dreams.

While the results are impressive, they do not just happen. Results which last are found by those who have learned how to balance the importance of following biblical truth and, at the same time, integrating it into both personal and organizational leadership.

This task is not an easy one. It is a necessary one. And there are thousands of people around the world who are part of this journey. Do educational and cultural differences provide a context which mediates results? Of course. Do denominational differences drive certain initiatives and hold back others? Certainly. Nevertheless, in country after country (and I have visited and discussed these ideas with leaders in dozens of countries around the world), effective integration of biblical truth with dimensions of both organizational leadership and personal leadership is making a difference.

When I first wrote *The Other Side of Leadership* (1987) and *Leading with a Follower's Heart* (1990), my experiential leadership context was primarily suburban American, evangelical, and connected primarily to Christian higher education. Those are very healthy contexts and I learned much from them. Even though my tradition is still evangelical, I now live in one of the urban capitals of the world with incredible diversity. As I have visited with Christian colleagues of multiple ethnicities from around the world, whether evangelical, historic Protestant, Orthodox, or Roman Catholic, I have seen God at work in wonderful and significant ways.

As a result, in all of these contexts, including many in the United States, I have carried on the discussion of the ideas you are about to read in this book. I am more convinced than ever that the models of leading and following which come to us from the Scripture are not only timeless, they are without geographical boundary.

For example, everyone is concerned about the public side of leadership. And there are public roles which must be played and functions which must be carried out. Everyone also desires and seeks to understand and practice the dimensions of private or personal leadership, about how to be a better husband or wife, or how to be a better father or mother, or simply, how to be a better person. Everyone understands yet a third component of leadership, the inner side of leadership, or as Willow Creek pastor Bill Hybels calls it, "Who Are You When No One's Looking."[1] As respected leadership author Stephen Covey puts it, "It is in this third area where the soul of leadership is best determined and developed. And both the public and private dimensions of leadership will be shaped by the kind of fire which is kept in this furnace."[2] And in a recent interview in *Chief Executive* with Frances Hesselbein, CEO of the Peter Drucker Foundation, she observed that the first challenge facing future leaders "is a matter of how to be — not how to do (leadership)."[3]

So, I went back to the drawing board, so to speak, and reviewed the ideas of my first two books, and concluded that they should be revisited, and for the most part, reaffirmed.

The ideas first presented now have an additional ten years of a dramatically expanded context and perspective. And those contexts and perspectives have been included. In addition, however, the material has been arranged to reflect both the public or organizational side of leadership and the private and inner dimensions of leadership.

In order to provide a context for what follows, it is important that you understand the framework of how I develop the ideas of the importance of both leading and following. Without this backround, the rest of the book has less significance.

In late 1995 Pope John Paul II, visited several cities in the Northeast, including New York City. In one of his interviews quoted in *U.S. News and World Report*, he said the following, "America needs much prayer, lest it lose its soul."[4] During this decade and in those which follow, Christian leaders must avoid losing the soul of leadership. For unless leadership is contexted biblically; and unless leaders pay as much time dealing with biblical claims and models as they do with other organizational literature, leadership will move independent of the necessity of being in tune and in touch with the Holy Spirit of God. And more professions of mere words, rather than sound practices of faith, will carry the day. That is a tragedy all of Christendom cannot afford.

1

Defining Leadership

EVERYWHERE I LOOK I see leaders. I see mothers and fathers who each lead in very important and distinctive ways. There's the mother who persistently encourages a hesitant son to strive for higher levels of achievement. And the father, who patiently practices with a sometimes discouraged daughter who later becomes a gifted athlete. I see leaders as choir directors, Sunday School teachers, pastors, business executives, faculty, and a variety of organizational presidents. I see people who have incredible influence over their peers. Most, if not all, people have a bit of leader in them.

This book, however, emphasizes a special kind of leader, a leader who understands what it means to both lead and follow. From the beginning, I want to note that my definition of "leader" is a broad one, not limited only to "an assigned role or title." I define as leaders those persons who believe they can and must make a difference in their organizations, their families, and their communities, and who do so by following biblical principles. In addition I believe that for the Christian who leads and follows, the ends or objectives aspired to in leadership must also be biblical.

Before we go further, I should note that Jesus was not excited about the term "leader." In fact, He argued against its use; "Nor should you be called 'Leader,' because your one and only only leader is the Messiah" (Matt. 23:10, TEV). This concern of Jesus' will be emphasized carefully throughout this book. Leaders must carry out their assignments with humility and great carefulness, submitting all actions to review by a Holy God, lest we tread in inappropriate ways on the options which belong exclusively to Him.

Harvard professor John Kotter makes the distinction between capital "L" leaders (of which there are not very many) and small "l" leaders (of which there are many). He notes that "it would help greatly (in terms of leadership development) if we could get more people to think about leadership in the small 'l' sense. . . ."[1] Unfortunately, many people think about leadership in only the capital "L" sense. Yet both capital "L" and small "l" leaders influence others toward a given end, goal, or purpose, whether the outcomes or objectives be positive or negative. And just as leadership outcomes can be negative or positive, so too can the processes or methods of leading be positive or negative.

Here then is a preliminary observation about leadership: it can be positive or negative; it can be slanted toward God's divine purposes or in another direction. It is leadership just the same. Jesus is the perfect example of positive leadership. Hitler is probably one of the best-known examples of negative leadership.

Positive and Negative Leadership

Scripture is filled with examples of those who led positively. And this book will look at many of them. But the Scripture also contains long lists of those who led negatively, of those who led people away from loving and serving God rather than toward doing so.

Negative Leadership

Probably one of the better examples of concern for negative leadership in Scripture is found in the Book of Ezekiel. In its own way it illustrates God's desire to have people who are deeply in love with Him. However, it primarily stands as a stark reminder that there are consequences for sin and disobedience to a loving Heavenly Father. The writer, Eze-kiel, is graphic in many of his descriptions of the sin of God's people and about His impending judgment on them. In the first part of chapter 34, Ezekiel communicates the word of the Lord, specifically targeting the shepherds or leaders of Israel, as follows:

"Mortal man," He said, "denounce the ruler of Israel. Prophesy to them, and tell them what I, Sovereign Lord, say to them: You are doomed, you shepherds of Israel! You take care of yourselves, but never tend the sheep. You drink the milk, wear the clothes made from the wool, and kill and eat the finest sheep. But you never tend the sheep. You have not taken care of the weak ones, healed the ones that are sick, bandaged the ones that are hurt, brought back the ones that wandered off, or looked for the ones that were lost. Instead, you treat-ed them cruelly. Because the sheep had no shepherd, they were scattered, and wild animals killed and ate them. So My sheep wandered over the high hills and the mountains. They were scattered over the face of the earth, and no one looked for them or tried to find them.

"Now, you shepherds, listen to what I, the Lord, am telling you. As surely as I am the living God, you had better listen to Me. My sheep have been attacked by wild animals that killed and ate them because there was no shepherd. My shepherds did not try to find the sheep. They were taking care of themselves and not the sheep. So listen to Me, you shepherds. I, the Sover-eign Lord, declare that I am your enemy. I will take My sheep away from you and never again let you be their shepherds; never again will I let you take care only of yourselves. I will rescue My sheep from you and not let you eat them (34:2-10, TEV).

Among others, this example of negative leadership identi-fies at least four characteristics of a negative leader:

Selfish ambition. The leaders' priority was taking care of themselves and their own needs rather than expressing care to and taking care of their flocks. The implication clearly seems to be that the shepherd must have as high a priority taking care of the flock as he has of taking care of himself.

Lack of caring. Second, these verses clearly suggest that there are specific ways in which the leader is supposed to be actively involved with caring for the flock: strengthening the weak, healing the sick, binding up the injured, bringing back the strays, and searching for those lost sheep. While each of these actions has its contemporary expressions, the idea of the leader caring for the sheep is very powerfully expressed here. Jesus' discussions of the shepherd and sheep in John 10:1-17; Matthew 18:10-14; and elsewhere illustrate the positive example of what a good shepherd does.

Brutality. Third, leaders are supposed to lead in specific ways: "You treated them cruelly" (Ezek. 34:4, TEV). We will see later that leaders are instructed to lead with a quality of gentleness. And however we define gentleness, it clearly seems to me that it doesn't mean "cruel."

Inability to unify. Fourth, negative leadership has consequences for the flock. The text notes that because of the poor care of the sheep by the shepherd, the flock wandered and was scattered. The implication is that a good shepherd keeps the flock together.

Negative leadership, not surprisingly, also has negative consequences for the leader: "I, the Sovereign Lord, declare that I am your enemy. I will take My sheep away from you and never again let you be their shepherds; never again will I let you take care only of yourselves. I will rescue My sheep from you and not let you eat them" (v. 10, TEV).

What really makes our discussion and observation of Christian leadership more difficult is the reality of knowing that we have people in formal or informal leadership roles influencing others toward ends and objectives which are not necessarily biblical. And if "the people being led" are biblically illiterate, that is, if they're not "examining the Scriptures every day to see if what the leader said is true" (Acts 17:11, my paraphrase), the followers are more capable of being misled by these Christian leaders.

It is clear that the Christian leader who aspires to leadership in the context of the Christian organization must reflect biblical objectives and purposes. Further, how one leads must reflect biblical processes and ways of dealing with people. And the motives, or the why of leading which drive one's leadership, must also be proper, reflecting biblical qualities.

Positive Leadership

Positive leadership includes leading and following as necessary parts of the same whole. Arguably, one cannot be a leader without having followers. I define a follower as being somewhat different than a subordinate. I view a subordinate as a person who, under the direction of a superior, carries out some kind of assigned role or responsibility. The subordinate can carry out this role or responsibility with great joy and eagerness or with great reluctance and a sense of burden. When I carry out my responsibility or role because I want to rather than because I have to, I move in the direction of being a follower. It seems to me that Christ wanted followers, not subordinates.

One of the great mistakes made by some leaders is their tendency to see "followers" as having little if any capacity to influence the direction of either the "problems" or the "opportunities" faced by organizations. Such leaders see themselves as the primary fountain of organizational truth and corporate enlightenment. Woe to any subordinate who "crosses" this kind of leader.

Carnegie Mellon professor Robert Kelley discusses this kind of leader this way: "We tend to think of followers as passive sheep." But, says Kelley, "Effective followers do question the judgment of leaders and compare their sense of what's right and wrong against what's asked of them."[2] I want to state Kelley's point even more strongly: Effective followers must question the judgment of leaders. To be sure, leaders do have insights about the organization and its vision. But so too do followers. An effective leader celebrates the "we-ness" not the "me-ness" of an organization's accomplishments. And an effective leader celebrates "the team as hero."

In the same way that subordinates can have the attitude of a follower, so too must a leader. Leaders can become followers by:

- submitting their ideas and plans to the review and input of their followers;
- actively learning from their followers;
- strongly committing themselves to the welfare of their followers.

By responding to input received from subordinates, a leader can greatly improve effectiveness. Thus leaders must constantly seek to serve their followers, yet at the same time maintain their leadership role. And it is those leaders, who have immersed themselves into the Scriptures and who have learned the true joy of serving, who have begun to discover the soul of leadership.

I am persuaded that seeking input from and being sensitive to the people I lead does not necessarily mean that I have abandoned an assigned leadership role. There are those who argue that being sensitive to the people in this followership role means that I have handed over my leadership role to the people. They believe that by doing so, I have doomed the organization to stagnation or even bankruptcy. However, an effective leader, even though a servant of the people, must help keep people moving along or toward a given course or direction. The shepherd, for example, doesn't serve the sheep well if the flock is permitted to move randomly in all directions at will. I like how former HEW secretary John Gardner expresses this: "The leader/follower relationship is at best mutually nourishing, mutually strengthening. It is not a bland relationship. It is not without tension and conflict. The ideal is leadership strong enough to propose clear directions and followers strong enough to criticize and amend—and finally, enough continuity of purpose to resolve disputes and move on."[3]

There are times when leaders must follow and followers must lead. Therefore an effective leader must be able to wear two different hats, so to speak. As an article in the *Harvard Business Review* points out, "Followership is not a person but a role, and what distinguishes followers from leaders is not intelligence or character but the role they play. Effective followers and effective leaders are often the same people playing different parts at different parts of the day."[4] So, rather than discussing only leadership, my preference is to analyze the concept of "leader-follower" in particular and the concepts of leading and following in general.

The "Leader-Follower"

Here then is an important distinction I want to make as we proceed: Whenever I talk about leaders throughout the course of this book, I do so in the context of the leader as being one who can both follow and lead. Whenever I discuss followers, I mean a follower who can both lead and follow.

In my work with a Christian organization, I am hired by a board of trustees. I follow their policies. But there are times when I must (and they desire me to) give leadership to the board, even though I am not a board member. I have a responsibility to lead the staff. Yet the reality is that the staff knows far more than I do in a variety of areas. For example, our information technology people and our financial people have considerably more expertise in these areas than do I. So in those areas and others I need to be a follower and learner. I need to provide leadership for staff; yet I must be attentive to their concerns, listening to their needs and the expressions of their desires as to how to make our organization more responsive to their needs. In that role I follow. I provide leadership for an administrative team, yet they are experts in the areas in which they provide leadership. So therefore I must follow their lead in many matters.

Again, one of the greatest mistakes made by leaders is for them to view themselves and to permit others to see them as the "only" leader and everyone else in the organization as the followers. Such an arrangement unduly and unnecessarily burdens the leader and limits the probability that the organization will achieve its goals. As Harvard professor Elizabeth Moss-Kanter has observed: "There are not enough creative geniuses to go around and there are too many problems in this era for them to afford to have only a handful of people thinking about solutions."[5]

Perhaps our most powerful example of "followership" comes from members of the body of Christ in the local church. In 1 Corinthians 12; 1 Peter 4; Romans 12; and similar passages, the sense communicated is that each person who is a member of the body of Christ has at least one gift and is therefore necessary for the body to properly function. And the "leader" of the local church who ignores utilizing each gift of each member of the church will probably not see the church reach its full potential. Just as the physical body does not function properly if some of its parts are not allowed to function, so too with the body of Christ. Paul hammers this home with great force in 1 Corinthians 12:12-31. "The body is a unit, though it is made up of many parts; and though all its parts are many, they form one body. So it is with Christ" (v. 12).

It is important for me to observe in this discussion about followership that the CEO-type in an organization, even though fully committed to the operative concept of followership, most likely still carries the ultimate operating authority (legally) for the organization.

Summary

During a trip to Egypt, I spent about ten days in Cairo. This is the city of pyramids and the Sphinx. The most prominent natural feature of that city is not the desert but the Nile River. You can't get to very many places without seeing or crossing or recrossing the Nile.

And seeing that river, it was difficult for me not to think a lot about Moses, that great reluctant leader of the Jewish people. Indeed, this was the very river that produced frogs and was turned to blood.

Moses is a great example of someone who first tried leadership by taking matters into his own hands. He followed the traditional way of leading (through the raw use of power) and it led to death and banishment from position. But it was in his banishment from Pharaoh's court to the desert that he discovered the soul of leadership. He didn't want the assignment and refused, initially, to take it from God. But in serving as a shepherd, he learned that there could be nothing more important than recognizing the holiness of God and then responding obediently to His call. However strong his own desires, Moses had learned that God's were the most important. However clever his former methods of controlling and leading, he learned that strength in leadership comes through continual, obedient trust in God and a willingness to serve others. And having rediscovered this difference, Moses' second leadership assignment was drastically different and far more effective.

While most of us have never served in Pharaoh's court or tended sheep in the desert for many decades, we can still learn the lessons of Moses . . . that only leadership that honors God and which comes from the soul is leadership which will be effective.

2

The Nine Tasks
of Leadership

MUCH HAS BEEN written about leadership without actually
defining what leadership is. I find it helpful to discuss leadership by focusing on its tasks, and there are many.

One of the most helpful lists is the one developed by
former HEW Secretary John Gardner. He has argued that a
leader has to deal with at least nine critical tasks.

The Nine Critical Tasks of a Leader

Envisioning Goals

First, the leader has the responsibility to "envision goals."[1]
By this he means the ability to set goals and to create a
vision of what the people or the organization can achieve.

Time and time again we see the leaders in the Old Testament envisioning goals for their people. When people saw
the walls around Jericho and complained, "No, we can't,"
Joshua said, "Yes, we can." When the Israelites were faced
with Goliath and said, "No, we can't," David responded with
a vigorous, "Yes, we can." When ten of the spies told the
Israelites they could not capture Canaan because of the
giants and other obstacles, Joshua and Caleb said, "Yes, we
can."

A colleague in Brazil had a dream for a multimillion dol-
lar printing/binding plant to produce Bibles for Brazil. In

that land of poverty and opportunity, because he made the initial question, "Where is God in this project?" a beautiful plant successfully operates. He was able to envision this project for countless people who then helped make it a reality.

Affirming Values

The second task Gardner identifies is the need for the leader to "affirm values."[2] As he observes:

A great civilization is a drama lived in the minds of a people. It is a shared vision; it is shared norms, expectations and purposes. When one thinks of the world's great civilizations, the most vivid images that crowd in on us are of the monuments left behind. . . . But in truth all the physical splendor was the merest by-product. The civilizations themselves, from the beginning to end, existed in the minds of men and women.[3]

The values shared by the people Moses led came from a variety of sources, the most important of which were the Ten Commandments. Over and over Moses had to remind the people not only of shared values but the sole foundation for those shared values—trust in the Almighty God. Moses had to maintain the vision God had imparted to him despite grumbling, murmuring, and insurrection. And contemporary Christian leaders are called to do the same thing.

Motivating

Gardner's third leadership task is that of "motivating."[4] Observes Gardner: "Leaders do not normally create motivation out of thin air. They unlock or channel existing motives."[5] It is for these reasons, for example, that a leader must attend to the goals, dreams, and needs of the people being led.

However, motivation cannot be superimposed on the group. "Any group," says Gardner, "has a great tangle of motives. Effective leaders tap those motives that serve the purposes of collective action in pursuit of significant shared goals."[6] One of the methods constantly used by Moses in this regard was to continually identify for the people the blessings which would result if obedience to God were forthcoming. "For I command you today to love the Lord your God, to walk in His ways, and to keep His commmands, decrees and laws; then you will live and increase, and the Lord your God will bless you" (Deut. 30:16). Just as important, however, were the negative consequences that would follow if obedience were not the chosen course. "But if your heart turns away and you are not obedient, and if you are drawn away to bow down to other gods and worship them, I declare to you this day that you will certainly be destroyed" (vv. 17-18). Negative motivations can produce positive actions as well as positive motivations can produce positive actions.

Gardner further observes that "positive views of the future must be tempered by a measure of tough-minded realism."[7] Neither Moses nor Joshua suggested, for example, that the Promised Land could be taken without some degree of difficulty, e.g., fighting. What they did assure the people, however, was that God was on their side and that they would prevail (31:3-6).

Managing

A fourth leadership task identified by Gardner is "managing."[8] While he doesn't necessarily see this as the primary role of leadership, Gardner does see it as an indispensable part of the task of leadership. Management items that he identifies, for example, include those of planning, priority-setting, agenda-setting, decision-making, and exercising political judgment.

In the Old Testament, for example, careful attention was given not only to the concept of worship, but also to how people were to worship. The various sacrifices, offerings, and procedures the people were to follow in a host of areas were painstakingly and meticulously spelled out. Many times, after consulting the Lord, Moses told the people how to get water and where to get bread. These activities are representative of basic management tasks.

Achieving Workable Unity

A fifth task of leadership is to achieve "workable unity."[9] Gardner does not suggest that this task will be achieved when total organizational uniformity is present or when there is a total absence of conflict. In fact, he believes that some conflict will be inevitable: "Indeed one could argue that willingness to engage in battle when necessary is a sine qua non of leadership." Gardner holds that this task includes the concern for and ability to resolve conflicts and the need to build trust in the organization.

The subject of unity in Scripture is a rich one. Many of Paul's letters discussed this very important topic. And Christ Himself, as expressed in His prayer to His Father just prior to His death, made the subject of unity a significant part of the prayer:

> My prayer is not for them alone. I pray also for those who will believe in Me through their message, that all of them may be one, Father, just as You are in Me and I am in You. May they also be in Us so that the world may believe that You have sent Me. I have given them the glory that You gave Me, that they may be one as We are One: I in them and You in Me. May they be brought to complete unity to let the world know that You sent Me and have loved them even as You have loved Me (John 17:20-23).

Indeed, He stated that the evidence to the world that He was sent by the Father would be to have the world see believers brought to complete unity.

Marylou and I were once walking by a softball field in Central Park. It was unlike any softball field I had ever seen because right in the middle of the outfield was a very large tree. Yet softball was being played with abandon. People simply learned to play in spite of the less than perfect conditions. Sometimes in leadership we miss opportunities because we insist on perfection which we might seldom achieve rather than taking and making the most out of workable opportunities. This is especially true when dealing with the matter of unity.

Explaining

A sixth task of leadership is that of "explaining."[10] By explaining Gardner suggests the need for sharing information about what is going on and why. Gardner sees a strong similarity between the explaining function of leaders and the teaching function of leaders: "Teaching and leading are distinguishable occupations, but every great leader is clearly teaching — and every great teacher is leading."[11]

One of the primary roles of Moses as a leader was Moses as a teacher. Time and time again he called the people together to teach them the ways of the Lord. And he called on the people to also be teachers — of their own children. Children likewise were to be attentive to their parents' instruction: "Listen, my son, to your father's instruction and do not forsake your mother's teaching" (Prov. 1:8).

Many leaders miss the mark on this one. They assume that because the memo has been sent, clarity of understanding results. They can't understand why people still have questions. I have found that regular open meetings with the president, where the agenda is what our staff wants to talk about, not what I want to talk about, help with this important task of explaining.

Serving as a Symbol

A seventh task of leadership is to "serve as a symbol."[12] Any leader — whether a pastor, CEO, foreman, or teacher, to name a few — has faced the issue of being identified primarily as a symbol.

My grade-school teacher was a symbol to me of every good thing there was to know about teaching and learning. When I saw her in the store she was still my teacher and I expected her to act in a certain way. The same could be said about a host of other leadership positions. The leader who refuses to recognize this symbolic role, who insists always on being his own person, will indeed face a rocky road. Observes Gardner: "Leaders can rarely afford the luxury of speaking for themselves alone."[13] Moses was very much aware of his symbolic role in this regard. So too were the high priests. When Moses went to the top of Mount Sinai, for example, he went there not just for himself but on behalf of his people. The commandments he received were not just for his benefit, but for all the people's benefit.

I have found this to be especially true in an international organization where there are a multitude of worldviews, ethnicities, and a variety of church traditions. Activities and practices which are perfectly acceptable in one culture are totally unacceptable in another. So this task of serving as a symbol becomes even more difficult and complex.

Representing the Group

The eighth task of leadership that Gardner identifies is that of "representing the group."[14]

A leader must be fully aware of the strengths and weaknesses of the organization and negotiate appropriately. The leader must also be aware of the needs and wants of the constituents and look out for their best interests. This representational function or task is probably most easily identified in the political realm when a leader from one country sits down with the leader of another country to negotiate some treaty or agreement. A ready illustration of this role in Scripture is when Joshua negotiated a treaty with the Gibeonites. God had instructed Joshua to wipe out the neighboring countries, yet the Gibeonites perpetrated a successful ruse which fooled Joshua. As the people's representative, however, he was bound, once the ruse was discovered, to abide by its terms.

In the case of Moses, this representational role was clearly identified by his father-in-law during a visit: "Listen now to me and I will give you some advice, and may God be with you. You must be the people's representative before God and bring their disputes to Him" (Ex. 18:19).

Renewing

The ninth task of leadership identified by Gardner is the task of "renewing."[15] What Gardner has in mind is that organizations are always changing. As a result, previously valid methods may, at some time in the future, be discarded.

He argues that because of change, the organization must always be seeking to be self-renewed so that its purposes and goals, even though achieved by different methods, will nevertheless remain intact. According to Gardner:

> Little by little, preoccupation with method, technique and procedure gains a subtle dominance over the whole process of goal seeking. How it is done becomes more important than whether it is done. Means triumph over ends. Form triumphs over spirit. Method is enthroned. Men become prisoners of their procedures, and organizations that were designed to achieve some goal become obstacles in the path to that goal.[16]

An extremely vivid illustration of this task relates to the New Testament shift to include the Gentiles in the church when previously only Jewish believers were included. Paul was more sensitive to the renewing function in this specific context than was Peter, but with the help of a heavenly vision, Peter also caught the message even though he continued to struggle with all of its ramifications.

As leaders and organizations prepare for the next millennium, there is probably no more difficult task than dealing with this renewing task. For example, all organizations will deal with changes outside of the organization over which the organization has no control, but which will dramatically impact organizations. A tax code which discourages charitable giving is one such example. The leader who succeeds in this task understands that "the future truly belongs to the learning, not the learned." Renewal of both the organization and its people will continue to be a very important task of leadership.

The Leadership Team

I want to note one other concept that Gardner identifies — the concept of the leadership team. He argues that a person will be a better leader if he or she is part of a leadership team: "Most of the leadership that can be called effective involves a number of individuals acting in a team relationship. Most ventures fare better if one person is in charge — but not as a solo performer, not as a giant surrounded by pygmies."[17]

Gardner argues for the leadership team concept for several reasons. First, just as the organization is constantly changing, so too is the leader. And the leader who is surrounded with a team of key players, each of whom possesses different yet complementary strengths, is well positioned to keep up with and ahead of the needs of the organization. Second, the leadership structure is constantly in a state of adjustment. While every organization has an official organizational chart, most members of an organization know the informal as well as the formal levels of access. As Gardner observes, "Everyone understands the 'kitchen cabinet' phenomenon."[18] Again, leadership that is dispersed is well positioned to deal with both this formal and informal structure. Third, just as people within the organization are changing, so too is the organization's external environment. And leadership that is dispersed can be in tune with these changes.

Summary

- Envisioning goals.
- Affirming values.

- Motivating.
- Managing.
- Achieving workable unity.
- Explaining.
- Serving as a symbol.
- Representing the group.
- Renewing.

Addressing these nine leadership tasks, then, and the need for the leader to develop a leadership team, are important elements in understanding and doing leadership. They are steps in the right direction. But if we are to handle these tasks properly, we must grapple with several additional concepts: those troublesome concepts of power and authority and the need for trust. How we deal with power and authority and trust will do much to help us understand the soul of leadership.

3

Power, Authority, and Trust

WE CANNOT VERY well discuss leadership without also discussing the concepts of power, authority, and trust, and that is the task of this chapter.

Leadership and Power

Kast and Rosenzweig, professors from the University of Washington, give us an excellent definition of power: "Power is the capability of doing or affecting something. It implies the ability to influence others. In its most general sense, power denotes (1) the ability—to produce a certain occurrence or (2) the influence exerted by a man or group, through whatever means, over the conduct of others in intended ways."[1]

Three Kinds of Power

According to Kast and Rosenzweig, there are three kinds of power: physical power, material power, and symbolic power.[2] Physical power is most readily thought of in the context of the police or a military organization. These types of entities have the power to harm, incarcerate, or even to take one's life in certain circumstances. An example of material power could be the leading financier of an organization. All CEOs know the power of a donor who insists on using a donation to manipulate the organization toward a particular direction or to pursue a particular purpose. An example of symbolic power would be the ability to motivate people to do their best in order to help the organization achieve its goals.

In the same way that he has written about leadership, John Gardner has also provided some useful analyses on the subject of power. He notes as follows: "Power is not to be confused with status or prestige. It is the capacity to ensure the outcomes one wishes and to prevent those one does not wish. Power as we are now speaking of it—power in the social dimension—is simply the capacity to bring about certain intended consequences in the behavior of others."[3]

God's View of Power

Simple reflection about the life and ministry of Christ on earth suggests that He not only had power, He exercised power appropriately and toward appropriate ends. His life provides the positive example about how power can be used and ought to be used. Before a leader uses power for selfish purposes, this question should be faced: "What would Jesus have done?" If a leader wants to use power to strike back at those who falsely and maliciously misrepresent, again, "What would Jesus have done?" Jesus' words recorded in Mark 10:42-44 bear repeating:

> You know that those who are regarded as rulers of the Gentiles lord it over them, and their high officials exercise authority over them. Not so with you. Instead, whoever wants to become great among you must be your servant, and whoever wants to be first must be slave of all.

It's not enough, however, for leaders to reject or run from power. As Gardner notes, "Power lodges somewhere."[4] The key issue, then, is to submit that power to the lordship of Christ, using it for God-honoring ends. Though the processes of how power is exercised is important, we must go past processes and also look at motive. Time and time again, "religious" leaders in the Old Testament were castigated by God for impure motives, despite the fact that they appeared, on the surface, to be exercising their power appropriately.

> I hate, I despise your religious feasts; I cannot stand your assemblies. Even though you bring Me burnt offerings and grain offerings, I will not accept them. Though you bring choice fellowship offerings, I will have no regard for them. Away with the noise of your songs! I will not listen to the music of your harps (Amos 5:21-23).

God is watching and judging everything I do, and is constantly weighing the thoughts and attitudes of the heart (Heb. 4:12, paraphrased). Therefore, as I exercise power in leadership, I need to be alert to my innermost motives governing its exercise, the ways in which its exercised, and the ends or purposes for which I want to use it.

Power and Accountability

It is vital, Gardner notes, to make sure that leaders hold and are held to high standards of accountability. He notes Acton's assertion: "Power tends to corrupt; absolute power corrupts absolutely."[5] He observes, and I want to underscore his emphasis, that because many in our society view power as the essence of wickedness, Acton's remark is generally misquoted as "Power corrupts" rather than quoted in its correct form: "Power tends to corrupt." Simply put, leaders ought to welcome efforts by boards to insist on leadership accountability, for accountability is an important control for making sure power and authority are properly handled. Alternatively, too many "safeguards" can make a leader totally ineffective. As Gardner notes, "When accountable leaders are stripped of power, the people lose power."[6]

In her very helpful book, *The Religion of Power*, author Cheryl Forbes discusses the concept of power. To her way of thinking, power is defined as follows: "Insistence on what we want for no other reason than that we want it; it means making other people follow us despite their own wishes. Power is assumed, insensitive, dehumanizing, and ultimately destructive."[7] Forbes sees power as something to be "delivered from" rather than to be sought after: "Christians must say no to power, individually and corporately. A decision for power is antithetical to a desire for God."[8] Conversely, she sees authority as "positive and usually involves a conferred right within strictly controlled bounds. It is a temporary recognition or a temporary state of 'inchargeness.'"[9]

Leadership and Authority

It is difficult to discuss the issue of power without also discussing the issue of authority, even though they are different concepts. According to Prison Fellowship Ministries founder, Charles Colson,

> Power and authority must not be confused. Power is the ability to affect one's ends or purposes in the world. Authority is having not only the power (might), but the right to affect one's purpose. Power is often maintained by naked force; authority springs from a moral foundation. Mother Teresa is the best living example. She spends her life helping the powerless die with dignity; yet few people command more authority worldwide.[10]

Colson cautions us that "worldly power — whether measured by buildings, budgets, baptisms or access to the White House — is more often the enemy than the ally of godliness."[11] The concept of authority, then, appears on the same continuum as power but at a different place. The relationship among power, authority, and leadership is important and quite complex. To paraphrase Gardner, neither authority nor power make one a leader. There are those who have both power and authority but who have no willing followers. Again, the comments of business professors, Pascale and Athos, are helpful:

> The consistent picture of the effective leader is the one who adopts the style of a "superfollower," who serves with his followers' blessing and consent, and who is able to inspire because he is first able to respond to their needs and concerns. Power in this context means the ability to get things done, to mobilize resources, and to draw on what is necessary to accomplish goals. Power is thus more akin to "mastery" than to "domination" or "control."[12]

The issue for Christian leaders, then, is neither an undue concern for power for its own sake nor authority for its own sake. Rather, the issue is, "How can I exercise God-given power and authority to help the organization which He has entrusted to me achieve His purposes and goals?" Again, how I use power and authority as a leader becomes just as important as the ends sought through the use of both power and authority.

Leadership and Trust

When one becomes a leader in an organization—any organization, whether a church, a college, or a business—there are a variety of voices saying, "Trust me." In a college situation, for example, the faculty want the trust of the administration and vice versa. The alumni want to be trusted by the administration and vice versa, and so on down the line. Everybody wants to be trusted. In other organizations the same "trust me" statements are made by staff, volunteers, and board members.

Biblical Christianity frequently asks that we trust the Lord:

Trust in the Lord with all your heart and lean not on your own understanding; in all your ways acknowledge Him, and He will make your paths straight (Prov. 3:5-6).

Trust in the Lord and do good; dwell in the land and enjoy safe pasture. Delight yourself in the Lord and He will give you the desires of your heart. Commit your way to the Lord; trust in Him and He will do this (Ps. 37:3-5).

When I trust someone, I am in essence saying that in matters affecting my welfare, I know the one trusted will be concerned about and will diligently work for my betterment. Furthermore, I need not use extraordinary measures in order for that commitment to be carried out. "A loyal constituency is won when people consciously judge the leader to be capable of solving their problems and meeting their needs."[13]

There is much to be gained for any leader in winning the trust of constituents. Leaders must not only forge bonds of trust between themselves and their constituents, they must create a climate of trust throughout the system over which they preside. Trust is not the only glue that holds a human group together, but when it dissolves, the capacity of the group to function effectively is seriously impaired.[14]

According to Louis Barnes of Harvard University, trust in an organization is more important to its functioning than is either authority or power. Further, trust is easily destroyed, but perhaps, just as importantly, trust can be easily created and/or restored.

Destroying Trust

According to Barnes, trust is readily destroyed when leaders hold to three seemingly harmless assumptions: First, that important issues naturally fall into two opposing camps, exemplified by either/or thinking; second, that hard data and facts are better than what appear to be soft ideas and speculation, exemplified in the "hard drives out soft" rule; and finally, that the world in general is an unsafe place, exemplified by a person's having a pervasive mistrust of the world.[15] It is Barnes' observation that while these assumptions seem simple enough, when leaders combine all three, the long-term organizational impact can be "very destructive" to the issue of trust.

Either/or thinking. According to Barnes, this assumption reflects the tendency to believe only two primary options exist for any decision. In reality a given problem may have multiple solutions. The organizational leader who is an either/or practitioner tends to limit the range of options for resolving difficulty. Furthermore, the options presented, usually only two, soon become symbols which can represent polarized entities. Thereafter, the polarization evolves into sides such as unions versus management, black versus white, theory versus practice, us versus them. In a church situation, the sides can take many shapes—the young versus the old, the big givers versus the small givers, and old-timers versus the newcomers. Barnes suggests by implication, therefore, that leaders need to avoid either/or thinking, not only to minimize the unnecessary polarization which results from symbolic concerns but, more importantly, so that the organization is open to and can consider other options.

Hard is better than soft. As an extension of either/or thinking, Barnes argues that this second false assumption is built around a premise something like the following: "If I have data for supporting my recommendation and you base your recommendation only on feelings or intuition, then my recommendation is superior to or better than your decision and my recommendation should prevail." Since I want my recommendations to prevail, I search for hard data or facts or numbers rather than searching my feelings or intuition or other more abstract, "soft" possibilities.

According to Pascale and Athos, the Western management mind-set is dominated by "hard" managers.

American managers tend to overfocus on the "hard" elements. Some of the best work done in business schools in recent decades has been in advancing our understanding of the "cold triangle" of strategy, structure, and systems. Each one and the relationships among the three are particularly susceptible to analytical, quantitative, logical, and systematic investigation. In short, "science" of one kind or another, rigorous observation and conceptualization—thinking, if you prefer—were required. That's what business schools value. That's how professors get rewarded. And that's what fits our culture's central beliefs about managing.[16]

What these authors observe is that Western culture is dominated by this "hard" mind-set while other cultures are more open to a "soft" mind-set. "Hard versus soft," then, is more a phenomenon of culture than it is a requirement for good management. Pascale and Athos, moreover, caution against ignoring the "soft" parts of organizational management: "In short, the soft elements can no longer be regarded as frosting on the corporate cake. They are indispensable parts of any corporate commitment to long-term success."[17]

I see these differences in many different countries. In some cultures, if there is no relationship between people, the figures or numbers don't matter. In others, the reverse is true. Our leadership responsibility is to balance these multiple issues in ways which are productive. Interestingly, trust appears to be a soft variable.

Mistrust of the world. This assumption "holds that the world is a dangerous place requiring that a person adopt a position of pervasive mistrust to survive."[18] In an organizational context, this view assumes Darwinian or "survival of the fittest" overtones: "I need to get the other person before that person gets me. Our organization needs to come up with the creative plan or program first; otherwise, our competitor, whether the church or the organization next door, will take away all our potential parishioners or potential gift income." Such an assumption negatively impacts the trust level within an organization.

Creating Trust

Barnes' research efforts suggest that one key variable in the ability of an organization to solve problems is a high level of trust. If this is the case, what can a leader do to create trust? According to Barnes, leaders need to abandon the three assumptions stated earlier and at the same time seek less rigid, more creative combinations.[19]

According to Gardner, "One of the most important prerequisites for trust in a leader is steadiness."[20] By steadiness, Gardner means predictability. Gardner also notes that another important element for establishing organizational trust is fairness: "fairness when the issues are being openly adjudicated but, equally important, fairness in the back room. Nothing is more surely stabilizing than confidence that the leader is unshakably fair in public and in private."[21]

Regrettably, many Christian leaders who hold visible positions of leadership and who are active in a local church separate what is expected of them in their personal walk with Christ from what is expected of them as Christian leaders in a corporate Christian context. It's ironic that while many Christian organizations insist on "statements of faith," far fewer insist on a "statement of practice." Yet our Lord was unimpressed with the words of people if they were not accompanied with properly motivated actions. In short, in our corporate expressions of Christianity we often neglect our corporate witness. We have said something to the effect that "it makes no difference that our corporate structures and the way we operate within them differ little from the typical secular corporate culture." The paradox is that Jesus strongly argued that people would be attracted to His cause because of the differences they would see in the actions of the corporate Christian community when compared with the actions of the secular world. This not only fails to produce trust in an organization, but further, the cause of the kingdom is significantly set back.

From this brief review, we see that the secular corporate world argues for high levels of trust in an organization. Trusting persons will be harder working people. Trusting persons will be more committed people. Trusting people will be more effective people. So it makes sense, after all, for the leader to manage and cultivate trust in an organization. And not only does it make good sense organizationally, but high levels of trust ought to characterize the organization which calls itself Christian. This is particularly the case where power, authority, and leadership are involved.

Summary

There is, after all, a difference between power (the actions and methods a person in a given position takes to effect a goal, whether or not authorized) and authority (what the "position" authorizes). Clearly, power is a broader term than authority. In organizational leadership, it is imperative that the power and authority of the leader be reviewed regularly by a board. Interestingly, leadership can take place whether or not one holds a position of power and authority. The overnight, God-ordained, rise of Joseph from prisoner (no power or authority) to prime minister (full power and authority), was connected in no small way to the leadership qualities the Pharaoh saw in Joseph.

And so too with building trust. Leaders who (1) provide and search for multiple options as potential solutions to problems or identify a variety of opportunities for the future do much to build trust in an organization.

Leaders who (2) insist on hard data but who also allow for prayer, the role of intuition, and other types of soft input, tend to end up with the most solid decisions. This is particularly true in a Christian organization which allows for and earnestly seeks the guidance of the Holy Spirit. Often, God's clear leading can't be quantified.

And leaders who (3) choose to take a positive view of the world and the people they lead end up looking for the best in people and situations, not the worst. Some would argue that this "lack of realism" will ultimately be in the worst interests of the leader. To the contrary, leaders who practice these three elements build trust and identify for followers multiple options for possible organizational futures.

Once again, we come full circle to the soul of leadership. People see power, position, and authority. David had none, yet he was chosen by God to lead because of his soul-qualities (he was a man after God's heart). And so too with Joseph and Moses and Peter and Paul and John the Baptist and yes, even Christ's own supreme example (Phil. 2:6-11, CEV).

4

Mind and Body

HEALTHY LEADERSHIP BEGINS with a healthy leader. I grew up in a conservative church which quite often had visiting evangelists. The basic thrust of their sermons was something to this effect—don't drink, don't smoke, don't dance; save others, witness, and avoid hell. I never heard any sermons pertaining to the care of my body, the dangers of overeating, and the importance of diet and exercise. One of the strongest advocates of the "don't drink or smoke" line was an evangelist who weighed over 300 pounds. It didn't dawn on me until later in life that the issue for the Christian leader is stewardship of the body, whether the problem is food abuse, drug abuse (e.g., pills, alcohol, coffee), improper rest, or lack of exercise.

My observation tells me that these are not only concerns personally ("Oh, what's so bad about carrying around an extra ten to fifteen pounds?" we rationalize), but often Christian culture tells me that slippage, or sin, in this area is not quite so bad as slippage, or sin, in other areas.

Take Care of Your Body

Paul reminds us in 1 Corinthians 3:16-17 that the body is God's temple: "Don't you know that you yourselves are God's temple and that God's Spirit lives in you? If anyone destroys God's temple, God will destroy him; for God's temple is sacred, and you are that temple."

As a result of my background, it was always easier for me to tolerate persons with weight problems than those who were alcoholics. Sadly, many in Christian organizations are substantially overweight. Given the frequent and seemingly never-ending schedule of travel, dinners, banquets, and homemade pies and cookies that must be sampled, it's very easy for the leader to struggle in this area. Yet proper diet, rest, and exercise are critically essential for the leader. While short-term neglect in these areas will not immediately produce negative results, long-term neglect may prove disastrous.

Oswald Sanders tells the following story of Robert Murray McCheyne: "When McCheyne was dying at the age of thirty-two — he had overspent himself in revival work and so forth — he told a friend at his bedside, 'God gave me a horse to ride and a message to deliver. Alas, I have killed the horse and I can't deliver the message.' " Sanders concludes, "I am not suggesting for a moment that you become oversolicitous for yourself or care for yourself too much or be afraid to spend. But there's a point when it is wise to stop and have a rest."[1]

Guidelines I try to follow include the following:

- get adequate rest (for me at least seven hours);
- participate in exercise that does not require a specified playing area (I try to jog 12–16 miles every week).

I enjoy basketball, but when I travel, it's hard to find a gym. Jogging, then, is a much better alternative for me, as I can usually find a street or a treadmill. For those who do little traveling, basketball, swimming, tennis, or racquetball may be good types of regular exercise. Whatever you choose, do something that you enjoy.

- Follow basic nutritional guidelines. Nutritionist Denise Webb, Ph.D., in her article, "The Power of Positive Eating,"[2] has provided good counsel:

DO snack regularly. Just do so intelligently, choosing low calorie, high-fiber foods like fruits and vegetables.

DO eat breakfast. Having a meal in the A.M. can minimize your appetite for lunch and prevent your metabolism from slowing down during the morning hours.

DO try some of the new reduced fat and fat-free products. These substitutes help you cut back on fat and calories without requiring mini portions.

DO read food labels. Most products in the supermarket provide nutrition information on the label. Choose foods that are as low in fat and high in fiber as possible.

DO boost your fiber intake. Health experts currently recommend eating at least six servings of grain products a day.

DO be sure to get at least five servings of fruits and vegetables each day. They're rich sources of beta carotene and vitamin C — nutrients thought to be important in warding off cancer and heart disease.

DO give in to cravings — occasionally. Struggling against yearnings is a surefire path to a binge. Try managing your craving with a small serving. Avoiding the tempting food completely only makes it more desirable.

DO banish guilt from your thinking. Berating yourself because you happened to overindulge only fosters feelings of failure and fuels the urge to give up altogether. Instead, accept your lapse and return to your new, healthier habits as soon as possible.

The point I make is simple to state but hard to practice: the proper care of one's body is critically important to the leader. There are enough other stress points in leadership. This ought not be one of them.

It's easy to slip back into old habits. I know what to do . . . so when I feel I'm out of control I have to stop, admit it, and begin again. I force myself to step on that scale and asses the "damage" and go on from there. The tendency is for me to avoid my regular physical exam, not wanting to hear about any area I need to watch. I realize the foolishness of that and take that step and make that appointment . . . and yes, find that I must watch that cholesterol, but in general things are great.

When I'm experiencing stress (and oftentimes I don't feel I'm stressed), my shoulder really gets tense. And here is where running helps me, as it reduces the stress level and provides the opportunity to think and pray. I once knew a professor who, in his consulting practice, told me he jogged regularly for the exercise, but also because it gave him uninterrupted "think" time. I, and others, have also gained new insights into problem/opportunity areas while "putting on some miles" and being alone with God in this way.

We can encourage others by our example in this area. I was recently challenged by one of our staff members to participate in a 5k run in Central Park. While I was walking regularly, I rationalized that I didn't have the time to "work out" in this way. But he insisted and I persisted. I ran in that race and in the process gained not only a new workout schedule, but I've also made new friendships with others in the Bible society who ran in that race who I didn't know were even runners. And "running and sweating" together created a new type of common ground that wouldn't have been possible otherwise. Paul's words in 1 Corinthians perhaps say it best: "Do you not know that in a race all runners run, but only one gets the prize? Run in such a way as to get the prize" (1 Cor. 9:24, TEV).

Take Care of Your Mind

Just as important as keeping the body in shape is continuing to "exercise" your mind. Many leaders stop growing intellectually after they achieve given positions of leadership. Degrees are earned and classes are taken primarily to present the proper set of credentials for the job. The leader who fails to aggressively pursue further cognitive development, however, will not long be an effective leader.

Education

While formal classwork is always an option, and I would add, I have always found it to be extremely stimulating, that is not the only option. One of the advantages of formal classwork is that it contains a built-in element of risk. After the degree is secured, it is very tempting to avoid placing oneself in a position again where academic failure can result. "After all, I have enough risks attached to leadership responsibilities. I don't need more." This kind of risk, however, can serve as a catalyst for growth. So from time to time formal coursework ought to be considered. Institutes and workshops may also be useful.

One wise thinker has said it well, "The future belongs to the learning, not the learned." All of us have experienced those no longer on the cutting-edge of their professions, the leaders resting on outdated degrees from the past. When I interview persons for positions of leadership, one of the questions I always ask is this one: How do you stay on the cutting-edge?

Management consultant Price Pritchett argues that those in leadership should be preaching the gospel of "employability security, not job security to staff." Simply put, if staff are encouraged to stay on the cutting-edge and given resources to do so, not only does the organization benefit, but so does the staff member. As a result, the staff member is highly employable, both within and without the organization. For this person, there are no "dead end" streets, only new opportunities. And so too for the leader; staying "fully alive" spiritually and physically; and staying on the cutting-edge of one's profession enhances not only the ability to lead, but also one's future employability.

Reading

Additionally, the leader ought to be an avid reader, both of works pertinent to leadership and others totally outside of one's given vocation, including those by secular as well as Christian authors. And I'm obviously assuming that this type of reading will not be in lieu of Bible reading and study.

According to Gordon MacDonald: "The development of the mind makes it possible for men and women to be servants to the generations in which they live. We do not develop our intellects merely for our own personal advancement, but we put our thinking power to work for the use of others. As my mind grows, it may make possible the growth of others."[3] And Oswald Sanders observes, "The man who desires to grow spiritually and intellectually will be constantly at his books."[4] Among other reasons for encouraging reading, Sanders notes the following: mental stimulation, cultivation of style, acquisition of information, and fellowship with great minds.[5]

Meditation/Reflection

It is also important for the leader to set aside time for what former colleague William Green calls reflective leadership. Much of leadership, at least in the organizational context, involves scheduling meetings, responding to complaints, and the like. Yet if the leader is to lead, time must be spent, repeatedly, away from the office, reflecting on the enterprise. One of the key responsibilities of a board is to make sure the leader takes time for reflective leadership.

My period for reflective leadership includes large doses of reading material, which obviously enhances cognitive development. Regularly scheduled days out of the office help me to do this.

Frequently leaders lose sight of the overall purposes and mission of an organization. Sustained quiet time for reflection outside of the office helps retain perspective in this important responsibility.

Summary

Once again, leadership is not a series of disconnected parts. Rather, as Covey states it, the spiritual, mental, physical, and social can be viewed as a series of overlapping concentric circles. And the central place, where all of these circles overlap, he calls "The fire within."[6]

For our purposes, this place of convergence, where good diet and exercise, and strong mental and social development, built on a strong spiritual foundation—where all of these converge together—in the center will be the Holy Spirit of God—directing, leading, empowering, and consoling. And it makes all of the difference in leadership.

5

Leadership and Family

DURING DISCUSSIONS IN our small fellowship group at church, the subject of leadership and the family often arises. As it usually does in these kinds of gatherings, a variety of perspectives were shared: success in the job but no real time with the children or, success in the job and time with the children, but nothing solid with the spouse.

All across the world, in diverse cultures, this question of leadership and the family comes up. From Egypt to Ecuador; from Santiago to Madrid; the questions are the same — when will the children get to know their mother or father? When will my husband/wife have time for me? And this dilemma cuts across most professions, including the church.

Jim Smith is thirty-eight years old. He has a pretty wife, two beautiful children, and is considered one of the outstanding pastors in his city. Jim and Jane were married while Jim was still in seminary. Their first child was born during his senior year. Jane never completed her college education but took a job to help Jim through seminary. Jim is an effective preacher and is greatly respected by both his assistant pastor and the congregation. He works hard on his sermons. His church is growing. Jim's wife will leave him next week.

But its not just the church where we find this problem. We also find it within many Christian organizations:

Bob Ramson is the executive director of Christian Commitment Abroad, which he founded twenty-two years ago. He has traveled all over the world and is a much sought-after speaker. After a shaky beginning, CCA began to grow rapidly about ten years ago. Much of its growth is due to Bob's high level of commitment and his willingness to give himself unstintingly to the work of Christ. Bob doesn't know it, but he left his wife and children eight years ago.

These two anecdotes, both from World Vision president emeritus Ted Engstrom and World Vision executive Ed Dayton's book, *The Christian Executive*,[1] aptly illustrate the situations too often faced by Christian leaders—they have failed in their marriages.

Leaders and Their Spouses

Paul's qualifications for overseers and deacons included the requirement that these leaders be "faithful in marriage" (1 Tim. 3:2, CEV). And just what kind of husband did he have in mind? He answers this in Ephesians 5:25-33, CEV:

A husband should love his wife as much as Christ loved the church and gave His life for it. He made the church holy by the power of His word and He made it pure by washing it with water. Christ did this, so that He would have a glorious and holy church, without faults or spots or wrinkles or any other flaws.

In the same way, a husband should love his wife as much as he loves himself. A husband who loves his wife shows that he loves himself. None of us hate our own bodies. We provide for them and take good care of them, just as Christ does for the church, because we are each part of His body. As the Scriptures say, "A man leaves his father and mother to get married, and he becomes like one person with his wife." This is a great mystery, but I understand it to mean Christ and His church. So each husband should love his wife as much as he loves himself, and each wife should respect her husband.

Clearly, the husband is to love his wife as Christ loved the church. He ought to love his wife as he loves his own body. Many leaders have an idolatrous relationship with another "mistress" called "the ministry." This "mistress" demands long hours, time away from home, and is used to justify all kinds of unbiblical priorities. This kind of idolatry must be labeled for what it is—sin. The illicit affairs with the corporate mistress have got to stop. God's priorities cannot be ignored. He expects leaders to love their spouses as He loved the church. And this requires that the leader not neglect the needs—all of them—of the spouse. As Engstrom and Dayton note:

> Some of us immediately respond in our own defense, "But this is the ministry to which God has called me! My wife understands that. That's one of the sacrifices we are making together." Perhaps. But perhaps that is your view of the situation, and although it may be outwardly shared by your wife, perhaps inwardly she feels quite differently. Too often the Christian wife is put in the position of appearing to oppose the will of the Lord if she does not feel at ease with the circumstance within which her husband is moving. Many men and women marry before they have a clear picture of the ministry to which they (or he) may be called. Too often they overlook what the Spirit may be saying to her and what gifts God may have bestowed upon her.[2]

If this kind of spousal relationship characterizes the life of the leader, we have done an absolutely dismal job of practicing Christlike love. We must start over. Too soon is not soon enough. In terms of family priorities, one's spouse must be made number one and the spouse must know it.

Make Your Spouse Priority One

Here are some suggestions to consider to help develop and strengthen the relationship with one's spouse.

Take regular vacations. Take these vacations several times per year, even if they are only day-long outings. I am amazed and surprised at how many leaders do not spend much time vacationing with their spouses. Vacation times without children are especially important for developing intimacy, both sexual and otherwise. Take time to have fun!

Do something special. These "special things" should be above and beyond help with everyday household chores. One of the habits suggested to me many years ago was to bring home cut flowers for my wife—every week if possible. I have not succeeded every week, but I hit that goal more often than I miss it. Early in our marriage, there were weeks when I would bring home a single carnation, for that's all the budget allowed for. But it was as meaningful as a dozen red roses, because it came from the heart with love. This small monthly expenditure was one of the best investments I could make in our marriage. Once in a while, slip in something additional, like new clothes or jewelry.

Make spiritual renewal as a couple a continuous journey. This is sometimes a sore spot with couples, as practices and recollections from home (often negative) are frequently brought forward into the marriage. Each person must learn and grow at his or her own pace. But growth eventually needs to take place together. Growing together, spiritually, enriches and deepens a marriage. Patience, consistency of words with actions, and much prayer are imperative on this journey.

Share your worlds. Often, many spouses outgrow each other and eventually grow apart. Make sure the world for each is properly understood and shared. Growing together, not apart, should be the perspective.

Spend time together. This means more than the occasional "quality time" slot between activities. If necessary, be prepared to discard all of your plans at a moment's notice. The issue of "when" has to be worked out by each couple, but don't let that keep you from finding the time to be together.

Share family financial information. Make sure your spouse understands the family financial situation and make sure she is financially cared for in the event of your death. Too many leaders keep their spouses uninformed in these kinds of matters. Discuss them openly and forthrightly. I've seen many husbands protect their wives from this "burden" only to have a greater burden emerge over the long haul. Money won't make the marriage, but sharing information can help keep communication lines open and avoid walls from going up.

Engstrom and Dayton offer additional suggestions: "Start asking your wife for dates, just the two of you together. Ask her to evaluate how she sees you spending your time. Try to fantasize what you believe would be the very best situation for you as individuals and as a couple ten years from now."[3] Don't believe the lie that your spouse will settle for "a little bit of quality time." The spouse appreciates quality time, to be sure, but large doses of quality time is what the spouse deserves. Just as our Heavenly Father desires significant amounts of both quality and quantity time of us, so too do our spouses.

Engstrom and Dayton provide another reminder to leaders: "God's work will get done without you. God is really not nervous about the future. Isn't He much more concerned with what you are than with what you accomplish, and isn't what you are demonstrated by the relationships you have? And isn't the most profound of those relationships the one you have with your wife? Have you left your wife? We pray she will take you back."[4]

Have You "Left" Your Spouse?

They also have provided the following checklist for leaders to test whether or not they have "left" their spouses. If you answer yes to most of these statements, perhaps you've already "left" your spouse or are in the process of "leaving":

How Do You Stand? Check All That Apply:
( ) I usually take work home at night.
( ) I haven't had a date with my spouse in two weeks.
( ) I don't have a date with my spouse listed in my appointment book.
( ) I usually work away from home more than ten hours each day.
( ) We have had two fights in the last two weeks.
( ) We haven't had a fight in five years.
( ) I have four or more years education beyond my spouse.
( ) We married before I was called to my present task.
( ) Our youngest child is 16–20 years old.
( ) My spouse hasn't been on a trip with me in four years.
( ) Most of our social relationships revolve around my work.
( ) The family dinner is often interrupted by phone calls for me.
( ) My spouse has little understanding of how my organization works.
( ) My spouse has had no additional formal education since we were married.
( ) My spouse does not have any career plans outside of our marriage.[5]

A concluding thought. Aside from the general observations identified thus far, this area of the spousal relationship is one in which the Bible does not provide many actual examples. In other words, Scripture instructs us how to properly love and care for our spouses, but it doesn't provide many cases of extended dialogue between husband and wife, especially about the kinds of issues which dominate contemporary marriage relationships. While we gain quite a few insights into the wives of Abraham, Job, and Jacob, we know little about the wives of Joseph, Peter, Joshua, and Moses. And we're in the dark similarly with Ruth, Esther,

Deborah, and Naomi. We don't know for sure just what roles they played in the ministries of their husbands.

Take Moses, for instance. We do know that when God called Moses to return to Egypt from his forty years of shepherding, he returned with his wife and two sons: "So Moses took his wife and sons, put them on a donkey and started back to Egypt. And he took the staff of God in his hand" (Ex. 4:20). But during the Exodus, Zipporah and her sons returned to her father in Midian and only occasionally did they visit Moses thereafter (see 18:2, 5). Why this arrangement? We are never told.

Leaders and Their Children

While donors, deacons, and many others can get the leader's attention with little effort, the leader's children often are not so fortunate. As a general observation, children can survive with minimal attention. And some get precious little from their leader/parent. Alternatively, children will take as much time as they are given.

The Biblical Perspective

Let's look first at some biblical observations about the leader's involvement with his children. According to the Old Testament, God clearly expected parents to teach children biblical truths because without them the nation of Israel would not long survive. They were to teach God's commandments to their children constantly, regardless of the situation. This included not only verbal instruction, but also instruction by example and by the use of visual aids.

Impress them on your children. Talk about them when you sit at home and when you walk along the road, when you lie down and when you get up. Tie them as symbols on your hands and bind them on your foreheads. Write them on the doorframes of your houses and on your gates (Deut. 6:7-9).

Teach them to your children, talking about them when you sit at home and when you walk along the road, when you lie down and when you get up. Write them on the doorframes of your houses and on your gates, so that your days and the days of your children may be many in the land that the Lord swore to give your forefathers, as many as the days that the heavens are above the earth (11:19-21).

Take to heart all the words I have solemnly declared to you this day, so that you may command your children to obey carefully all the words of this Law. They are not just idle words for you — they are your life. By them you will live long in the land you are crossing the Jordan to possess (32:46-47).

This concern for children is additionally set forth in Psalm 78:4: "We will not hide them from their children; we will tell the next generation the praiseworthy deeds of the Lord, His power, and the wonders He has done."

In brief, a leader has a responsibility for the biblical education of his family. Good books which provide input for parents on the subject of rearing children are numerous. The purpose of this discussion is not to duplicate them. Instead, I want to set forth some of the ways the leader might work at this important priority.

Be flexible. Leaders might not be able to follow some formalized plan. What worked with our children when they were preschoolers, for example, will not work as they have become young adults. Not only have we changed, but they have also changed and so have our schedules.

When our children were younger, much of my schedule change was driven by my position as a college president and by the accelerated number of after-school and weekend activities the children found themselves involved with. However, we always found that the four teachable moments mentioned in Deuteronomy 6 (when we get up in the morning, at mealtime, when we take trips together, and at bedtime) remained teachable moments regardless of the children's ages. Teachable moments were not always capable of being scheduled. They presented themselves at various times and in various ways.

Our goal as parents, therefore, was to be with our children as much as we could (both individually and together) to make the most of those teachable moments. We also discovered a number of other practical things which worked well for us as a family. First, we tried to have breakfast out with one of the children each Sunday morning before church. Since we have three children, I would take each one for three weeks and then my wife would do likewise. We did this for more than ten years. It was fun for us to see the changes in the nature of conversation. The children always looked forward to that special alone time with each of us.

Find common interests. Take up some family recreational activities that you all can enjoy together. For example, our family enjoys snow skiing and water sports. It's one thing for parents to drag children forward into an adult world. It's quite another to actually enter theirs. Our children loved camping. Our preference would have been a nice quiet motel (safe from all of the elements . . . rain, cold, dampness). They loved the adventure and the constant activity. Effort must be taken to find commonness. Relationships with children take on new dimensions and are enriched as both parents and children strive to live in each other's worlds.

Keep home and office separate. Avoid taking work home from the office. I mean this in two ways. First, I mean it psychologically. Leaders have to work hard to make sure the problems of the office don't become the problems of the home. Second, I refer to physical work—I usually don't bring home a briefcase stuffed full of office business every night.

When the children were much smaller, they couldn't understand why Daddy couldn't play when he was home. Somehow, I was unable to translate "I must study" or "I have this report to complete" into "children-ese." As a result, I changed my habits so that when I was home from the office I was usually available to spend time with my family.

Emphasize the positive aspects of leadership. Repeatedly emphasize the nonmaterial benefits of leadership to your family. Often it's easy to focus on the detriments of being a leader. To be sure there are many. But benefits also abound.

Our children, for example, have gotten to meet many interesting people whom we have hosted in our home. They have often traveled with us to speaking engagements, and we have taken side-tours of interest to them. Plus, we've had the additional benefit of uninterrupted "talk" time which travel affords.

Plan for the long term. Raise your children to be independent self-starters. Start this training at an early age, gradually giving them more and more autonomy as they mature. Some have argued that children should be capable of being fully independent of their parents by age eighteen. There are major differences in North America on this point as in many other parts of the world, the young person doesn't leave home until married.

I share these observations about children knowing full well that being parents who desire godliness for their children does not necessarily assure godly children. There are frequent Scripture references, for example, where a godly leader was followed by an ungodly son who was followed by a godly son and so on. Just reread 1–2 Kings or 1–2 Chronicles and you'll get the picture! As leader/parents, then, all the Lord asks is that we simply do our best and continually cast our children on Him and His grace.

Summary

There are fewer higher priorities for the leader than caring for and helping to encourage one's children and spouse. People know this and yet proceed otherwise. Why? Somehow, the task comes across as burdensome. To be sure, work is required. However, love is the most important ingredient. We are to love our spouses as Christ loved the church.

6

Dealing with Sexuality

DIVORCE AND MARITAL infidelity claim an increasing number of Christian leaders each year. The purpose of this chapter is not to identify names or to assign blame. All leaders, however, probably have to admit, at least to themselves, that this issue is a troubling one. As John Stott has observed, "Nobody (with the sole exception of Jesus of Nazareth) has been sexually sinless. There is no question, therefore, of coming to this study with a horrid 'holier-than-thou' attitude of moral superiority."[1]

Modern culture oozes with the overtones of sexuality—and Christians have not escaped its pervasive influence. Indeed, it has even invaded the executive suite. As author Cheryl Forbes has observed:

> Sexuality is one of the oldest means to power. Kings, and the occasional queen, have used it, as have the common husband and wife. It operates in businesses and schools, wherever people intermingle. Of all the means to power—intellectual, financial, psychological—it is the most basic. Everyone practices it, Christians and non-Christians alike. No matter how much we want to avoid it, we cannot talk about power without talking about sex.[2]

Sexuality is part and parcel of almost all television shows, movies, and songs. The Christian response has typically been to ignore the issue of sexuality. We feel comfortable discussing God's love, but quite uncomfortable discussing the love between man and woman. Rarely does one hear a Christian song about love and marriage on religious radio. Thankfully an increasing number of Christian books deal with the subject.

Many Christian organizations are almost totally devoid of women in the executive suite. In the university as well as the business world, Christian or otherwise, women tend not to be in visible positions of leadership in great numbers. Other Christian nonprofit organizations reflect a similar pattern. Why? Part of the problem may be the belief, by some, that God may have distributed His gifts on the basis of sex. Another element in not having women in the executive suite may be in part related to sexuality. Men in the Christian culture have not been used to having to compete with women as peers. What's more, women in the executive suite may create uncomfortable situations when typical professional assignments, such as overnight travel to meetings and conventions, are necessary.

Dealing with Sexuality

Though others are more qualified to write about this subject, I would nevertheless like to offer a few observations. First, leaders must accept and harness their sexuality. Stott notes:

> We are all sexual beings. Our sexuality, according to both Scripture and experience, is basic to our humanness. Angels may be sexless; we humans are not. When God made humankind, he made us male and female. So to talk about sex is to touch a point close to the center of our personality. Our very identity is being discussed, and perhaps either endorsed or threatened. So the subject demands an unusual degree of sensitivity.[5]

We can't deny the way God made us. The sexual drive is a powerful one. Accordingly, the leader who takes the attitude, "I never have to worry about that," is quickly going to be in trouble. Indeed, the intensity of this normal part of who we are should prepare us to be on our guard about sexual improprieties.

Adultery — The Causes

In my discussions with leaders who have failed in this area, they usually observe that sexual sin is not always premeditated. Further, it doesn't always result from a lack of love or affection for one's spouse. Rather, it results from the frequency of contact and time spent together on the job. As Forbes observes: "Sexual response between men and women is always present and nearly automatic. We need to recognize this, and though we can't dispel it completely, we can avoid deliberately using sexuality for power."[4]

The secular literature, for example, when describing the boss/secretary relationship often refers to the secretary as the "office wife." As Pascale and Athos note, "One's secretary is often one's lone outpost of the personal in an otherwise largely impersonal organizational world."[5] This is not to suggest that the sexual intimacy of the husband/wife relationship is present, but other similarities to the husband/wife relationship certainly may be. The exhortation to the leader then, "Be on your guard," is highly appropriate.

I want to make it clear that I am not assigning culpability for sexual sin only to the "other women," or the "other man" a leader works with. Obviously, the responsibility to be prudent is both on the leader and on those being led. Many male leaders, for example, tend to place the blame for their sexual downfall on other women: "My wife failed to meet my needs," "I was seduced." Unconsciously, many male leaders hold to the assumption: "If women aren't seducing righteous men of God now, they are at least destroying their sexuality and weakening their wills."[6] As

Forbes notes, "The excuse is as old as Adam, and just as morally corrupt now as it was then."[7]

Just Say No

Leaders—both men and women—simply have to say no to sexual temptations. They must remember that God is not in the business of tempting people:

> When tempted, no one should say, "God is tempting me." For God cannot be tempted by evil, nor does He tempt anyone; but each one is tempted when, by his own evil desire, he is dragged away and enticed. Then, after desire has conceived, it gives birth to sin; and sin, when it is full-grown, gives birth to death (James 1:13-15).

Biblical Examples of Moral Failure and Its Consequences

The models of leadership in Scripture, particularly in the Old Testament, suggest that the issue of sexuality has been a problem throughout history. God's Word on the issue, however, has always been clear. Don't do it. The Bible is filled with examples of moral failure in leadership. For example, King David's act of adultery with Bathsheba. Here, David's consummated lust produced tragic consequences for his family and others, a poor example that was followed countless times by his descendants, always with the same result.

> This is what the Lord says: "Out of your household I am going to bring calamity upon you. Before your very eyes I will take your wives and give them to one who is close to you, and he will lie with your wives in broad daylight. You did it in secret, but I will do this thing in broad daylight before all Israel.... But because by doing this you have made the enemies of the Lord show utter contempt, the son born to you will die" (2 Sam. 12:11-12, 14).

Not content with only one woman, David's son Solomon took his father's sexual proclivities ad extremis. Predictably, Solomon's excessive preoccupation with sex and women led to his downfall:

King Solomon, however, loved many foreign women besides Pharaoh's daughter—Moabites, Ammonites, Edomites, Sidonians and Hittites. . . . He had seven hundred wives of royal birth and three hundred concubines, and his wives led him astray. As Solomon grew old, his wives turned his heart after other gods, and his heart was not fully devoted to the Lord his God (1 Kings 11:1, 3-4).

There are many other examples of leaders in the Bible who played "fast and loose" in the area of sexuality, and all were eventually punished for their sinfulness. The Bible is clear on the subject of sexuality—intimacy should take place only in the context of marriage. The Bible gives numerous, clear warnings against sexual sin. When confronted with sexual temptation, the believer must also rely on the Holy Spirit. This Spirit, and the wisdom provided, gives the Christian the insight necessary to look beyond the temporary pleasures of the visible world to the eternal rewards that obedience to God's will brings.

Wisdom will protect you from the smooth talk of a sinful woman, who breaks her wedding vows and leaves the man she married when she was young. The road to her house leads down to the dark world of the dead. Visit her, and you will never find the road to life again (Prov. 2:16-19, CEV).

The words of an immoral woman may be sweet as honey and as smooth as olive oil. But all that you really get from being with her is bitter poison and pain. If you follow her, she will lead you down to the world of the dead. She has missed the path that leads to life and doesn't even know it. My son, listen to me and do everything I say. Stay away from a bad woman! Don't even go near the door of her house. You will lose your self-respect and end up in debt to some cruel person for the rest of your life (5:3-9, CEV).

You should be faithful to your wife, just as you take water from your own well. And don't be like a stream from which just any woman may take a drink. Save yourself for your wife and don't have sex with other women. Be happy with the wife you married when you were young. She is beautiful and graceful, just like a deer; you should be attracted to her and stay deeply in love. Don't go crazy over a woman who is unfaithful to her own husband! (vv. 15-20, CEV)

The point, again, is for the leader to be ever alert in this area. No leader is immune from temptations, and each must always be prepared with a biblical response. Some leaders handle other kinds of temptations very well; they struggle, however, when dealing with sexual temptation. Perhaps as Paul prayed for deliverance from his "thorn in the flesh," deliverance in this area can likewise be sought. The words of Paul in response to his unanswered prayer are still alive with power:

Three times I prayed to the Lord about this and asked Him to take it away. But His answer was: "My grace is all you need, for My power is greatest when you are weak." I am most happy, then, to be proud of my weaknesses, in order to feel the protection of Christ's power over me. I am content with weaknesses, insults, hardships, persecutions, and difficulties for Christ's sake. For when I am weak, then I am strong (2 Cor. 12:8-10, TEV).

Practical Guidelines for Dealing with Sexuality

What are some practical guidelines that might help combat sexual temptation?

Divert Your Eyes

First, since the eyes and the mind are critically involved with lust, leaders ought to avoid, for example, "stopping to gaze" at hotel and airport newsstands. Buy the newspaper and run.

Watch Television with Caution

When in a hotel room, consider not turning on the TV and rely instead on a radio. Too many times I have found myself tempted to watch an HBO movie ("Of course I can handle it!"), so I have learned that the best defense is simply not to watch the TV. It is important to face the possible temptation and to do what will work to avoid the temptation.

Avoid the Appearance of Impropriety

Always keep your spouse informed of time spent out of the office with a member of the opposite sex, whether at lunch, on a business trip, or otherwise. Your spouse will appreciate your honesty and by so doing you will have achieved a built-in accountability against "secret" meetings.

Sometimes, a "Third Wheel" Is Good

When possible, and when a business trip requires time together away from the office (especially for overnight trips), make sure a third party knows about it, and if possible, make sure another person goes along. The business trip does not always require that "just the two of you" go. Indeed, if you want it to be "just the two of you," perhaps this is an indication that the relationship is already more than just a business one.

Select Movies Which Feed the Soul

Oftentimes, temptation is encouraged by a trip to the theater. And the movie which is receiving all of the awards may often produce some malnutrition while fueling lust. Spouses can be of tremendous help in encouraging the best choices, not necessarily the popular ones.

Other guidelines could be suggested, but my chief point is this: in order to reflect sexual purity in lifestyle, the leader must be especially alert to and avoid sexual temptation. As Paul admonished us:

> You also say, "Food is meant for our bodies, and our bodies are meant for food." But I tell you that God will destroy them both. We are not supposed to do indecent things with our bodies. We are to use them for the Lord who is in charge of our bodies. . . . Don't you know that a man who does that becomes part of her body? The Scriptures say, "The two of them will be like one person." But anyone who is joined to the Lord is one in spirit with him.
>
> Don't be immoral in matters of sex. That is a sin against your own body in a way that no other sin is. You surely know that your body is a temple where the Holy Spirit lives. The Spirit is in you and is a gift from God. You are no longer your own own. God paid a great price for you. So use your body to honor God (1 Cor. 6:13, 16-20, CEV).

While this chapter may make some uncomfortable, the issues raised are real. And leaders and spouses need to squarely address both the opportunities for success and failure.

Leaders need to take every reasonable step to ensure the integrity of the soul in this particular area. To be sure, forward visionary leadership is enhanced by the inner qualities of the soul.

Yet as important as this issue is in both marriage and leadership, there is sometimes reluctance to face it. Perhaps there is not time. Perhaps fear prevents disclosure. As my wife Marylou has written:

Lack of time is a real problem. Consequently, the "hot issues" get set aside. Since it takes too much time and energy to work through these tough and sometimes painful issues, [couples] avoid them and keep conversation at the "safe" level. But below the surface lies a dangerous faultline, and pressure is building.[8]

Paul's words or caution and encouragement in Galatians 6, bear repeating:

My friends, if someone is caught in any kind of wrongdoing, those of you who are spiritual should set him right; but you must do it in a gentle way. And keep an eye on yourselves, so that you will not be tempted, too. Help carry one another's burdens, and in this way you will obey the law of Christ" (Gal 6:1-2, TEV).

This is particularly good advice to husbands and wives and leaders in this important area.

7

The Personal Burden of Leadership

IN CHAPTER 18 I will explain that one ought not be in a position of leadership without a clear sense from the Lord that he or she is God's choice for the position. The burdens are too great and the stress too significant. If the leader is considering a formal leadership function, then the question must be asked: just what are the burdens of leadership and who has the responsibility for them?

This issue was squarely faced by Moses in Numbers 11. It seems that the Exodus from Egypt was certainly nothing to write home about. Even though the people were initially delighted to leave the land of bondage, they soon began to compare their enslaved lives in Egypt with their nomadic existence in the desert. They had complained about food so the Lord provided manna. Indeed, it must have seemed to Moses that all the people found time to do was complain:

The people began to complain to the Lord about their troubles. When the Lord heard them, He became angry and sent fire on the people. It burned among them and destroyed one end of the camp. The people cried out to Moses for help; he prayed to the Lord, and the fire died down. So the place was named Taberah, because there the fire of the Lord burned among them.

There were foreigners traveling with the Israelites. They had a strong craving for meat, and even the Israelites themselves began to complain: "If only we could have some meat! In Egypt we used to eat all the fish we wanted, and it cost us nothing. Remember the cucumbers, the watermelons, the leeks, the onions, and the garlic we had? But now our strength is gone. There is nothing at all to eat—nothing but this manna day after day!" (Num. 11:16, TEV)

Further, the complaining was not just an isolated event, for the Scripture states that "Moses heard all the people complaining as they stood around in groups at the entrances of their tents" (v. 10, TEV). Knowing they don't have the ability to meet every "need" presented to them, few things discourage leaders more than being constantly reminded of all that the organization ought to be doing but is not. This is particularly the case since words of praise or appreciation are infrequently shared with leaders. Again, people ought to have opportunities to make ongoing suggestions for improvement.

One of the priorities I try to regularly engage in at the Bible Society is to provide time for staff to meet me in open sessions to raise issues/questions which are on their minds. While I enjoy being with staff, the sessions usually produce many more concerns than they do praises. And this seems to be true no matter how much progress is or isn't being made. I've also experienced this with other organizations. And yet these kinds of opportunities are vital because they give staff the opportunity to "vent" and that is very important for enhancing staff morale. As one of our staff said to me as I closed one of these sessions, "Thanks for listening and for giving us the opportunity to share concerns." In these kind of sessions, I find that it is important to keep people focused on issues and not on people. I want us to be tough on issues yet tender with people. We should also recognize that organizational satisfaction may mean complacency, thus making it more difficult to change and go after organizational excellence.

Dissatisfaction: The Basis of Leadership Excellence

Consultant Lawrence Miller has argued that: "Satisfaction and excellence are inherently in conflict. Satisfaction implies acceptance of things as they are. And Harvard professor John Kotter argues that it's difficult for organizations to go forward with change where there is sense of satisfaction with the status quo. Dissatisfaction is the source of motivation. It leads to actions to change that which is the source of discomfort. The achievement of excellence can occur only if the organization promotes a culture of creative dissatisfaction."[1] According to John Stott, without this kind of creative dissatisfaction, there may not be any organizational vision:

So what is vision? It is an act of seeing, of course, an imaginative perception of things, combining insight and foresight. But more particularly, in the sense in which I am using the word, it is compounded by a deep dissatisfaction with what is and a clear grasp of what could be. It begins with indignation over the status quo, and it grows into the earnest quest for an alternative.[2]

Creative Dissatisfaction versus Negative Complaining

Leaders, then, ought to value expressions of creative dissatisfaction. The Israelites, unfortunately, were not involved with the expression of creative dissatisfaction, but of negative complaining. Indeed, their complaining had a devastating effect on Moses. He told God, in fact, that if He didn't have a better idea, he wanted to be put to death. He expressed his frustration to the Lord this way:

Why have You brought this trouble on Your servant? What have I done to displease You that You put the burden of all these people on me? Did I conceive all these people? Did I give them birth? Why do You tell me to carry them in my arms, as a nurse carries an infant, to the land You promised on oath to their forefathers? Where can I get meat for all these people? They keep wailing to me, "Give us meat to eat!" I cannot carry all these people by myself; the burden is too heavy for me. If this is how You are going to treat me, *put me to death right now* — if I have found favor in Your eyes — and do not let me face my own ruin (Num. 11:11-15, italics added).

Leaders today ask the very same questions. "Lord, why did You bring me to this place? Lord, how come I did not know everything that was wrong with this place when I said yes to Your call? Lord, I want to be someplace else, someplace better — and someplace that doesn't have these kinds of problems." God must smile sometimes as He sees us go through periods like these. He knows, as do we, that He's in the business of delivering us in our circumstances, not from them. He wants us to remember His words to Israel:

But now, this is what the Lord says — He who created you, O Jacob, He who formed you, O Israel: "Fear not, for I have redeemed you; I have called you by name; *you are Mine.* When you pass through the waters, *I will be with you;* and when you pass through the rivers, they will not sweep over you" (Isa. 43:1-2, italics added).

His answer now is the same as His answer to Moses then: "Is the Lord's arm too short? You will now see whether or not what I say will come true for you" (Num. 11:23). Just what did He do for Moses? How did He deal with Moses' burden? God responded in two ways. First, He agreed to a plan of dispersed leadership (a concept discussed in chap. 1 of this book) by changing the organizational flowchart:

The Lord said to Moses: "Bring Me seventy of Israel's elders who are known to you as leaders and officials among the people. Have them come to the Tent of Meeting, that they may stand there with you. I will come down and speak with you there, and I will take of the Spirit that is on you and put the Spirit on them. They will help you carry the burden of the people so that you will not have to carry it alone" (Num. 11:16-17).

In essence, God identified other persons who could help Moses, the leader, carry the load.

The second way God responded to Moses' plea regarding his burden was by providing a tangible answer to a tangible need. The people clamored for meat and God provided meat. God still is in the business of responding to tangible needs. Numerous Christian leaders could testify as to how God has tangibly met the needs of their organizations. I count myself among them.

This, then, needs to be emphasized: The organizational burden is not solely the leader's; it is also the Lord's. The solution for carrying the burden might include institutional reorganization, delegation, and greater attention to dispersed leadership. And we see that God may respond directly to the need which triggered the "complaint" in the first place.

The Art of Carrying Burdens

The desire to have a burden-free existence is noble but, at the same time, naive. The record of Scripture constantly presents examples of leaders with burdens of various kinds. Alternatively, from Adam to Abraham, from David to Daniel, we see a God who is constantly at work delivering people, not from their circumstances but in them.

The burdens of leadership are no different. There is then no such thing as problem-free leadership or problem-free organizations. The question then becomes, how do we cope?

Cast Your Burdens on the Lord

First, we are told to cast our burdens on the Lord. We are told to commit our ways to the Lord: "Commit your way to the Lord; trust in Him and He will do this" (Ps. 37:5). We are told to acknowledge Him in all our ways: "With all your heart you must trust the Lord and not your own judgment. Always let Him lead you, and He will clear the road for you to follow" (Prov. 3:5-6, CEV).

All of you young people should obey your elders. In fact, everyone should be humble toward everyone else. The Scriptures say, "God opposes proud people, but He helps everyone who is humble." Be humble in the presence of God's mighty power, and He will honor you when the time comes. God cares for you, so turn all your worries over to Him (1 Peter 5:5-7, CEV).

Share Your Burdens with Others

Assuming I have done this, then what? Several other suggestions are appropriate. First, we are to share our burdens with others: "Help carry one another's burdens, and in this way you will obey the law of Christ" (Gal. 6:2, TEV). I can't have someone else help me with my burden if I don't share it, and not very many leaders are good sharers of burdens. Why? Probably one reason is that they have gotten "burned" for having done so.

This is why accountability groups are so important in leadership. It is necessary to be in a group where leaders and leader-couples can be accountable to one another and where leaders can be candid and frank. A second suggestion is that leaders are not to carry burdens that they ought not deal with in the first place. Many leaders, for instance, "carry the world on their shoulders" when all God wants them to do is carry a small piece of it. Many leaders worry or carry "wrong" burdens when God wants them to carry "right" burdens. For example, note the following verses:

Don't worry about anything, but pray about everything. With thankful hearts offer up your prayers and requests to God. Then, because you belong to Christ Jesus, God will bless you with peace that no one can completely understand. And this peace will control the way you think and feel (Phil. 4:6-7, CEV).

I don't believe these verses tell me that I should be unconcerned or unburdened about a world which has no hope. I don't believe these verses tell me I should have no concern for my children, my wife, or for the organization I lead. Paul, for example, lists his burdens in 2 Corinthians 11. After enumerating a long list, he notes the following additional one: "And not to mention other things, every day I am under the pressure of my concern for all the churches" (v. 28, TEV). Many leaders could make similar statements. I believe the point of the Philippians passage, then, is that we are to focus our concerns on the right burdens, burdens which God will help us carry, burdens such as those represented by the following verses:

Then you will live a life that honors the Lord, and you will always please Him by doing good deeds. You will come to know God even better (Col. 1:10, CEV).

In conclusion, my friends, fill your minds with those things that are good, true, noble, right, pure, lovely, and honorable. Put into practice what you learned and received from me, both from my words and from my actions. And the God who gives us peace will be with you (Phil. 4:8, TEV).

You have been raised to life with Christ, so set your hearts on the things that are in heaven, where Christ sits on His throne at the right side of God. Keep your minds fixed on things there, not on things here on earth (Col. 3:1-2, TEV).

What kinds of concerns are we to avoid? Jesus gives us one such list recorded in Matthew 6:25-34 (TEV):

This is why I tell you: do not be worried about the food and drink you need in order to stay alive, or about clothes for your body. After all, isn't life worth more than food? And isn't the body worth more than clothes? Look at the birds: they do not plant seeds, gather a harvest and put in barns; yet your Father in heaven takes care of them! Aren't you worth much more than birds? Can any of you live a bit longer by worrying about it?

And why worry about clothes? Look how the wild flowers grow: they do not work or make clothes for themselves. But I tell you that not even King Solomon with all his wealth had clothes as beautiful as one of these flowers. It is God who clothes the wild grass — grass that is here today and gone tomorrow, burned up in the oven. Won't He be all the more sure to clothe you? What little faith you have!

So do not start worrying: "Where will my food come from? or my drink? or my clothes?" (These are the things the pagans are always concerned about.) Your Father in heaven knows that you need all these things. Instead, be concerned above everything else with the Kingdom of God and with what He requires of you, and He will provide you with all these other things. So do not worry about tomorrow; it will have enough worries of its own. There is no need to add to the troubles each day brings.

In short, the list includes our lives (though it doesn't follow that we should be reckless or abuse our God-given temple), food and drink, and the kind of clothes we wear. We're also told not to worry about the burden of tomorrow. When we couple our faith in the power of Christ with the burden we carry, we practice conscientious Christian living. When we carry our burden without coupling it to faith in an all-powerful God, we'll end up being preoccupied with worry.

The exhortation "not to worry" in the Philippians passage follows with ways to make sure that we don't. First, we present our burdens to the Lord in prayer or petition. We give them to Him. Second, we wrap those petitions with praise or thanksgiving. When Hezekiah was faced with the burden of seemingly insurmountable odds militarily, he had no other option than to give the situation to God:

And [Hezekiah] prayed, "Almighty Lord, God of Israel, seated above the winged creatures, You alone are God, ruling all the kingdoms of the world. You created the earth and the sky. Now, Lord, hear us and look at what is happening to us. Listen to all the things that Sennacherib is saying to insult You, the living God. We all know, Lord, that the emperors of Assyria have destroyed many nations, made their lands desolate, and burned up their gods—which were no gods at all, only images of wood and stone made by human hands. Now, Lord our God, rescue us from the Assyrians, so that all the nations of the world will know that You alone are God" (Isa. 37:15-20, TEV).

And God gave him a tremendous victory. Jehoshaphat faced similar adversity with similar results:

Jahaziel said, "Your Majesty and all you people of Judah and Jerusalem, the Lord says that you must not be discouraged or be afraid to face this large army. The battle depends on God, not on you. . . . You will not have to fight this battle. Just take up your positions and wait; you will see the Lord give you victory. People of Judah and Jerusalem, do not hesitate or be afraid. Go out to battle, and the Lord will be with you!" (2 Chron. 20:15, 17, TEV)

Leaders often have no other option but to give their burden to the Lord. This is what God desires all along. When we who are leaders give our burdens to the Lord, the Philippians passage suggests that we will experience the peace of God, and further, that that peace will transcend all our understanding. And neither our hearts nor our minds will be preoccupied otherwise. Indeed, when burdens are given to Him, we can sigh with relief. This is the only way a leader can keep a "cool head," so to speak, during a particularly burdensome time.

Write Down "Your" Burdens

I have faced many tough issues in leadership. I have spent sleepness nights praying for and struggling with potential answers. Almost in every instance, it has helped to write down my concerns. There are times when an early morning/ late night memorandum to "file" has brought great clarity and perspective to an otherwise hopeless situation.

Be Prepared to "Walk Away from" the Problem

For some leaders, knowing that they have the option to walk away from a position of leadership is a tremendous help. By "walking away" I mean moving on to a different activity to totally change the mental landscape. This provides both freedom and clarity. Attending a concert, taking time off, a short vacation, and similar activities are what I have in mind here. I once had a staff member who "walked away" on weekends by resigning on Friday night and unresigning on Monday morning — all along keeping this decision solely to himself. This "walking away" provided wonderful release and perspective which allowed for appropriate progress the next week.

I cannot close this chapter without noting that sometimes God chooses to increase, rather than decrease, the complexity of issues or burdens, so that it forces us to totally depend on Him for solutions. A clear biblical example of this is Gideon, where God had him reduce the already outnumbered army still further. Why? So there would be no mistaking that God was the source of deliverance (Jud. 7).

I remind myself of this and then refocus myself accordingly. He really does want the burdens of leadership. I must remember that the more grave the situation, the more willing I must be to turn the burden over to Him. The result? The greater the praise and glory which goes to the Heavenly Father when victory results.

> The burdens laid upon us were so great and so heavy that we gave up all hope of staying alive. We felt that the death sentence had been passed on us. But this happened so that we should rely, not on ourselves, but only on God, who raises the dead (2 Cor. 1:8-9, TEV).

8

Personal Renewal

THE BURDEN OF leadership can cause quite a drain on one's peace of mind, so in this chapter we want to look at personal renewal in leadership. In particular, I want to discuss the subject of the Sabbath as a potential key to personal renewal.

The Bible offers numerous examples that help our perspective on personal renewal. Paul, for example, had as a driving concern a desire for spiritual renewal. He desired that those who knew Christ would be transformed by the renewing of their minds (Rom. 12:2). Paul knew that being committed to Christ would change the way people lived. And the rest of Romans 12 spells out some of the evidences of spiritual renewal.

Reasons We Need Renewal

If we were to list danger points in contemporary Christian leadership, inattention to personal renewal would come very high on the list. For many leaders, the norm would probably look like this: neglected family priorities, neglected physical fitness priorities, and neglected spiritual priorities. I have talked with enough people in organizational leadership to know that this is a monumental problem. Few leaders will lie on their deathbed wishing they had spent more time in the office and less time with their families.

Fewer still will be able to identify with Paul's statement that he stayed the course of his calling. We all know of our need for renewal, yet we neglect it. Why? Better yet, why do we have these concerns for personal renewal in the first place?

John Gardner, in his classic, *Self-Renewal*, suggests that we all stagnate as people if we don't involve ourselves in activities of renewal:

> "Keep on growing," the commencement speakers say. "Don't go to seed. Let this be a beginning, not an ending." It is a good theme. Yet a high proportion of the young people who hear the speeches pay no heed, and by the time they are middle-aged they are absolutely mummified. As we mature we progressively narrow the scope and variety of our lives. We become caught in a web of fixed relationships. We develop set ways of doing things. The most stubborn protector of his own vested interest is the man who has lost the capacity for self-renewal.[1]

Personal experience affirms Gardner's observations. We need to be pursuing personal renewal because some would say that leadership is tougher now than in earlier generations. They argue that the complexity of the leadership challenge is continuing to accelerate. A recent comment by Harvard professor John Kotter illustrates this view. Addressing the personal requirements needed for leaders, he states: "Even in the simplest conditions a variety of things are needed to create the vision and strategy, and to elicit the teamwork and motivation. But simple conditions are not the norm any more. *Complexity is the norm*" (emphasis mine).[2] He then notes the varying degrees of incremental complexity given the nature of the organization, the number and kind of people involved, and the technology used.

Further, longevity in a significant position of organizational leadership, whether as pastor of a church, president of a nonprofit organization, or head coach of an athletic team, tends to be the exception, rather than the rule. Kotter observes that one of the key ingredients in effective leadership is "a tremendous energy level and a deep desire to use that energy for supplying leadership."[3] Anyone who has held or who holds a position of leadership knows the need for high energy. And a tired or exhausted leader will rarely be effective.

As my wife, Marylou, has expressed it, "Leaders tend to be high-energy, workaholics. . . . They thrive on challenges, on giving that extra surge of adrenalin to attack one more problem, schedule one more meeting, make one more trip. 'I'll rest later,' they say. And the world rewards this behavior — 'The more you do, the better you must be.' "[4]

Factors Which Prevent Renewal

Why do we leaders in organizations struggle so much with personal renewal? Some of the most common reasons include fear of failure, greed, pressure to succeed, and the need for prestige.

Fear of Failure

First, there is the press of our egos. No leader wants to fail or to be involved with what management consultant, Kets de Vries, calls the "F-dimension (failure factor)."[5] So all of our personal time and energy is spent on the organizational agenda and its health rather than incorporating and merging together our personal and family agenda.

While personal family failures become more and more acceptable in society, few leaders want to say, "And the organization lost its way during my administration." And every leader wants to be seen as deserving the trust the organization has given.

In spite of religious rhetoric such as "God has called me elsewhere," leaders look for the right opportunity to leave "failing" organizations. Few leave thriving enterprises that are financially solid and spiritually sound. People want to be part of a "winner." Leaders are no different. And many are driven by ego to make sure their organization stays or becomes a "winner." Many do so at great personal and physical cost. Many leave their organization hoping naively that a change of scenery, problems, and people will help them become renewed.

Greed

One of the unspoken rules in an organization is that enough is never enough. If the organization is a church, a better and bigger building, more programs, more staff and, obviously, more money are needed. The same can be said about almost any other kind of Christian organization. We assert our belief in a God who claims He is capable of meeting our needs. Yet we always need more! As a result, no matter how long leaders work, "they" never get everything done.

Christian leaders pick up on this "but more is needed" philosophy and become enslaved to it. Since there are so many needing spiritual help, I must always say "yes" to invitations to speak. Since money is always needed, I must make all the fund-raising calls I can. I must get into as many churches or homes as I can. Church families need me; staff need me; donors need me; and the list continues. Pastors and other leaders willingly spend this time for the organizations they serve, convincing themselves that the shepherd is to lay down his life for the sheep. The extreme needs of the church "justify" less attention to family needs. The wife of a leader friend of ours told us that she and her husband seldom spent alone time. Even on vacations there were calls to make, people to see, for the organization. As one writer has put it, "You as the leader have such a heavy responsibility of daily prayer for your people that you may have to limit the amount of time you pray for yourself and your own family."[6]

Pressure

The press of the job is a third reason for personal burnout. Leadership responsibilities have become more complex, so more time is needed just to stay on top of the job. Seldom is the "learning" finished, the planning completed, or the envisioning finalized.

One of the practices I had followed for years was going to the office on Saturday mornings to do creative work—to write and to dream. Yet during my years as a college president, I regularly went to the office on Saturdays just to catch up. Many leaders can identify with this sense of being consumed by the job. And the danger from this can be deadly when the work holds a high enjoyment level.

Prestige

A fourth reason we fail to pursue personal renewal is that we have a seemingly built-in drive for promotion and prestige. We become uncomfortable with our "current situation in life" and therefore want to "minister" at a bigger church, or a bigger organization. We want the prestige that comes from working somewhere (anywhere other than where we are) that the secular world thinks is "big time." And we know that we won't be recognized for our achievements (by another organization elsewhere) if we don't overachieve in our current position. So we work excessive hours to try to prove to others that we not only are worthy of the position we hold, but also to demonstrate that we deserve to be given a chance at something "bigger" and "better."

This attitude, and all of us have battled it at one time or another, ignores the biblical teaching that our work is always done for the Lord, not for an organization. John also cautions us about a preoccupation with "the pride of life" or the "boastings of what he has and does." Such thoughts come "not from the Father but from the world" (1 John 2:16).

One of the best stories I have heard on this topic was told by a veteran missionary who protested the fact that God had called him to the mission field, and apparently into seeming oblivion, while all of his friends back home were "achieving" more important and "recognizable" things. As this dear saint listened for God's answer to his tired protest, the response that he heard from the Lord was something like this: "My son, your responsibility is to concern yourself with the depth [what God thinks of you] of your walk with Me. It is My responsibility to handle the breadth [what man thinks of you] of your walk with Me." King David said it this way: "In Your hands are strength and power to exalt and give strength to all" (1 Chron. 29:12). Simply put, a selfish desire for promotion and recognition and the false need to keep proving yourself to others are seldom if ever excuses to ignore personal renewal. Now, where does all of this lead?

The Sabbath and Personal Renewal

While trying to avoid being simplistic in an effort to address this concern for personal renewal, I believe one significant way of approaching this issue of personal renewal is to review the concept of the Sabbath. One of the Ten Commandments, the Sabbath, is a concept Jesus practiced and appeared to both honor and accept (though He did not necessarily follow all of the legalistic requirements that people had added to it).

Many of us grew up at a time when little attention was given to the Sabbath. Other than infrequent references to the fact that Sunday needed to be different, one heard little about this important biblical concept.

After all, the "Sabbath" was an Old Testament concept given under Law, and modern, enlightened Christians are under grace. But upon review, the Scripture (only a small number of illustrative verses will be referred to here) presents the Sabbath as having several important goals that we ought to consider.

The Sabbath As a Day of Rest

The idea of the Sabbath as a day of rest comes to us early in Scripture, starting in Genesis 2:2-3, TEV:

By the seventh day God finished what He had been doing and stopped working. He blessed the seventh day and set it apart as a special day, because by that day He had completed His creation and stopped working.

We don't know why God rested. It was obviously not because He was tired or burned out. But He rested on the seventh day; He blessed the seventh day; He made it holy. So we know from the beginning of Creation that the seventh day was to be different based on what God Himself said about it.

This day-of-rest concept begins to acquire additional meaning in verses like Exodus 20:8; 23:12; 34:21; and 35:1-3. In the first instance — as part of the Ten Commandments — the instruction comes to us that people are to labor and to do all of their work in six days. This applied to families, servants, and to animals as well. The reason for this commandment appears to be God's example in resting on the seventh day of Creation.

Exodus 23:12, TEV suggests "rest" both for people and animals as being one of the results of the Sabbath: "Work six days a week, but do no work on the seventh day, so that your slaves and the foreigners who work for you and even your animals can rest." In this regard I would note that while refreshment may not be the sole purpose of the Sabbath, it is at least one of the purposes for it. Additional Scriptures (here I have in mind verses like 31:12-14 and Lev. 23:3) expand the significance of the Sabbath Day concept to include the covenant God made between Himself and the people. The reference in Leviticus includes the idea of it being a "day of sacred assembly."

For our limited purposes I want to highlight only the rest and refreshment aspects of the Sabbath Day. Whatever else may be its significance, one main purpose of the Sabbath is that once every seven days there ought not be any work done of the type one normally does the other six days.

Outcomes of the day include rest (both personal and corporate), refreshment, and sacred assembly before the Lord.

It's interesting to note that in other parts of the world this day of rest has a decidedly different focus. In Egypt, for example, when I asked why there were no young people in the morning service, I was told that Sunday was a school and workday in this predominately Muslim country. And in Russia and Ghana, the day is used to celebrate the goodness of the Lord with other members of the church. And many times the whole day will focus on this time together with the family of God.

Yet in the West, sometimes leaders dread Sundays. Why? Because for many, Sunday is a day of exhaustion. Invitations to speak at churches take leaders away from their family for the whole day (as well as away from the local church) and often the Saturday night before if the church is some distance away. And often, the days away fall on family days of celebration.

I am not prepared to make a long list of suggestions about Sabbath Day activity other than to note that as we approach our Sabbath, we need to have answers for questions such as these: Will what we have planned for our family produce rest and refreshment for us? Will our plans include seeing this day as holy to the Lord (I don't intend to suggest here that other days ought not be holy or further suggest a secular/sacred dichotomy) and as a day of blessing? How will we address the need for sacred assembly? How will we make sure we will not be doing "work" normally done on the other six days of the week on this one? As I wrestled with these types of questions as a younger leader, I reduced outside Sunday speaking engagements at other churches and began to enjoy even more being in our local church on Sundays. Taking the Sabbath more seriously has provided personal renewal for us. For those such as clergy who are busy and at work on this seventh day, an alternate day might result in similar benefits. Perhaps the words of Christ need to be heard once again: "The Sabbath was made for the good of human beings; they were not made for the Sabbath" (Mark 2:27, TEV).

The Sabbath As a Year of Rest

The Scripture also presents the concept of Sabbath as a year of rest for the land. We see this in passages like Leviticus 25:1-7, particularly verses 4 and 5, TEV: "But the seventh year is to be a year of complete rest for the land, a year dedicated to the Lord. Do not plant your fields or prune your vineyards. Do not even harvest the grain that grows by itself without being planted, and do not gather the grapes from your un-pruned vines; it is a year of complete rest for the land."

God gave these commands to the Israelites as they looked forward to going into and caring for the Promised Land. Interestingly, those involved with agriculture today likewise talk about the need to rest the land and to rotate crops. Further, we don't know how following this commandment altered the people's lifestyles during this year of rest for the land. Presumably they still did work, but not in the fields. Perhaps they rebuilt their houses. Perhaps equipment was repaired and new clothes were made. It is not farfetched to suggest that, at a minimum, the Sabbatical Year for the land changed people's routines, work habits, and schedules.

Again, I'm not prepared to make a long list of sugges-tions as to how this might have relevance, if any, to our discussion about personal renewal. However, I have dis-cussed this matter with enough people to know that signifi-cant periods of time, whether one month or several, or indeed up to one year, away from the regular work habit, schedule, and routine can play a very significant part in personal renewal. Aside from all of the many job-related benefits, giving people "sabbaticals" provides opportunities for reflective thinking that otherwise is not possible or prob-able in the usual routine. A sabbatical provides enhanced opportunities for stillness (see Ps. 46:10), quietness, and heightened spiritual awareness.

The education profession in many parts of the world

probably does a better job at providing opportunities for personal renewal than do other professions. "Time off" during the summer provides for changes in routine and schedule. Many educational organizations provide time off through a "sabbatical" program after a requisite number of years of service.

Some countries take this "time off" for renewal with great seriousness. During a trip to Australia, I was interested to learn that, as a matter of public practice, if not policy, persons who have been employed for approximately ten years by the same employer are usually given three months off, fully paid, as a "long service leave" benefit. I believe as Christians we need to address more completely the matter of personal renewal through sabbaticals. I am not arguing for a specific length of sabbatical. What I am suggesting is that the concept of the Sabbath in the Scripture (and I haven't mentioned the related concept of the "Year of Jubilee" set forth in Lev. 25:8-55), both with regard to the "day" and the "year" gives strong biblical precedent for "time off" to be involved with a different routine as necessary for rest and refreshment. Yet if those in positions of leadership don't believe this is important or take personal renewal seriously, then for certain, neither will the people "being led."

The New Testament Concept of Rest

Jesus urges His disciples in Matthew 11:28-30: "Come to Me, all you who are weary and burdened, and I will give you rest. Take My yoke upon you and learn from Me, for I am gentle and humble in heart, and you will find rest for your souls. For My yoke is easy and My burden is light." Additional key references to "rest" are found in the Book of Hebrews, particularly chapter 4. There appear to be several levels of meaning to the biblical concept of rest:

Spiritual Rest As God's True Salvation

First, there is the idea of spiritual rest as God's true salvation is compared with the false religion and burdens of the

Pharisees. Knowing God provides a rest for our souls that can't be satisfied by things or money, power or prestige, or mere religious practices.

Spiritual Rest As Communion with Christ

Second, there is the idea of rest as a daily resting in Christ. As I give my burdens to Him, He gives me rest. As I hide myself in the God of Creation, my perspective changes and so too does my life. This kind of rest doesn't mean we simply stop our work and rest. Rather, it's part of the process of casting our cares on Him and learning from Him, knowing He cares for us. This kind of spiritual rest restores our souls and our minds.

Spiritual Rest As Simple Relaxation

Third, the idea of rest includes the idea of cessation of normal activities and refocusing our time and energies more intently on the Living God. This is in part the kind of rest associated with the Sabbath we talked about earlier. It provides spiritual and physical refreshment.

God desires workers and leaders who are personally refreshed and renewed. Obedient practice to what Jesus Himself modeled in this area will do much to help us in our ongoing pursuit of personal renewal.

Summary

One of the best biblical case studies involving exhaustion, rest, and renewal comes from 1 Kings 18—the story of Elijah. He had performed a powerful miracle involving the prophets of Baal; predicted and was the instrument God used to end a three-year drought; and raced a chariot (and won!). Yet, having experienced these victories, a queen's death threat sent him running for his life. All leaders know the experience of seeing tremendous victories followed by the usual valleys. Elijah was so discouraged that he asked God to: "Take away my life; I might as well be dead" (19:4, TEV).

God intervened directly into the process of renewal for Elijah. First, Elijah slept. Sometimes rest does wonders for renewing the body and spirit. Second, God gave him food to eat (v. 6) and it was a simple meal. Sometimes our tiredness is because of poor eating habits and poor diet. Third, Elijah went back to sleep again. Fourth, he again was awakened and again told to eat and drink and to prepare to take a forty-day journey to Sinai, the mountain of God.

Thus far, Elijah experienced a variety of the steps we have previously discussed:

1. He got away from the busyness of his life;
2. He rested;
3. He ate properly;
4. He engaged in exercise.

All of these are good as far as they go. But the important element in renewal was yet to come and it was this: he had a fresh encounter with the Living God.

And while God comes to us in a variety of ways, and we usually want it to be spectacular, here, God came to Elijah in "the soft whisper of a voice." The important point is that Elijah had positioned himself to hear this "soft whisper." Often we don't experience God because we expect Him to meet us on our terms, not His. And so we miss the word from God because we're in the wrong place and not listening. Both are critical for those who will lead.

The final result? Elijah, after about six weeks "away from his work," and after a fresh encounter with God, was ready once again for service. His example is one from which all of us could benefit.

9

Pursuing Excellence

THE IDEA OF excellence and quality is linked to everything from books and beverages to ball clubs and banks. As one writer has put it:

Excellence is "in"! It is now fashionable to be excellent. Corporations, colleges, and football coaches proclaim their commitment to excellence, while television extravaganzas celebrate what they claim to be examples of excellence. Everyone loves excellence and shuns mediocrity.[1]

Just what is excellence or even Christian excellence? Does it differ from the concept of success? Does it have relevance to leaders of Christian organizations? If so, in what ways? These questions are crucial and it's to their discussion that I now turn.

Excellence Revisited

In recent years probably nothing has done more to trigger widespread discussion of the term excellence than the popular business book by Peters and Waterman, *In Search of Excellence*.[2] To be sure, the book has a number of interesting points. For instance, I like its emphasis on process and people, items which are readily reflected in the book's eight basic principles. I say a hearty "amen" to its observation that "the real role of the chief executive is to manage the values of the organization."[3] And the concept of "management by wandering around" is one that an effective leader is advised to pursue.

As much as I enjoyed reading this book, however, there are parts I struggled with. For example, the authors don't really define what they mean by excellence. My sense is that they are using the term excellence to be synonymous with the term success, and success is defined in fairly straightforward terms—higher profits and better products. In Peters and Waterman's view, by following eight basic steps, a company would be more capable of achieving the kind of success it desired. In essence, these steps become means to the ends of excellence and success—the epitome of corporate achievement. In this domain, excellence has a single dimension that must be served. Obviously, this is not necessarily wrong, because all of us have pursued this kind of "achievement excellence" through accomplished goals—the achievement of a college degree sufficing as but one example.

John Gardner is another who has written extensively on this subject of excellence. In his books *Excellence*[4] and *Self-Renewal*[5] Gardner tends to take a somewhat broader view of the concept of excellence and suggests that it exists in all facets of our society and in a variety of ways.

> There are many varieties of excellence. In the intellectual field alone there are many kinds of excellence. There is the kind of intellectual activity that leads to a new theory and the kind that leads to a new machine. There is the mind that finds its most effective expression in teaching and the mind that is most at home in research. There is the mind that works best in quantitative terms, and the mind that luxuriates in poetic imagery. And there is excellence in art, in music, in craftsmanship, in human relations, in technical work, in leadership, in parental responsibilities.[6]

Gardner suggests that whatever one does should be characterized by a high level of energy and technical competence. One of his more famous quotes in this regard illustrates the point:

An excellent plumber is infinitely more admirable than an incompetent philosopher. The society which scorns excellence in plumbing because plumbing is a humble activity and tolerates shoddiness in philosophy because it is an exalted activity will have neither good plumbing nor good philosophy. Neither its pipes nor its theories will hold water.[7]

High Standards as the Basis of Excellence

Gardner makes several other substantive observations which I believe are useful for this discussion. First, he suggests that there can be no excellence without standards or benchmarks:

Our society cannot achieve greatness unless individuals at many levels of ability accept the need for high standards of performance and strive to achieve those standards within the limits possible for them. We cannot have islands of excellence in a sea of slovenly indifference to standards.[8]

Professor and author Gary Inrig argues correctly, in my opinion, that setting "excellence as the standard is not enough. What is the standard of excellence? How do we identify and measure it?"[9] Discerning the relationship between standards and excellence seems to be one of our primary tasks. We not only have to grapple with the concept of standards in our personal lives (e.g., level of degrees sought after, physical fitness, involvement with family, etc.), but we also have to grapple with it in an organizational setting (e.g., do all personnel, for example, require the same degree of rigor in pursuing excellence in a given task?). Probably many of us can remember experiencing at one time or another during our student days the sense that "I'd rather have a B from her than an A from him." This search for standards, then, particularly in the context of the Christian organization, is one of the most important concerns for leaders. Do we put our emphasis on externals or input standards (e.g., quality of staff, dollars raised), or do we focus on output standards? (e.g., number of people served, etc.)

Two cautions are in order. First, leaders need to beware of searching only for "either/or" solutions because our emphasis should include both types of standards—input and output. Second, leaders must not avoid such a search simply because of its degree of difficulty. Indeed, leaders must be careful not to confuse the "degree of difficulty" and "degree of impossibility." And we must certainly guard against assuming that because certain externals or input standards are present that the standard of excellence is satisfied. Third, we must avoid believing that because we describe ourselves or our organizations as "Christian," that excellence automatically results. We must take the words of the late Quaker philosopher Elton Trueblood to heart: "Holy shoddy is still shoddy."

To summarize, Peters and Waterman, and dozens of other writers, see success as the end result. Excellence is primarily seen as achievement. If it is excellent, success will result. Gardner sees excellence as both means and ends, based on high standards and characterized by self-renewal.

Excellence: A Christian Perspective

There are others who have dismissed "achievement" as the route to success. For example, in *The Success Fantasy*,[10] Anthony Campolo argues that worldly success generally means wealth, power, and prestige with all of its pejorative trappings. He sees this type of success as inconsistent with the teachings of Scripture.

Robert Sandin's *The Search for Excellence*,[11] while not defining excellence or clearly stating standards, implies that excellence, at least in the university world, is characterized by certain external standards. In listing "benchmarks of quality" he includes items such as an institution's finances, its library, instructional, and physical resources, and concludes that colleges with less of these kinds of things, "are . . . less prepared to meet the educational and economic competition of our times."[12]

Two other books by Christian authors are Gary Inrig's *A Call to Excellence*[13] and Jon Johnston's *Christian Excellence*.[14] Inrig notes that excellence is a multidimensional concept that great thinkers have approached from several diverse perspectives. Social excellence involves the proper pursuit of talents and achievements that have social utility.[15] Human excellence involves the development of man or woman as human.[16] Personal excellence reflects the psychological jargon of the self-actualization seekers so prevalent in our culture.[17] Utilitarian excellence is the pursuit of those things that are external ends, such as material possessions or public notoriety.[18] Finally, Inrig discusses technical excellence as levels of skills whether in music, art, science, athletics, etc.[19] He ends up suggesting that excellence for the Christian should focus more on qualities of character represented by the fruit of the Spirit and other such spiritual traits than on pursuing the more worldly, achievement-oriented definitions of excellence.

Johnston juxtaposes success with excellence and argues that Christians ought to be pursuing excellence, not success. For him, "Success is attaining cultural goals . . . and . . . is reserved mostly for those who have made or who are making it big. These people wear clothing with the right labels, eat at the best restaurants."[20] Whereas success is reserved for only the few, excellence can be achieved by everybody. The differences between success and excellence for Johnston are obvious:

Success bases our worth on a comparison with others. Excellence gauges our value by measuring us against our own potential. Success grants its rewards to the few but is the dream of the multitudes. Excellence is available to all living beings but is accepted by the few. Success focuses its attention on the external—becoming the tastemaker for the insatiable appetites of the . . . consumer. Excellence beams its spotlight on the internal spirit. Success encourages expedience and compromise, which prompts us to treat people as means to our ends. Excellence cultivates principles and consistency. . . ."[21]

Inrig sees excellence as characterized by qualities such as the fruit of the Spirit, whereas Johnston's metaphor is agape love.

Excellence and Success in Scripture

Success is not viewed as with disdain in Scripture. In fact, on a number of occasions people were promised success if they remained true to God. For example, God promised Joshua success and prosperity if he followed certain biblical guidelines. Clearly, the kind of success Joshua experienced reflects achievement in the best sense of that word.

Military success. First, Joshua achieved military success. He had the kind of reputation with his people that many leaders hope for but never experience, for it is written: "What the Lord did that day made the people of Israel consider Joshua a great man. They honored him all his life, just as they had honored Moses" (Josh. 4:14, TEV).

Material success. Joshua was also successful materially, for later we read: "When the people of Israel finished dividing up the land, they gave Joshua son of Nun a part of the land as his own. As the Lord had commanded, they gave him the city he asked for: Timnath Serah, in the hill country of

Ephraim. He rebuilt the city and settled there" (19:49-50, TEV).

Many leaders would value what was said of the organization under Joshua's leadership — Israel — to be said of their own leadership efforts:

> So the Lord gave to Israel all the land that He had solemnly promised their ancestors He would give them. When they had taken possession of it, they settled down there. The Lord gave them peace throughout the land, just as He had promised their ancestors. Not one of all their enemies had been able to stand against them, because the Lord gave the Israelites the victory over all their enemies. The Lord kept every one of the promises that He had made to the people of Israel (21:43-45, TEV).

Spiritual success. Joshua achieved success because it was given to him by the Lord. He achieved success because he was committed to doing God's work God's way. He was careful to obey the Lord's command laid out at the beginning of his leadership career:

> Be sure that the book of the Law is always read in your worship. Study it day and night, and make sure that you obey everything written in it. Then you will be prosperous and successful (1:8, TEV).

Elsewhere in the Old Testament, we are challenged to reflect excellence in our speech: "Excellent speech becometh not a fool: much less do lying lips a prince" (Prov. 17:7, KJV).

The Leader and Excellence

Thus far we have examined excellence from two viewpoints: the secular perspective and the Christian perspective. Now we ask the question, "How can these two perspectives help the Christian leader pursue excellence in leadership?" There are at least four ways.

Leaders Need to Pursue Excellence in Preparation

God puts His future leadership choices through an extended period of preparation. Joseph and Moses are but two examples. From his youth Joseph felt that God had called him to be a leader. Indeed, he was so outspoken about this calling that his father admonished him to quit talking about it so much. But leadership did not come early or easily for Joseph. During his teens and twenties, hard circumstances befell him in order to prepare him for his future role. Joseph was educated in cisterns, the slave market, and finally, in prison. Hardly a course of training and development to suggest to anyone who wants to be a senior-level government official.

Yet while Joseph was being prepared for a subsequent leadership assignment, we note two curious observations. First, we find no evidence that Joseph was dissatisfied with God's conditions of preparation for leadership. Second, we see no evidence that Joseph tried to accelerate God's timetable.

Moses' life provides a similar example of hard preparation for leadership. Some writers have suggested that Moses' life can be thought of in three periods of approximately forty years each—forty years as one of Egypt's best and brightest; forty years as a caretaker of sheep; and forty years as a shepherd of God's people. Moses' early years would be viewed by many as a proper preparation for leadership. Educated in the best schools of Egypt, and as the son of Pharaoh's daughter, he had it made. By our standards he would have been a graduate of Harvard, summa cum laude. As Stephen noted, "Moses was given the best education in Egypt. He was a strong man and a powerful speaker" (Acts 7:22, CEV). In short, he was on the way to becoming successful in the best sense of that word. Yet God had other plans involving Moses' preparation for his leadership. God's plan included Moses' abandoning the good life he had in Egypt, shepherding in the wilderness, then wandering in the desert with a rebellious and stubborn people.

I believe God wants leaders who diligently work at achieving excellence in the quality of their preparation, whether through degrees or experience. But we see from these two examples of biblical leaders that preparation for leadership involves more than degrees or position. It also involves contentment in circumstances and an awareness that God's timing is never late. Striving to lead in the big church or to serve as president of a large organization may not be evidence of impure motives. Forcing God's timetable, coupled with an attitude of discontent while serving the smaller out-of-the-way organization, most assuredly is.

Leaders Need to Pursue Excellence in Christian Character

The expression of excellent character qualities is found in the fruit of the Spirit: "Love, joy, peace patience, kindness, goodness, faithfulness, humility, and self-control. There is no law against such things as these" (Gal. 5:22-23, TEV). Leaders need to reflect these qualities not only in their own lives, but they need to encourage and promote these qualities in job-related assignments.

Decisions regarding the initial hire, promotions, and subsequent decisions to retain an employee might well take into consideration these types of character qualities as well as the other more traditional performance standards of the job. And leaders should compliment an employee's quality of self-control and/or kindness just as regularly and frequently as job performance accomplishments. The leader should attempt to have the organization reflect the positive character qualities of its employees. Organizations, just like people, have personalities. Churches, for example, tend to be identified as "cold" or "warm" churches. Organizations are often described with words such as "Over there they care about people"; "At that place people feel important." I believe it's possible for an organization to reflect, through its people, biblical qualities. If persons within the organization reflect these qualities, it would seem logical to assume that so too would the organization where those persons work. We go full circle then to the earlier comment—an organization's employees need to be encouraged, through the positive example of leaders, to reflect biblical qualities of character.

Leaders Need to Pursue Excellence in Organizational Structure and Processes

Organizational processes and structures need to be regularly reviewed. In organizations, there are often too few procedures pertaining to how things are done. As a result, too much organizational time is spent trying to ascertain just how things should or ought to happen. I like to tell our staff that organizations should be tough on issues; tender with people; clear on processes; and inherently and fundamentally fair. While we have made some progress in this, the long-term direction has been established.

Because human beings are creatures of habit, elements of process can do much to contribute to a stable organizational environment. On the other hand, some organizations are too preoccupied with organizational procedures. In this kind of organization, the way things are done assumes a greater prominence than the ends sought. As Gardner notes:

This concern for "how it is done" is also one of the diseases of which societies die. Little by little, preoccupation with method, technique and procedure gains a subtle dominance over the whole process of goal seeking. How it is done becomes more important than whether it is done. Means triumph over ends. Form triumphs over spirit. Method is enthroned. Men become prisoners of their procedures, and organizations that were designed to achieve some goal become obstacles in the path to that goal.[22]

Leaders Need to Pursue Excellence in Organizational Vision

Too few leaders give careful attention to the cultivation and nurture of the organizational dream. In a church setting, many pastors sometimes forget to emphasize to their parishioners that invitations to sing in the choir, teach a class, or help in the nursery are not more things to add to an already crowded schedule. Rather, they are opportunities for service and worship.

In Christian organizations, people ought to be presented with the challenge that they have the opportunity to exercise their spiritual gifts for the good of the church; they have the opportunity to be colaborers with God in the very important task of kingdom building. Are laborers laying bricks or building cathedrals? Are farmers pulling weeds or preparing for a harvest? Leaders have the responsibility to cultivate vision in the organization. As Proverbs 29:18 says, "Where there is no vision, the people perish" (KJV).

While efforts are sometimes made to separate achievement (in the way we have used the term here) from excellence, the organizational reality is that both must be integrated together. Settling for achievement or excellence will most likely create problems.

For example, excellence of character and in processes are terribly important for people and organizations. Yet if the organization does not achieve its mission and remain fiscally healthy, problems will result. So the wise leader will pursue and encourage both. Achieving excellence the right way is an end worthy of any leader and organization.

10

From Personal to Organizational Leadership

ONE OF THE difficulties of having an inclusive definition of leadership is that it tends to overlook the unique needs and expectations of organizational leadership. By "organizational" I'm talking about an entity that is voluntarily brought into existence by a group of people to achieve a given purpose or need, and which usually tends to be incorporated legally. Christian colleges, mission agencies, parachurch organizations, and an "organized local church" (as compared with the church) tend to be the kinds of organizations I'm referring to.

Differences between Personal and Organizational Leadership

What are some of the distinctives or tendencies of organizational leadership? While similarities are many, I believe there are some differences between personal and organizational leadership. I want to suggest several.

Organizational Leadership Has a Primary Focus on Interacting with People within the Organization

In an organization, one must practice leading and following. Whether with family or company personnel, the leader of an organization has as a primary mandate the development and care of people and the provision of a healthy culture where work can be done.

Organizational Leadership Has a Commitment to Achieve a Purpose or Mission

Organizations are brought into existence not just to exist but with a goal in mind. For example, students are educated; the hungry are fed; Bibles are distributed, and missionaries are sent. Further, nonvolunteer personnel expect to be paid for their services at regular time periods. So however good might be the leader's skills at getting along with people, however personable, these other organizational ends also need to be met. Further, actions taken and policies developed must reflect consistency with biblical means and ends.

In Organizational Leadership, One's Call to Leadership Must Be Continually Confirmed

Few persons who hold positions of authority will see subordinates become followers if in fact the people refuse to confirm one's leadership. Examples abound in both secular and Christian organizations where this confirmation did not take place. Further, this confirmation must be ongoing for leadership to be effective. The fact that I begin my leadership assignment to the usual fanfare and accolades of followers is no guarantee that it will continue.

The Organizational Leader Has to Guard Against Being Consumed by the Needs of the Organization[1]

While there are burdens to be sure in personal leadership, they are intense in organizational leadership. There are the burdens of personnel decisions. There are the burdens of finance—making sure bills are paid and paychecks issued on time. Knowing that hundreds of families are depending on the "right decision" is of significant concern to the leader. Some of Christ's most encouraging and comforting words for leaders and followers are found in Matthew 11:28-30:

> Come to Me, all you who are weary and burdened, and I will give you rest. Take My yoke upon you and learn from Me, for I am gentle and humble in heart and you

will find rest for your souls. For My yoke is easy and My burden is light.

Jesus Christ gives rest to all of the burdened and weary. As we take on His yoke (way) and as He teaches us, we find inner rest for our souls. His yoke is easy and His burden is light. What refreshing news and comfort for leaders and followers. These words make it easier for both.

Defining Organizational Leadership

Before exploring the various other relationships involving the leader and the organization, I want to probe further the concept of organizational leadership. Just what is organizational leadership? How does it differ from managership, and what might be its relationship to power and authority?

To flesh out our definition, a variety of literature will be explored. According to Arthur Schlesinger, Jr., leadership is "the capacity to move, inspire, and mobilize masses of people."[2] Former U.S. Supreme Court Justice Arthur Goldberg defines leadership as "great ability and great opportunity greatly employed—an art, not a science and . . . largely intuitive."[3] Some see leadership as pyramidal or hierarchical: "In this classic view, a chain of command lies at the heart of the operation. Information flows up the chain, orders come down. Obedience becomes the primary obligation of the employee and the giving of orders the responsibility of the leader."[4] This view is reflected in the observations of a Harvard Business School student as he describes his perceptions of the kind of business leader most admired by his colleague students: "the tough, hands-on manager, someone who justifies his or her high pay by being the crisis-solver, the problem-fixer, the head-basher."[5] However rigorous might be the attempt to define leadership, one must realize that the concept of leadership is not an exact science; if anything, it's like an inexact art. Gardner, for example, observes that:

Any attempt to describe a process as complex as leadership inevitably makes it seem more orderly than it is. Leadership is not tidy. Decisions are made and then reversed. Misunderstandings are frequent, inconsistency inevitable. Most of the time things are out of hand. No leader enjoys that reality, but every leader knows it.[6]

Gardner defines leadership as "the process of persuasion and example by which an individual (or leadership team) induces a group to take action that is in accord with the leader's purposes or the shared purposes of all."[7] The story of Moses leading the people from Egypt, for example, would fit this definition. The people to be led certainly desired to be out from under their Egyptian bondage. They had no plan, however, to effect this purpose until Moses, God's handpicked leader, came on the scene. Nehemiah also fits this description of leadership. In chapter 2 of the book which bears his name, he returned to Jerusalem to help complete a God-given task. It can be implied from this story that God's people desired to see the walls rebuilt, but the task remained undone until this leader came on the scene.

It's important to note from the accounts of Moses and Nehemiah that neither imposed himself on the people by a simple fiat such as, "God has appointed me to be your leader; now you be my followers." Rather, each provided evidence for the group about how he was called by God and equipped for the task. Moses could share his desert experience, including his confrontation with the Living God at the burning bush. Nehemiah could share how King Artaxerxes had endorsed his mission in response to God's answered prayer.

Leading versus Managing

An important leadership distinctive which Gardner addresses is a substantive difference between "managers" and "leaders." Some argue that one fundamental difference is that managers focus on making sure that things "get done right" while leaders focus on making sure that the "right things get done." Gardner is not so sure that indeed a major difference exists between managers and leaders. As he observes:

Many writers on leadership are at considerable pains to distinguish between leaders and managers. In the process leaders generally end up looking like a cross between Napoleon and the Pied Piper, and managers like unimaginative clods. This troubles me. Every time I encounter an utterly first-class manager he turns out to have quite a lot of the leader in him.[8]

Gardner, however, then proceeds to identify six ways in which leaders and leader/managers distinguish themselves from the general run of managers:

- *They are long-term thinkers;*
- *They look beyond the unit they are heading and grasp its relationship to the overall organization;*
- *They reach and influence constituents beyond their jurisdictions and boundaries;*
- *They put heavy emphasis on the intangibles of vision, values, and motivation, and understand intuitively the nonrational and unconscious elements in the leader-constituent (follower) interaction;*
- *They have the political skill to cope with the conflicting requirements of multiple constituencies;* and
- *They think in terms of renewal.*[9]

Katz and Kahn on Leadership

One of the foremost sources on the nature of the organization in the context of leadership is the classic, *The Social Psychology of Organizations* by Daniel Katz and Robert Kahn.

This book is highly recommended for those who aspire to and/or who serve in a position of organizational leadership. One basic assumption in much of their work is that the study of leadership is incomplete without an understanding of how organizations function as organizations. The leader who understands how organizations function, and more specifically, how his or her organization functions, enhances the probabilities for effective leadership.

As Katz and Kahn discuss leadership, they identify the three ways the concept has typically been presented: "as the attribute of a position, as the characteristic of a person, and as a category of behavior. To be a superior is to occupy a position of leadership, and to be a company president is to occupy a position of greater leadership."[10] They also suggest that leadership is a relational and interactive concept — "the influencing agent and the persons influenced. Without followers there can be no leader."[11] Further, they suggest that leadership is more than role performance. They see the organizational leader as one who is willing to (and usually does) go far beyond the usual expectations of role performance: "We consider the essence of organizational leadership to be the influential increment over and above mechanical compliance with the routine directives of the organization."[12] These authors identify several reasons why leadership is needed.

Organizations Need Structure

Any kind of organization has an incomplete structure. People usually know the difference between how the organization is supposed to work and how in fact it does work.

Unless one is committed to a multivolume description of organizational rules and procedures (and some Christian organizations are), there are usually some gaps between practice and structure that require ongoing interpretation, adaptation, embellishment, or omission. The effective leader helps in this process.

One of the primary concerns of Jesus as presented in the

Gospels was that the Jewish leaders had gone overboard in this area. Their efforts to be precise and tight with their religious regulations—to make everything nice and neat—took the heart and reason out of the purpose for the regulation in the first place. As Katz and Kahn observe: "The concrete case always needs something of interpretation and adaptation, embellishment or thoughtful omission."[13] Jesus did this as a leader and it got Him into trouble. As a leader, however, He thought it well worth the trouble.

External Conditions Are Constantly Changing

A second reason for leadership in an organization, according to Katz and Kahn, is that the external conditions under which the organization must function are always changing.[14] The leader then serves as a viable link to the outside boundary areas or conditions.

Organizations, including churches, are vitally impacted in their programs by things that happen beyond their walls or even communities. Mission programs and the need to feed the hungry are but two examples. Concern about legislation, whether on the topic of pornography or abortion, is another. One of the Apostle Paul's functions and priorities was to keep geographically distant groups of Christians aware of each other's needs. He was always pleased when he saw a generous response on the part of one group to the needs of another. In this role Paul served as a leader.

Organizations Are Constantly Changing

New goals and strategies are identified, new priorities and strategic plans are established, and adjustments to organizational structure usually follow.[15] One of the needs for leadership is to coordinate and direct this change. When the early New Testament church was getting started, it had to make a distinction between elders and deacons because of rapidly changing needs and new priorities. Moses had to reorganize his management because of the changing needs of the people he led.

According to Katz and Kahn, the initiation of change within an organization "is the most challenging of all organizational tasks and rarely occurs without strong pressure outside the organization."[16] Pressure from outside the organization can come in a variety of ways — a vibrant competitor opens across the street; the old stodgy church gets a dynamic new pastor; or a financial crisis occurs. Those leaders who have been effective at organizational change possess two qualities, one cognitive — systemic perspective, and the other affective — charisma.[17] Systemic perspective means the ability to see the way each part of the organization relates to the others and how the organization itself relates to the larger world beyond. Systemic perspective is important for leaders, and critically important if change is desired.

With regard to charisma, as Katz and Kahn note: "The top organizational leader, who possesses legitimate power and controls rewards and sanctions, can mobilize more support for policies if he or she can generate charisma, that magical aura with which people sometimes endow their leaders."[18] Many times people assume that a leader is charismatic, meaning that he or she is "blessed" with a given personality type. Noncharismatic leaders look almost with envy at this type of personality and secretly wish that it was theirs as well. Few people, however, view charisma as something that the people themselves give to the leader and further, that charismatic leadership is characterized by abdication of responsibility on the part of the people and psychological distance between leaders and followers. It shouldn't come as a surprise that many leaders who are described as charismatic maintain distance between themselves and their followers. They do so because, "Day-to-day intimacy destroys illusion."[19]

Katz and Kahn share Gardner's ambivalence about whether or not there is a crystal clear distinction between the leader and the manager/administrator. As they note: "Organizations do not achieve greatness on the basis of their adequacy in handling daily administrative chores, but

unless these are taken care of, the organization deterio-
rates."[20] They also observe the neglect in given organizations "in which the top leaders spend almost all their time
discussing policies and plans and are out of touch with the
daily requirements of organizational life."[21] They state that
one key difference between those organizations that are successful and those that are not is that the leadership function
is dispersed throughout the organization. As they note:
"People have greater feelings of commitment to decisions in
which they have a part . . . and the wide distribution of the
leadership function is likely to improve the quality of
decisions. . . ."[22]

Moses was preoccupied with running the whole show until
his father-in-law Jethro paid him a visit. Jethro observed the
situation, assessed it properly, and said Moses' workload
was too heavy:

> You are not doing this right. You will wear yourself out
> and these people as well. This is too much for you to
> do alone (Ex. 18:17-18, TEV).

As a result, he suggested a new dispersed leadership
structure in which Moses became an even more effective
leader:

> "But in addition, you should choose some capable men
> and appoint them as leaders of the people: leaders of
> thousands, hundreds, fifties, and tens. They must be
> God-fearing men who can be trusted and who cannot
> be bribed. Let them serve as judges for the people on a
> permanent basis. They can bring all the difficult cases
> to you, but they themselves can decide all the smaller
> disputes. That will make it easier for you, as they share
> your burden. If you do this, as God commands, you
> will not wear yourself out, and all these people can go
> home with their disputes settled." Moses took Jethro's
> advice (vv. 21-24, TEV).

Alternatively, Joshua apparently did not effectively use a dispersed leadership style because after he was off the scene, the very things he stood for vanished, and a generation grew up who knew not God. Who says it can't happen again? Leaders who are committed to a long-term view of the organization will be practitioners of dispersed leadership.

What, then, is the connection between personal and organizational leadership? First, leaders, whether or not in an organization, must give special attention to all of the expectations of the Scriptures for godly living. Qualities of character, personal renewal, family priorities, intense spirituality — these, and many more, are important in personal leadership.

Organizational leadership, then, builds on these personal dimensions of leadership and attempts to integrate them into an organizational context so that the organization's mission can be achieved. It is to these organizational ends and tasks that the next several chapters will be focused.

11

Followership

MANY PERSONS WOULD agree that one of the earliest lessons taught by society is that we're to be followers. I well remember my childhood days in school and the teacher's constant reminders to make sure I followed the directions. One of the games we played during recess was "Follow the Leader." One of the marks of a good teacher in those days was to make sure young students knew how to make a line, stand in line, and follow whoever was at the head of the line — and to do all of this in an orderly fashion.

Forty years later the emphasis on being a follower has become much more subtle if not totally nonexistent in our Christian culture. The focus of our efforts is on leadership. As Gardner notes: "We expect our leaders to be sensitive to and to serve the basic needs of our constituents, expect them to have faith in their constituents and a caring concern for them."[1] Churches are seemingly forever offering seminars on leadership. Universities proudly proclaim their positions as preparers of future leaders. Christian periodicals carry the same emphasis.

I don't object to an emphasis on leadership; it is important. Alternatively, there has not been an equally important emphasis on followership. I have rarely seen any kind of conference on followership. Yet, as Engstrom has observed: "What most of us need is more training in how to follow."[2] Paradoxically, many who believe they are followers are in essence leaders. As has been noted elsewhere, it is rare that one is a leader in all dimensions of life or a follower in all dimensions of life. The reality is usually that, during any given week, one serves, alternatively, and in a variety of roles, as both leader and follower. When professors Katz and Lazarsfeld were doing research which was ultimately reported in their book, *Personal Influence,*[3] they attempted to locate opinion leaders. As might be expected, they found opinion leaders in official positions of responsibility. But they also found them in a variety of followership roles: "Unofficial leaders lead without benefit of authoritative office: here are the key men of a work gang, the spark plugs of a salesman rally, the elder statesmen who sit on park benches talking for newspapers."[4] These opinion leaders, then, lead in their own way, perhaps not as a Churchill would, but they nonetheless still have followers.

The focus of this chapter deals with the subject of followership. Just what is a follower? What are the responsibilities of followership? What are the privileges of followership? What ought to be the relationship of followers to leaders? Leaders to followers? And how shall we decide who to follow?

A Biblical Perspective on Followership

Scripture gives us many good examples of people who were effective followers. It also provides us with many different ways in which the idea of following can be used. Here are just several of the ways it's used.

All these officials of yours will come to me, bowing down before me and saying, "Go, you and all the people who follow you!" After that I will leave (Ex. 11:8).

The idea of "follow" here is that of walking along side of, and includes the idea of endurance.

Another use of "follow" occurs in Acts 12:8, which is a description of Peter's miraculous escape from prison:

Then the angel said to him, "Put on your clothes and sandals." And Peter did so. "Wrap your cloak around you and follow me," the angel told him.

Here, the meaning of "follow" includes the idea of "accompaniment," to be in the same way with, "union." It implies clear direction as well as close proximity between the leader and follower. A similar meaning is found in Jesus' words recorded in Matthew 8:22:

But Jesus told him, "Follow Me, and let the dead bury their own dead."

Still another use of "follow" appears in 4:19: "Come, follow Me," Jesus said, "and I will make you fishers of men." The context here suggests physical presence but not on an equal footing. In short, I am to remain close to the leader, but I am clearly to remain behind because I'm not in charge. This is the sense of Psalm 119:59: "I pay careful attention as You lead me, and I follow closely" (CEV).

Again, there are multiple case studies which could be done on biblical characters who were superb followers. Elsewhere I have written about Abel, Noah, and Job; Joseph and Daniel; and Peter and Paul. But again, I'm drawn to the character of Moses, for we see the hand of God on him from the time he was drawn from the Nile until he died before God. And while Moses was often an imperfect creation of God, there burned in his heart a desire to know God and to obey God. He was a learner and a shepherd in the desert; he was a reluctant servant of God as he confronted the Pharaoh; he was the reluctant leader as he strove to keep his followers from dissension and disobedience; he was the one who received the Ten Commandments; and he led his followers in and around the desert because of their, not his, disobedience. Even though Moses was denied the chance to experience the "Promised Land" because of one failure in learning obedience, Moses nevertheless stayed true to his calling and totally obedient to God, because he understood, as must we, that the first call on leadership is to be a follower.

Both the Old and New Testaments identify telling similarities between leadership and followership:

- both leadership and followership can be intensive;
- there need not be a gap between those leading and those following; and
- leadership involves showing someone the way and teaching, while following involves attention to modeling.

Other Perspectives on Followership

According to Gardner, "Leaders are almost never as much in charge as they are pictured to be, followers almost never are as submissive as one might imagine."[5] Further, and reflecting on the work of George Simmel (1858–1918), Gardner notes that "followers have about as much influence on their leaders as their leaders have on them. Leaders cannot maintain authority . . . unless followers are prepared to believe in that authority. In a sense, leadership is conferred by followers."[6]

Gardner further argues that the success or failure of the leader is dependent as much as, if not more, on the followers than on the leader: "Good constituents produce good leaders. They not only select good ones, they make them better by holding them to standards of performance."[7] Many times "leaders" assume that because they hold a given position, therefore, they are leaders. Not so, says Gardner:

The assumption by line executives that, given their rank and authority, they can lead without being leaders is one reason bureaucracies stagnate. They are given subordinates, but they cannot be given a following. Surprisingly, many of them don't know they are not leading. They mistake the exercise of authority for leadership, and as long as they persist in that mistake they will never learn the art of turning subordinates into followers.[8]

What is it, then, that followers want from a leader? According to Gardner,

Followers do like being treated with consideration, do like to have their say, do like a chance to exercise their own initiative — and participation does increase acceptance of decisions. But there are times when followers welcome rather than reject authority, want prompt and clear decisions from the leader, want to close ranks around the leader. The ablest and most effective leaders do not hold to a single style; they may be highly supportive in personal relations when that is needed, yet capable of a quick authoritative decision when the situation requires it.[9]

Additionally, followers desire "effective two-way communication," and significant face-to-face communication. As Gardner notes, "Wise leaders are continuously finding ways to say to their constituents, 'I hear you.' "[10] Furthermore, followers readily pick up and respond to nonverbal communication. According to Gardner, "Truly gifted leaders know not only what constituents need but what they fear, what they long to be, what they like best about themselves. Woodrow Wilson said, 'The ear of the leader must ring with the voices of the people.' "[11] Leaders ought to be followers of the people they lead because Christ commands us to be followers of Himself and followers in the sense of putting the needs of those we lead before our own.[12]

Followership Qualities

Engstrom and Dayton identify nine followership qualities.

- *Commitment.* "Our commitment is first to the person we work for, second to our fellow workers and third to the organization."[13]
- *Understanding.* "We know the task, our role in it, how we relate to others, whom we will be working with, their style and goals, and a host of other data."[14]
- *Loyalty.* "We will represent our leader fairly and carefully. We will protect his or her reputation."[15]
- *Communication.* We have elsewhere discussed the need of the leader to communicate with followers. The focus here is the follower communicating with the leader and with others who work with that same leader. Complete information should be provided, rather than giving only what one might think the leader wants to hear.
- *Competence.* "If you don't have what is needed to do a job, there is no way you can be a follower in that situation. . . . It's all right to stretch ourselves, but there are times when we have to say honestly and forthrightly, 'I don't think I can do that job adequately.' "[16] In my experience with a variety of organizations, rarely have I had persons admit to me that they did not possess the competence to do the job. Yet it had become clear to everyone, except the person involved, that such was lacking. When the person involved, in addition, is unwilling to grow or learn, the situation becomes even more difficult.
- *Promise keeping.* "Good followers do what they say (promise) they will do. When they recognize that they are not going to be able to keep the promise to their leader or their teammates, they immediately let the others know."[17]
- *Participation.* "Good followers understand where they fit in the larger whole. They recognize that a failure (to participate) on their part can jeopardize everyone else. That is why commitment to others beside the leader is so important."[18]
- *Getting along.* This quality focuses not only on the importance of participation but also on how one participates with others.

Getting along means spending time with others when what they are doing may seem frivolous or unnecessary. . . . Getting along is recognizing that often our own feet seem to be made of clay and others have something to tell us. Getting along means allowing others to help us, compliment us and sometimes criticize us.[19]

- *Sacrifice.* "We often talk about the cost of leadership. Seldom do we hear about the cost of followership—'take up his cross daily.' Following has about it a willingness to accept the possibility of our own execution. . . . It may be the execution of personal dreams and aspirations. It may be the execution of our own highly held opinions. It may be the offering up of our individualism for the good of the cause of which we are a part. . . . We discover that being a good follower calls for sacrifice we never imagined."[20]

The Failures of Followers

The literature of Christendom is filled with accounts of leaders who failed. Given our earlier discussion, however, of the almost symbiotic relationship between leaders and followers, almost by definition, then, the failure of leaders must be in some way connected to the failure of followers. But, where is the literature on the failures of followers? As Gardner has observed:

There is a vast literature on the failures of leadership— on the abuse of power, injustice, indecisiveness, shortsightedness, and so on. Who will write the essay on individual and collective failures among followers?[21]

Gardner then proceeds to identify three "failings of followers." First, he discusses the failure of noninvolvement such as "apathy, passivity, cynicism and habits of spectator-like noninvolvement which invite the abuse of power of leaders."[22] The concern here, of course, is that proper followership insists on leadership accountability. If followers don't insist on accountability, it is more likely that the leader will abuse and/or misuse power.

A second failure of followers is to "collaborate in their own self-deception." As Gardner notes, "A citizenry that wants to be lied to will have liars as leaders."[23] This type of deception often takes place when followers are unwilling to face facts. Organizational growth and the fixing of major problems will not take place if self-deception is practiced by both leaders and followers. A third failure of followers is "the failure of group cohesion among the followers—a circumstance that makes leadership very difficult indeed."[24]

When Do We Stop Following?

Because every leader is a follower, and every follower a leader, this question must be generally faced by all. When do I stop following the leader?

At first glance, the answer appears to be easy. Using our previous definitions, it would seem that one stops following when the leader stops leading. This answer, admittedly subjective, suggests that when the leader stops meeting the needs of the follower, following stops. While I, as a follower, may still be subordinate to a position of authority, the fact that I am a subordinate doesn't make me a follower. In essence, I can stop following, but still retain my position as a subordinate within the organization.

Another principled option I have, however, and one not readily chosen by those persons who stop following, particularly during times of economic tightness, is to leave the organization and go elsewhere. Perhaps this is the most honest option for the follower. Furthermore, since leaders are also followers of people they lead, leaders ought also to have the option to stop following the people. If the people being led are absolutely opposed to the direction a given leader might suggest, then the leader must carefully evaluate future effectiveness in other areas as well.

Both leaders and followers must candidly admit that there are times when it is right for the followers to stop following and/or for the leader to stop leading. The ideal situation would be one where both affected leaders and followers would draw this conclusion on their own initiative without someone else drawing those conclusions for them. Occasionally followers must have the integrity to admit that they wholeheartedly disagree with a general but substantial organizational direction, and that they would be better off becoming a supportive subordinate or going elsewhere. What happens many times, however, is that followers stop following and then become unhappy subordinates. As a result, they do everything in their power to get rid of the current leader. But unless the leader is clearly violating some clearly stated biblical principle, this kind of personal organizational agenda may run afoul of Scripture.

If the follower cannot become either a contented subordinate or is not willing to work for change in a proper manner, then I would argue that such an individual should leave the organization and go somewhere else where the organizational agenda would be more compatible with his or her personal agenda.

While leadership, especially the right kind of leadership, is important, so too, followership is important to the health of an organization. We must remember that this includes the leader who too is a follower — of the people being led.

The relationship between leaders and followers is an interactive and mutually dependent one. And both roles, not just that of the leader, must be carefully attended to. Without good leaders the organization, most likely, will not experience growth and development. Without good followers holding leadership accountable, the organization may lose its collective soul and commitment to mission. When leaders and followers, who both follow and lead, work together, each recognizing biblical claims and each striving to understand the organizational dimensions of what it means to "Honor Christ and put others first," then there is the likelihood that tremendous and dynamic organizational development will occur.

12

Confrontation

ONE OF THE most important yet one of the most difficult assignments of organizational leadership is the task of confrontation—both of issues and of people. When one thinks about the concept of confrontation, a number of scenarios come to mind—labor versus management, parent versus child, country versus country. In spite of the difficulties involved with confrontation, leaders know that in order to be faithful both to the responsibilities of the position and to the commands of Scripture, the leadership function cannot be properly carried out without a willingness to be involved with confrontation.

And, since confrontation usually involves personnel decisions, it is all the more difficult to carry out. Yet, confront we must if we are to be effective leaders. Fred Smith, a Christian businessman from Dallas, offers this insight:

> Whenever I am tempted not to act in a difficult personnel situation, I ask myself, "Am I holding back for my personal comfort or for the good of the organization?" If I am doing what makes me comfortable, I am embezzling. If doing what is good for the organization also happens to make me comfortable, that's wonderful. But if I am treating irresponsibility irresponsibly, I must remember that two wrongs do not make a right.[1]

Options to Confrontation

Professor David Augsburger, in his book *Caring Enough to Confront*,[2] states the various options to confrontation.

- *Ignore the problem.* First, the leader can choose to ignore the problem. This option is your basic "head-in-the-sand" approach. Perhaps the problem will go away if nothing is said or done.

Surprisingly, many times this is the best option to consider. Leaders many times elevate insignificant incidents to the status of significant problems simply by agreeing to discuss the matter further. Since most leaders are not looking for additional work, this option to confrontation can be indeed useful. The insightful leader needs to be sensitive regarding which incidents ought to be handled this way and when.

The Old Testament story of Eli and his family is an illustration of the first option. God sent judgment to the house of Eli because of his wicked sons. Eli himself was judged "because of the sin he knew about; his sons made themselves contemptible, and he failed to restrain them" (1 Sam. 3:13). This was clearly a case where Eli ignored the problem.

- *Attack the problem mercilessly.* A second option to confrontation is the winner-take-all option. In this situation, there is no such thing as compromise. There is always a winner and there is always a loser. No middle ground is allowed. I either win big or I lose big. America's frontier heritage characterized by the "shootout-at-OK-Corral" mentality has glamorized this approach to confrontation.

One example of this option from Scripture is the story of Absalom and David. As one of David's younger sons, Absalom probably realized that he would not be a likely candidate to succeed his father as king. So he set out on his "winner-take-all" game plan which included "stealing the hearts of the people," open sexual immorality with his father's wives, and open warfare against his father. Had he won by following this approach, the kingdom would have been his. He failed in his attempt, however—losing the war, his dignity, and his life.

Experience suggests that many in the Christian world use this option to deal with problems. It's characterized by an attitude that says, "Let's not discuss our concerns or deal with them forthrightly. Rather, let's start a new church, change churches or jobs, or move away." The landscape of various Christian communities is littered with the remains, both psychological and physical, of persons who chose this method of dealing with problems and who, having lost the battle, ultimately dropped out of the war.

- *Capitulate.* A third option to confrontation is to capitulate or give in to the concern. This alternative assumes basically the opposite of the second option. I accede to the request and respond to the demands. I give them what they want.

A biblical example of this situation is found in 1 Kings 3. Two prostitutes, who shared the same house, came to Solomon with their tale of woe.

Solomon, depending on God-given wisdom, knew that on some issues capitulating is not going nearly far enough. He knew that sometimes the person who has truth on his side will not just give in. This story, then, illustrates both the dangers of acceding to a given request and the potential limitations of using this option to alleviate confrontation.

- *Compromise.* A fourth option to confrontation is the "I'll-go-halfway-if-you'll-go-halfway" approach. This option suggests that I have something worth hanging onto and I will work hard to hang onto my 50 percent. As long as I am able to hang onto part of my ideas or arguments, that is enough. I don't need to be the total winner. As a result, I don't need to be the total loser. Each side retains its dignity, so to speak. Each side is willing to compromise.

Probably one of the best biblical examples of using this approach for dealing with difficult issues is found in Acts 15, the story of the Jerusalem Council. A conflict had arisen about whether or not the new Gentile Christians had to submit to all of the Jewish traditions, such as circumcision, now that they had become believers. This issue was a highly emotional one and had the potential to splinter and fragment the early church, since many Jews were struggling with the concept of Gentiles being Christians in the first place.

Peter, who himself struggled with this issue, could have argued that the Jewish traditions were hopelessly out-of-date. Perhaps that position would have best satisfied Paul. Peter, however, didn't set forth that argument. Perhaps he knew that such a proposal would never have been agreed to by the Council. So instead, he suggested a Spirit-led compromise, one wherein the Jewish traditions would remain in place for Jews but the new Gentile believers would not be subject to them (vv. 7-10). Peter's proposal apparently was still too radical for the Jewish brethren, because what they ultimately agreed to was that Gentile Christians would still have a partial yoke, that is, they would have a list of Jewish traditions, even though shorter, to adhere to.

Even though it does not appear that Gentile Christians were present at this Council, those that ministered to them were. And it appears that this compromise solution was acceptable, for no dissent is recorded. In essence, what the Council agreed to was two different sets of church membership requirements, one for Jews and one for Gentiles. The singular success of this method for dealing with difficult issues suggests that it bears close consideration for use within our organizations. While each of these options may sometimes be used appropriately by the leader, there is a fifth option: the way of confrontation. As I use the term confrontation, I mean a willingness to look at an issue without a vested interest in the outcome, looking out always for the best interests of others. It may mean that my view won't be the prevailing one. It may mean that I'll "lose." But it also means that by involving myself in confrontation, I commit myself to a higher standard than simply winning or losing.

Why Confront?

A Christian leader has a twofold responsibility — not only to be effective in the leadership responsibility, but also to be faithful to the commands of Scripture. As Christians, we confront not to embarrass, belittle, tear down, or humiliate. We confront because of our commitment to help others reach their potential, including continued Christian development. Paul had to say some very difficult things to the readers of his letters, but it was because of his unwavering bottom-line commitment to people:

> Then you will live a life that honors the Lord, and you will always please Him by doing good deeds. You will come to know God even better (Col. 1:10, CEV).

Forms of Confrontation

In some professions, one of the distinctions frequently made regarding evaluation is the difference between "formative" confrontation and "summative" confrontation.

Formative Confrontation

Formative confrontation is the process of giving ongoing feedback to an individual, thus enabling him to make appropriate midstream corrections to do a better job. "John, we need to place more emphasis on that item rather than this one." "Mary, let's use more written work rather than solely oral reports."

Summative Confrontation

Summative confrontation has more of a sense of finality to it. "John, as of May 1, you will no longer have a job here." "Mary, your contract will not be renewed after it expires this year."

Both types of confrontation are helpful and each has its champions. In some ways, formative evaluation is a type of coaching. Certainly, summative confrontation will at times be necessary but rarely should it be the first-strike response of the Christian leader.

My experience with Christian organizations is that very little formative confrontation is done and an overemphasis is placed on summative confrontation. It is not unusual for an individual to be fired and not have any idea why. When reasons are given, they usually have not been preceded by the employer's earlier expressed concerns. Thus the individual goes without opportunity for adjustment and without organizational resources necessary to see improvement.

With these preliminary thoughts out of the way, let's now look at some biblical perspectives on this difficult subject.

Perspectives on Confrontation

Without question, confrontation is hard. I have yet to meet the Christian leader who relished the opportunity to confront difficult situations or difficult people. Indeed, the person who enjoys firing people needs to ask why. This kind of motivation may be a problem. Since termination usually has a variety of negative ramifications for the organization and for the leader (e.g., morale, economic, psychological, legal), if a leader tells me that firing people is one of the more enjoyable parts of the job, I become worried, not only for that leader but also for the organization being led.

Paul, on several occasions, discusses the difficulty of confronting people. Notice, for example, this passage:

> God is my witness that I stayed away from Corinth, just to keep from being hard on you. We are not bosses who tell you what to believe. We are working with you to make you glad, because your faith is strong.
>
> I have decided not to make my next visit with you so painful. If I make you feel bad, who would be left to

cheer me up, except the people I had made to feel bad? The reason I want to be happy is to make you happy. I wrote as I did because I didn't want to visit you and be made to feel happy. At the time I wrote, I was suffering terribly. My eyes were full of tears, and my heart was broken. But I didn't want to make you feel bad. I only wanted to let you know how much I cared for you (2 Cor. 1:23–2:4, CEV).

Make no mistake—for Paul and for many leaders, confrontation of people is painfully difficult.

One of the important tasks of the leader is to create an environment wherein both leader and followers are prepared—indeed, expect—to be confronted. Scripture is very clear on this principle.

Accept correction, and you will find life; reject correction, and you will miss the road (Prov. 10:17, CEV).

To accept correction is wise, to reject it is stupid (12:1, CEV).

Fools think they know what is best, but a sensible person listens to advice (12:15, CEV).

Stupid fools learn good sense by seeing others punished; a sensible person learns by being corrected (19:25, CEV).

Don't refuse to accept criticism; get all the help you can (23:12, TLB).

Listening to good advice is worth much more than jewelry made of gold (25:12, CEV).

In the end, people appreciate frankness more than flattery (28:23, TLB).

Contrary to what might be expected, the sense of these verses suggests that people not only ought to be ready for confrontation but that they should be eager to receive it. The idea seems to be, "I'll be less than effective as a leader if I fail to develop an organizational climate where persons feel free to confront me." As one staff member has noted with regard to confrontation, "It's more blessed to receive than to give." In short, by establishing a climate conducive to healthy confrontation, both individuals and the organization have the potential for positive growth.

Of course, people will not always respond to confrontation the way we would like, as Scripture plainly indicates:

Good people are remembered long after they are gone, but the wicked are soon forgotten (10:7, CEV).

Further, Paul records the reactions of the Corinthians to some of his more difficult, confrontive letters:

I don't feel bad anymore, even though my letter hurt your feelings. I did feel bad at first, but I don't now. I know that the letter hurt you for a while. Now I am happy, but not because I hurt your feelings. It is because God used your hurt feelings to make you turn back to Him, and none of you were harmed by us. When God makes you feel sorry enough to turn to Him and be saved, you don't have anything to feel bad about. But when this world makes you feel sorry, it can cause your death. Just look what God has done by making you feel sorry! You sincerely want to prove that you are innocent. You are angry. You are shocked. You are eager to see that justice is done. You have proved that you were completely right in this matter (2 Cor. 7:8-11, CEV).

These verses and others suggest that we should be alert to the fact that people who care about us and the organization we lead will be confronting us. When that happens, we should look for the good in it and learn from it — even though sometimes the confrontation may not be totally on target.

Like it or not, confrontation, whether its called by another name such as accountability, is essential to effective leadership. And knowing that confrontation pursued either the wrong way or with the wrong motive will produce organizational and personal disaster, here is yet another reason why the inner soul of the leader is so important. The leader who schemes to "get" a person who is not liked or who causes discomfort will almost always have that decision backfire. So approach this important task with great carefulness, humility, and with the right motive. Only then can we be sure that the results we hope and pray for have a chance to occur.

13

Perspective and Planning

SOME VARIABLES OF leadership, including those presented elsewhere in this book, enhance the leadership role, but their absence is not necessarily fatal to the enterprise. However, the leader who lacks an objective perspective, or "vision," will inevitably fail. As John White notes:

> People do not follow programs, but leaders who inspire them. They act when a vision stirs in them a reckless hope of something greater than themselves, hope of fulfillment they had never before dared to aspire to.[1]

Perspective is tied directly to several things, including planning and direction. Numbers 13 gives a good example of goal-setting and planning. When the Israelites finally reached the Promised Land, Moses appointed a group of fact finders (spies) to go into the land and to bring back their assessment of what lay before them. His instructions were as follows:

> "Find out what kind of country it is, how many people live there, and how strong they are. Find out whether the land is good or bad and whether the people live in open towns or in fortified cities. Find out whether the soil is fertile and whether the land is wooded. And be

sure to bring back some of the fruit that grows there."
(It was the season when grapes were beginning to rip-
en) (Num. 13:18-20, TEV).

As the story developed and the spies returned home, they
ended up giving a "mixed report." The majority of the fact
finders made the following observations:

We explored the land and found it to be rich and
fertile; and here is some of its fruit. But the people
who live there are powerful, and their cities are very
large and well fortified. Even worse, we saw the descendants of the giants there (vv. 27-28, TEV).

The minority report, filed by Caleb and Joshua, had a
different focus:

The land we explored is an excellent land. If the Lord
is pleased with us, He will take us there and give us
that rich and fertile land. Do not rebel against the
Lord and don't be afraid of the people who live there.
We will conquer them easily. The Lord is with us and
has defeated the gods who protected them; so don't be
afraid (vv. 14:7-9, TEV).

In essence, the majority said, "Wow, what a terrific place!
But how can we ever handle the price it will cost us to
secure it? Indeed, we can't." The minority said something to
this effect: "Wow, what a terrific place! The cost to secure it
may be steep, but with God's help we can do it." But which
side was right? Both had seen the exact same things. Yet
why did the majority give a negative report and the minority such a positive one? In organizations of all sizes, with
persons presumably viewing the "same" set of facts, more
times than not, leaders are faced with a majority and a
minority report. How does the leader know which one is the
correct analysis?

I'd like to suggest that in the story of the spies, one reason for the difference in viewpoint was godly perspective. One side saw the situation from only the human perspective while the other side saw the situation from God's perspective. Having a godly perspective is absolutely critical to leadership, because at times a situation looks absolutely hopeless from a human standpoint. But just how does a leader go about getting a biblical perspective on a given situation?

Perspective and Goal-Setting

First, in order to maintain a godly perspective, leaders must start with God-given goals. What is it that God desires for the organization He has called me to lead? Does He want more buildings? More members? More programs? More endowment? Does He want improved character in the persons associated with the organization? These and other questions are the beginning points in the search for biblical perspective.

Many times Christian organizations set their own goals. Then God is asked to bless them. In the case of Moses and the spies, the key to knowing which report was the proper one was a clear understanding of God's goals for the organization. With these goals clearly in mind, discernment of other matters came much more easily. Caleb and Joshua were able to see the situation from God's perspective for several reasons. First, they understood that God was going to give them the Promised Land: "He will take us there and give us that rich and fertile land" (v. 8, TEV). Further, they understood that God would be their protection and would be with them: "The Lord is with us and has defeated the gods who protected them; so don't be afraid" (v. 9, TEV). In brief, though they had seen the same walls and giants, their outlook was influenced more by the promises of God and their understanding of how God had previously worked in history. If that were not so, they too would have struggled with the right perspective.

In the pursuit of the proper perspective, the leader must be diligent in the search for God-given goals. Without such vision, the perspective will be missing and the people will perish—something that indeed happened to the Children of Israel who refused to view the Promised Land situation with the right perspective. Godly perspective, then, is related to God-given goals. Further, the leader must surround himself with persons who share this same commitment to God-given goals. As these persons, together, then, wrestle with what ought to be the God-given goals of the organization, the Spirit of God is able to make clear what He intends for us to accomplish—together. In my search for perspective, this must be my starting place. I will seldom be able to effectively understand or ascertain God-given goals if I am insensitive or out of tune with God-given purposes for both myself and the organization. Here is yet another reason why God's heart and my heart must be in tune. The soul of the leader is often where this process occurs.

In addition, the beginning points for these kinds of goals ought always be the achievement of the goals God has for me personally—goals such as reflecting the fruit of the Spirit in my life and refusing to abandon my "first love" (see Rev. 2:4). Until this kind of Christlike influence pervades every fiber of my being, I will fail to grasp a situation through His eyes.

Perspective and Planning

Good planning helps maintain godly perspective. Leaders must commit themselves and their organizations to developing a good planning process. Too many Christian organizations see planning as a waste of time. "Why plan?" they argue. "We can't predict the future. Besides, Scripture tells us to 'take no thought for the morrow.' Furthermore, planning takes away time that could be better used in the organization." These arguments, either explicit or implicit, are often heard by the leader.

After Moses had outlined Israel's goal—to enter the Promised Land—he began gathering information about Canaan and its inhabitants. Moses wanted this information so he could formulate a plan. By gathering information about the strength and location of the current inhabitants, as well as the quality of the land's natural resources, he could develop an effective strategy to conquer the Canaanites.

However, Moses' planning was only supplementary to the Lord's work. The Lord would do the majority of the work of defeating the Canaanites; Israel would only "mop up" after Him (Ex. 23:20-21). That doesn't mean Israel's part was unimportant, but it was mainly secondary to the Lord's, like infantry supporting a tank division. Therefore, their role in the conquest of Canaan still required meticulous planning. In like manner, we need to recognize that some sort of organizational planning is unavoidable. But the question remains as to whether leaders will affect the future with purpose or at random. Both Paul (Rom. 6:15-23) and Peter (2 Peter 2:19) suggest that people are slaves to that which masters and controls them. While professing freedom from slavery of one type, we can become victims of another. The same is true of planning. While professing freedom from the bondage of planning, we can become enslaved to the tyranny of the results of not planning. What's more, planning ought to be seen as a legitimate function of biblical stewardship.

Those who work within any organization, Christian or secular, work with at least three key resources—money, abilities, and time. Scripture has a lot to say about each of these. With regard to money and possessions, Jesus taught, "Anyone who can be trusted in little matters will be honest in important matters" (Luke 16:10, CEV). With regard to abilities, Paul wrote extensively about those skills and gifts bestowed on every believer. We read in 1 Corinthians 4:2, for example, "Those who have been given a trust must prove faithful." Finally, regarding the proper use of time, Proverbs 18:9 tells us, "One who is slack in his work is brother to one who destroys." As followers of Christ, we believe that we have a stewardship responsibility for all the resources that God has given to us. In brief, we believe we cannot practice good stewardship unless our planning helps us make the most of our resources.

Exhortations relating to stewardship appear throughout Scripture.

> The wise man looks ahead. The fool attempts to fool himself and won't face facts (Prov. 14:8, TLB).

> Plans go wrong with too few counselors; many counselors bring success (15:22, TLB).

> What a shame—yes, how stupid!—to decide before knowing the facts! (18:13, TLB)

> Don't go ahead with your plans without the advice of others (20:18, TLB).

> Any enterprise is built by wise planning, becomes strong through common sense, and profits wonderfully by keeping abreast of the facts (24:3-4, TLB).

> A sensible man watches for problems ahead and prepares to meet them. The simpleton never looks, and suffers the consequences (27:12, TLB).

With these observations providing some background, what follows are several guidelines for planning. I've used Numbers 13 as my context (the Promised Land and Moses).

Planning Must Reflect Previously Established Goals

The chapter (Numbers 13) begins with a clear statement of affirmation that the Promised Land was not Moses' idea but God's. And Moses was assured that the land of Canaan was going to be a gift from God ("Choose one of the leaders from each of the twelve tribes and send them as spies to explore the land of Canaan, which I am giving to the Israelites," v. 2, TEV). So there was no question about either the direction or the goal in this instance.

Often, leaders cannot point to a Scripture text to support a goal which needs to be achieved or pursued. This is why leaders need to be followers of both board and staff, as the Holy Spirit of God can speak to each. But establishment of goals is critical to leadership. If it doesn't matter where we end up, we can pursue any path. We have the same option if we draw the target after we take the shot. Unless we want to affect the future at random, we start with goals.

Paul was committed to "run toward the goal, so that I can win the prize of being called to heaven. This is the prize that God offers because of what Christ Jesus has done" (Phil. 3:14, CEV). These people had goals which they diligently pursued. We should do the same in our planning.

Priorities Must Be Developed among Given Goals

Moses had the option to select any approach to pursue the overall goal. But he first chose to organize a group of scouts or spies and then he gave them clear directions for actions. Moses made choices based on his priorities. And so too must leaders. Seldom are all choices worthy of praise. And certain choices or preferences do lead to different results and consequences.

Planning Requires Knowledge of the Facts As They Exist and Not As We Wish Them

First we have to know the facts and the realities. Moses was aware of the importance of facts in determining strategies or options. And that's why he wanted to know about the potential obstacles, such as walls and defenses. But he also wanted the facts about geography and agriculture. Too often leaders don't know the facts, or if they know, refuse to deal with their reality.

Planning Doesn't Discount the Past But Is Definitely Future-Oriented

Moses, knowing how God had worked in the past, could confidently handle the unknowns of the future. So while obviously celebrating the past, he eagerly looked forward to the future. He wanted to know God's next step and lived with that kind of anticipation. The past provided context and the future provides direction and hope. And the leader who gets into the past by going through history, as Moses did, is perhaps the leader who will have the most fulfilling journey. This is also the balance reflected by Paul: "The one thing I do, however, is to forget what is behind me and do my best to reach what is ahead" (Phil. 3:13, TEV).

In brief, we believe that for any Christian organization planning is a biblically endorsed function and process which leads not only to improved stewardship of available resources, but also to the accomplishment of goals. These goals reflect the tasks God has given us. In saying this, the leader must be aware that "the Lord builds the house" (Ps. 127:1) and that "we may make our plans, but God has the last word" (Prov. 16:1, TLB; cf. James 4:13-16).

14

Forgiveness

A LEADER WHO has not learned to be a good forgiver will not be as effective a leader as one who has. Leadership affords too many uncomfortable incidents, too many inaccurate accusations, and too little time to keep track of everyone who has "wronged" you.

To place the subject of forgiveness in some kind of a context, pretend for a moment that next week the local community auditorium will feature a dramatic presentation of your life story. The story will feature everything you've ever done. Everything! Nothing will be left out. In addition, the story will feature everything you've ever said. Everything! To make it even more spectacular, it will feature everything you've ever thought. Everything! Not very many leaders I know, including me, would want to come forward after a presentation like that to take a bow. Most of us would probably beat a path to the door as quickly as possible and vanish from sight.

Some leaders are probably thinking, "I'm sure glad nobody has a recorded story like that of my life." The truth of the matter, however, is that Somebody does have that story—unless we've experienced the forgiveness of Christ in our lives. The psalmist states that "as far as the east is from the west, so far does He remove our sins from us" (Ps. 103:12, TEV).

At the heart of the Gospel of Jesus Christ is forgiveness.

Christ died for our sins even while we were yet sinners. Because He paid the penalty for sin, I have experienced His forgiveness. And each time that I sin, I continue to seek His forgiveness. I'm told that "he who conceals his sins does not prosper, but whoever confesses and renounces them finds mercy" (Prov. 28:13). And in the New Testament: "But if we confess our sins to God, He can always be trusted to forgive us and take our sins away" (1 John 1:9, CEV). Simply put, as a forgiven person, and as a leader, I must be a forgiving person.

The idea that comes to us from the pages of Scripture features a two-dimensional concept of forgiveness. First, and as already has been noted, we need to experience forgiveness at the vertical dimension — between ourselves and God. Second, God wants us to experience forgiveness at the horizontal level — person to person. As we'll see, failure to forgive persons at the horizontal level produces a devastating impact on our relationship with God on the vertical level. This chapter will thus deal with such questions as why we must forgive, who is responsible to initiate forgiveness, how many times we must forgive, what does forgiveness involve, and what if I don't want to forgive.

Why Must We Forgive?

One of the fundamental arguments for horizontal forgiveness is that we are to forgive one another because Christ is our example. Note Paul's instructions:

> Put up with each other, and forgive anyone who does you wrong, just as Christ has forgiven you (Col. 3:13, CEV).

> Instead, be kind and merciful, and forgive others, just as God forgave you because of Christ (Eph. 4:32, CEV).

What Paul clearly commands is this: you have been forgiven by Christ, so you should forgive others. Simply put, a leader does not have the option not to forgive others. We are to forgive because Scripture commands it.

Who Is Responsible to Initiate Forgiveness?

Without question, the person responsible for causing the offense in the first place has a responsibility to initiate the forgiveness process. In other words, if I, as the leader, have done something to offend someone, I have a responsibility to go to that person and ask forgiveness. This assumes, of course, that I know that I have been the source of offense. Jesus talked about this type of situation in the Sermon on the Mount:

> So if you are about to offer your gift to God at the altar and there you remember that your brother has something against you, leave your gift there in front of the altar, go at once and make peace with your brother, and then come back and offer your gift to God (Matt. 5:23-24, TEV).

The idea is this. I'm standing in front of the altar getting ready to offer my sacrifice when I remember that someone has something against me—presumably because of something I've done. What am I to do? As important as sacrifice and religious ceremony are, Jesus says that it is even more important to be at peace. Therefore, I am to leave my gift or sacrifice at the altar, go seek forgiveness, and return to finish offering my sacrifice.

With regard to forgiveness, time is of the essence. We need to keep short accounts. So if we have to choose between going to church on Sunday morning or going to seek restoration with a friend, we are to first seek restoration. Notice, however, that Jesus doesn't provide an either/ or choice. He doesn't say, "Choose religious ceremony or pursue forgiveness." Rather, He seems to be suggesting that horizontal forgiveness ought to come before religious ceremony, and further that our willingness to participate in the forgiveness process will affect our ability to worship.

I believe that Scripture also teaches that the one offended has a responsibility to initiate the forgiveness process. Two texts which illustrate this principle are Mark 11:25-26 and Luke 17:3-4. In the Mark text, Jesus taught: "Whenever you stand up to pray, you must forgive what others have done to you. Then your Father in heaven will forgive your sins," (CEV). Whereas the Matthew 5 text was addressed to those who had offended someone else, this text is addressed to those who had been offended by someone else, whether or not the offender is aware of it. Unlike the Matthew text, where the offending one had the responsibility to take the initiative, this text simply suggests that if I am offended by something you've done, whether or not you know I'm upset about it, I have the responsibility to forgive you. If my forgiving you is primarily attitudinal, perhaps I don't even need to tell you about it. The point is, the one offended does not have the option to wait until the alleged offender initiates forgiveness. The one offended is also obliged to make things right.

If any doubt existed about what Jesus intended to say about the responsibility regarding the one offended, He made the point quite clear when He said to His disciples:

> So be careful what you do. Correct any followers of Mine who sin, and forgive the ones who say they are sorry. Even if one of them mistreats you seven times in one day and says, "I am sorry," you should still forgive that person (Luke 17:3-4, CEV).

How Many Times Must We Forgive?

Jesus apparently anticipated this kind of question because He addressed it on several occasions. In the Luke 17 passage, He observed that if a person sins against another seven times in one day and yet repents seven times, forgiveness must be extended. Peter was probably counting the number of times he had forgiven someone because according to Matthew 18:21-22 (CEV) he wanted to clarify the issue with Jesus: "Peter came up to the Lord and asked, 'How many times should I forgive someone who does something wrong to me? Is seven times enough?' " Jesus in essence told Peter to quit counting and learn once and for all that extending forgiveness to others needs to be viewed as a way of life for the Christian, no matter how many times he has been wronged: "Jesus answered, 'Not just seven times, but seventy-seven times!' " (v. 22, CEV)

What about "Bad" Sins?

Does the leader (and others, for that matter) have to be forgiven "bad" sins? The obvious inference here is that there are "good" sins, which are not worthy of significant organizational response and which can be forgiven. And then there are "bad" sins, which, if committed by the leader or others, and even when forgiveness is extended, will almost surely result in dismissal.

These kinds of issues are seldom discussed in Christian publications. Sins relating to sexuality (particularly affairs and divorce) and criminal conduct figure prominently as "bad" sins. Leaders and others who commit them, even when all parties extend and are extended forgiveness, can count on job-hunting. Why? Perhaps the matter would not be so troubling if the reason for the decision to dismiss were tied to matters such as "holiness of life" and organizational purity. Many times, however, the reason for the dismissal is based primarily on the rationale that continued employment "will be bad for our ministry. After all, people won't support our ministry if a forgiven check bouncer serves as our leader. Monetary gifts would stop and, obviously, the organization needs money to operate." And the organization definitely doesn't want its supporters to think it is "soft on sin." "Look how God punished Achan" (see biblical references such as Josh. 7), proponents of this view say. But what about David and the abominable sins he committed—lust, adultery, and murder? Did God remove him from office? The answer, obviously, is no. Of course, even though David confessed his sin and was forgiven by God, there were still consequences for his sin. Nathan the prophet announced God's judgment:

> "Now, in every generation some of your descendants will die a violent death because you have disobeyed Me and have taken Uriah's wife. I swear to you that I will cause someone from your own family to bring trouble on you. You will see it when I take your wives from you and give them to another man; and he will have intercourse with them in broad daylight. You sinned in secret, but I will make this happen in broad daylight for all Israel to see." "I have sinned against the Lord," David said. Nathan replied, "The Lord forgives you; you will not die. But because you have shown such contempt for the Lord in doing this, your child will die" (2 Sam. 12:10-14, TEV).

Because of David's sin, his son died and internal warfare within the royal family resulted. However, David was not removed from his position of leadership. Again, the question is raised—why not?

Perhaps the contemporary Christian organization has made one of its highest priorities keeping its constituency happy and the religious influencers satisfied rather than having Christ be its guide and example. Did not Jesus have His harshest criticism for the religious community? If David were a contemporary leader in a leading Christian organization and, assuming he genuinely confessed his sin, would there be doubt in anyone's mind that he would have been removed from his position of leadership? Why would God not remove David and why would we? Perhaps it's because we yet fail to understand how God works within His people and what forgiveness really involves.

What Does Forgiveness Involve?

According to a noted counselor, forgiveness involves at least three facets.

- *Don't keep bringing it up.* First, when I forgive, in essence I say that I will not raise the matter again. Our example, again, is the person of Christ and His relationship to me. When He forgives me, He obliterates the record.

- *Don't tell others about the problem.* Extending forgiveness means that after forgiveness has been extended, I will not tell other persons about the previously committed wrong. The matter of offense becomes a closed one between the two parties.

- *Don't dwell on it — let it go and move on.* After forgiveness has been extended, I will not dwell on the matter myself. The person who says, "I'll forgive you but I'll never forget it" has not really extended forgiveness. Granted, I may have to work at forgetting, but work at it I must. In the Parable of the Unmerciful Servant, Jesus addressed this issue in part by stating that forgiveness had to eventually affect the heart: "Unless you forgive your brother *from your heart*" (Matt. 18:35, TEV, italics added).

What If I Don't Want to Forgive?

If something is done without feeling, does that make the action ungenuine? No, I think not. Frequently the leader is called to do things that he or she may not feel like doing. The same is true in my personal life. For example, I don't feel like getting up early every morning, yet I do. Does that make me a hypocrite? Surely not. What would make me a hypocrite is going around telling everyone how much I enjoy getting up early in the morning. Some of Jesus' harshest words were targeted toward the Pharisees who constantly were trying to project an outward image to the people that didn't match their heart attitude.

In the context of forgiveness, if someone has offended me, it is not necessary that I feel like forgiving him in order to extend forgiveness. That is not hypocrisy. What would make the act hypocritical would be for me to state how much I've enjoyed extending forgiveness when in fact I've hated doing so. Time and time again, the leader is called to go against feelings to be a responsible leader and a responsible Christian. And when dealing with the issue of forgiveness, many times the leader may have to go against feelings. In the Luke 17 passage examined earlier, Jesus seems to be saying, "Don't even consider the fact that I ask you to forgive and forgive and forgive to be a big deal. Rather, consider your response to be analogous to the hired hand who is simply doing his duty."

Earlier discussion of the Parable of the Unmerciful Servant (Matt. 18:23-25) suggested that failure to forgive produced dire consequences. Mark 11:25 makes clear that our failure to forgive others results in the Heavenly Father's failure to forgive us. Given these dire consequences regarding the failure to forgive, it is shocking and surprising to witness the number of grudges, infightings, and political battles that many times plague Christian organizations. Perhaps one of the most important responsibilities of leaders is not only to make sure that accounts are kept short between them and others, but also to endeavor to ensure that forgiveness is practiced throughout the organization. Given the biblical emphasis on unity, and Jesus' statement that the world would know His disciples by the love they had one for another, it is not extraordinary that His teaching on the subject of forgiveness is so powerful and that the consequences of failing to follow this instruction are so extreme.

15

Compensation, Transitions, and Vulnerability

THERE ARE SEVERAL things about organizational leadership which are important to effectiveness in leadership. Most people understand the importance of leadership and planning; managing culture and developing people; and setting up structures and the importance of accountability. But as Christian leaders, the three items discussed in this chapter are often not mentioned in leadership books. Yet they are important to both leaders and followers. And it's the approach one takes to compensation, transitions, and vulnerability which often determines effectiveness in leadership.

Compensation

While not often verbalized, at least not initially, the issue of "how much will I get paid?" is an important question of the potential leader. As the unwritten rules of the hiring process are now set forth, it's not appropriate for the leadership candidate to raise pecuniary issues until at least final interviews take place, or preferably, once an offer is extended. Then and only then should financial discussions take place.

My assertion for the remainder of this discussion is that "leaders chosen by God" should seldom if ever raise concerns, other than perhaps for purposes of clarification, pertaining to the economic issues of their employment. I'll give my reasons later.

Many leaders negotiate or bargain for a "top" salary/benefits package and only accept "if the price is right." The assumption which underlies this kind of thinking is that the organization should take care of the leader's needs and then the leader will take care of the needs of the organization. And since the pressure of leadership is so great, a large salary, presumably to compensate for this stress, is called for. This attitude seems to be the reverse of that presented in Scripture, which is: if I'm called by God, I have a responsibility to take care of the needs of the people (remember our earlier reference to the leader as a shepherd?) and then God and the people will take care of my needs. If I have negative stress, God tells me to "cast my care on Him," not ask for more money and benefits. The actions of both Joshua and Nehemiah are once again instructive for leaders.

As mentioned earlier, the Book of Joshua is a story of success and victory. Because of their dependence on God, rarely did the Children of Israel meet defeat. Note the following:

So the Lord gave to Israel all the land that He had solemnly promised their ancestors He would give them. When they had taken possession of it, they settled down there. The Lord gave them peace throughout the land, just as He had promised their ancestors. Not one of all their enemies had been able to stand against them, because the Lord gave the Israelites the victory over all their enemies. The Lord kept every one of the promises that He had made to the people of Israel (Josh. 21:43-45, TEV).

Interestingly, we're also told about how the spoils of victory were allotted to the various tribes. Only after each tribe had received its inheritance did the Israelites turn to the matter of compensating their leader.

When they had finished dividing the land into its allotted

portions, the Israelites gave Joshua son of Nun an inheritance among them, as the Lord had commanded. They gave him the town he asked for — Timnath Serah in the hill country of Ephraim. And he built up the town and settled there (19:49-50). In other words, Joshua did not get his inheritance until after the others, the people he was leading, received theirs. Obviously, current practice is many times just the opposite. We have previously set forth the story of Nehemiah. He too chose not to receive the "entitlements" as governor.

> During all the twelve years that I was governor of the land of Judah, from the twentieth year that Artaxerxes was emperor until his thirty-second year, neither my relatives nor I ate the food I was entitled to have as governor. Every governor who had been in office before me had been a burden to the people and had demanded forty silver coins a day for food and wine. Even their servants had oppressed the people. But I acted differently, because I honored God. I put all my energy into rebuilding the wall and did not acquire any property. Everyone who worked for me joined in the rebuilding (Neh. 5:14-16, TEV).

Yes, Nehemiah could have had more, but he chose to have less because he wanted nothing to do with "lording it over the people." Several other biblical observations might also be of help. The Apostle Peter, for example, reminds us that as leaders we are not to lord our position over those we lead nor are we to be greedy for money:

> Be shepherds of God's flock that is under your care, serving as overseers — not because you must, but because you are willing, as God wants you to be; not greedy for money, but eager to serve; not lording it over those entrusted to you, but being examples to the flock (1 Peter 5:2-3).

Peter also reminds us of leadership's true reward: "And when the Chief Shepherd appears, you will receive the *crown of glory* that will never fade away" (v. 4, italics added). Elsewhere, we leaders are told, "Do your work willingly, as though you were serving the Lord Himself, and not just your earthly master" (Col. 3:23, CEV).

Transitions

Transitions in leadership tend to be awkward at best and divisive at worst — even within Christian organizations. Followers tend to become committed to a given leader and when that person is no longer the leader, for either voluntary or involuntary reasons, a certain amount of organizational tension is inevitable.

Some argue that once a leader retires or is "retired," that leader should no longer remain in the same geographical area. The reason for this is that if a retired popular leader remains in the same area, people within the organization will not transfer their loyalties to the new leader. The opposing argument, particularly with the case of the retired popular leader, is that since the retired person has built up a residual base of goodwill, the successor proceeds at his or her own peril if that expertise is not used for the good of the organization.

As a general operational guideline, transitions in leadership ought not be left to happenstance. Indeed, transitions ought to be well-planned long in advance. In *The Art of Japanese Management*, business professors, Pascale and Athos list the five key ingredients necessary "to build a great corporation that persists across time, especially after its builders are gone."

It takes first, a long time. Second, it takes constant socialization of new people and constant training of those who keep moving higher. Third, it takes endless articulation and reinforcement of what the institution honors, values, and believes. Fourth, it takes obsessive attention from the CEO. And fifth, it takes careful planning for (leadership) succession long in advance.[1]

Indeed, for transitions to be effective, the goodwill of both the retiring incumbent and the successor leader is essential if the work of the organization is to continue unabated. Some have argued that one of the most important legacies a leader can leave an institution is a smooth transition in leadership, where organizational allegiance can be quickly and readily given to the new leader.

John Gardner argues that a good leader constantly insists that followers will look to their own resources and their own initiatives rather than always look to the leader for direction:

The purposes of the group are best served when the leader helps followers to develop their own initiative, strengthens them in the use of their own judgment, enables them to grow and to become better contributors.[2]

However, there are also leaders "who diminish their followers, rendering them dependent and childlike, exploiting their unconscious need for the godlike magic helper of their infancy."[3] He observes that James Jones of Jonestown worked systematically to obliterate adult judgment and create dependency among his followers.[4] What Gardner is in essence suggesting is that a leader must always be asking the question: what effect will my departure, involuntary or otherwise, have on the continuing stability of the organization? Have I made my constituents or followers so dependent on me that they are unable to support a new leader, whether pastor or president? This consideration, then, leads us back again to the issue of transitions in leadership.

Michael Youssef shares several helpful suggestions on this subject of transitions. First, he notes that "one characteristic of good leaders is that they prepare others to take over. They don't just prepare their followers to 'do well,' but prepare them to do everything they are doing themselves."[5] He further suggests that current leaders help in the process of preparing other leaders by giving others "responsibilities before they're ready for it" and "before they ask for it."[6]

Scripture itself gives us several case studies on leadership transitions. We'll focus on the transition from Moses to Joshua. In the latter chapters of Deuteronomy, God had made it clear to Moses that he was no longer to be the leader of Israel, and that Joshua was to be his successor. Since we're told that when Moses died, "his eyes were not weak nor his strength gone" (Deut. 34:7), God had other reasons for desiring a new leader. Fortunately, Moses did not fight the changeover but worked hard at making the transition effective. Notice his charge to Joshua:

> Then Moses called Joshua and said to him in the presence of all the people of Israel, "Be determined and confident; you are the one who will lead these people to occupy the land that the Lord promised to their ancestors. The Lord Himself will lead you and be with you. He will not fail you or abandon you, so do not lose courage or be afraid" (Deut. 31:7-8, TEV).

The next step in the transition was that God took Moses out of the picture. After the charge had been given to Joshua, on that same day God spoke to Moses:

> Go to the Abarim Mountains in the land of Moab opposite the city of Jericho; climb Mount Nebo and look at the land of Canaan that I am about to give the people of Israel. You will die on that mountain as your brother Aaron died on Mount Hor, because both of you were unfaithful to Me in the presence of the people of Israel. When you were at the waters of Meribah, near the town of Kadesh in the wilderness of Zin, you

dishonored Me in the presence of the people. You will look at the land from a distance, but you will not enter the land that I am giving the people of Israel (32:49-52, TEV).

In these verses we see not only Moses immediately being taken out of the picture, but we also see the awesome price for failure in leadership (the problem of incomplete obedience). Finally, we see the positive response of the people to the leadership change:

Joshua the son of Nun was filled with wisdom, because Moses had appointed him to be his successor. The people of Israel obeyed Joshua and kept the commands that the Lord had given them through Moses (34:9, TEV).

We will obey you, just as we always obeyed Moses, and may the Lord your God be with you as He was with Moses! (Josh. 1:17, TEV)

Then and now, transitions in leadership continue. The future of most organizations, and the role that these organizations perform as part of the work of the kingdom, depend on how well these kinds of transitions in leadership are handled.

Vulnerability

"Why are leaders so elitist?" It's a question often asked by followers in an organization. Followers want leaders who are reachable, not leaders who are so "high and mighty" that one can't climb the pedestal to reach them. From my perspective, the issue is not so much one of "perceived elitism" as much as it is one of vulnerability. How vulnerable do leaders make themselves to the persons they lead? By vulnerable, I don't mean that leaders ought to go around "hanging out" all kinds of soiled laundry. Rather, I mean the ongoing demonstration and expression of basic human qualities, qualities such as anger, disappointment, and pain. This complex issue has been debated from various perspectives. On the one hand, some argue that it is absolutely essential for leaders to maintain distance between themselves and those they lead. Note the words of former university president and now consultant James Fisher:

> Distance has characterized effective leaders throughout history. And there need be nothing dishonest or unethical in its practice; it is simply unwise for a college president to establish intimate relationships with members of the faculty he or she must serve.[7]

As the argument is developed, Fisher points out that the people being led refuse to accept the leader as a regular person. Accordingly, invitations to social occasions (other than business) are rare. What's more, followers have a tendency to view the leader as "better than I am." In other words, the follower can have a given hang-up or weakness, but the leader had better not have one. Vulnerability, therefore, is to be avoided at all costs for, if the leader is perceived by followers as just a regular person, he may be unfit for leadership. As Fisher observes:

> Leaders are idealized as those whose strength enables them to assume the responsibility for their followers and who can devise better solutions and direction. Indeed, in this idealization, followers deny that leaders experience doubts, insecurities, or weaknesses. Followers react to their leaders' human foibles with astonishment, dismay, and even anger to an exaggerated degree, as if to say, "If you are not totally dependable, then you may not be dependable at all."[8]

The leader, in this view, is in a Catch-22. According to

Pascale and Athos, Japanese managers are more apt to exhibit vulnerability than are their Western counterparts:

> He is more likely to reveal his weaknesses and idiosyncrasies to his subordinates. In fact, many Japanese managers feel that by revealing their vulnerabilities they are better able to enlist assistance. Contrast this to subordinates in the West, who often have to discern a superior's weakness through a veneer of pseudo-competence. We are often inhibited from directly offering to help a boss because we are supposed to accept the "superior" image he is trying so hard to portray.[9]

If distance is maintained, the leader may be perceived as aloof and arrogant. If the leader becomes vulnerable, and shares weaknesses and other human tendencies, he or she is not worth following. Every leader has experienced this tension and seeming paradox.

On the other end of the spectrum is the position that it's OK for a leader to be vulnerable. Psychologist James Carr represents this viewpoint:

> As a premise of leadership, "familiarity breeds contempt" is a cop-out. It may serve a purpose, but does it serve the cause of leadership? By waving your degrees, your rank, your authority in the face of your subordinates and keeping them at arm's length, you can avoid the bother of knowing them . . . or caring about them. You can prevent their knowledge or caring about you as well and thus evade the responsibility that involvement implies. But what is teamwork without involvement?[10]

There seems to be little question that Scripture gives us a picture of Christians working together to reflect the bodily qualities of unity or teamwork. Certainly this concept of working together in unity is conducive to encouraging vulnerability in leadership. Note, for example, the following New Testament references:

If you have any encouragement from being united with Christ, if any comfort from His love, if any fellowship with the Spirit, if any tenderness and compassion, then make my joy complete by being like-minded, having the same love, being one in spirit and purpose. Do nothing out of selfish ambition or vain conceit, but in humility consider others better than yourselves (Phil. 2:1-3).

Finally, all of you should agree and have concern and love for each other. You should also be kind and humble (1 Peter 3:8, CEV).

God is the one who makes us patient and cheerful. I pray that He will help you live at peace with each other, as you follow Christ (Rom. 15:5, CEV).

Love each other as brothers and sisters and honor others more than you do yourself (12:10, CEV).

As a leader reviewing these verses, I ask myself this question: do these passages and scores of others like them suggest vulnerability or distance? The answer, to me at least, seems rather clear—when Christians are working together, as is the case in the Christian organization, vulnerability, not distance, ought to be the operative expectation. Indeed, in Paul's letter to the Galatians, he instructed them as follows: "Help carry one another's burdens, and in this way you will obey the law of Christ" (Gal. 6:2, TEV). Bearing someone else's burdens in a corporate context presupposes each party has knowledge of those burdens. And if I'm not practicing vulnerability, then both I and the people I lead will not be able to practice what Scripture asks us to do.
But how vulnerable should a leader be? As Navigator

president Jerry White has written: "People in ministry become closed because they have had friendships betrayed. They share their heart with somebody and say, 'We are really struggling in our marriage . . .' and before they know it, The board starts inquiring."

Being vulnerable with the more personal struggles of life doesn't mean that "everybody" need know of them. Other people usually don't share "everything with everybody." Alternatively, leaders ought to be regularly in touch with a small group of friends who can both share burdens and insist on accountability. The leader in isolation is a leader in trouble. The leader's spouse can also be of tremendous help in this area.

Finally, being vulnerable doesn't mean explicit garbage dumping. Leaders should exercise discretion in sharing details. Asking for prayer regarding "the family fight" might reflect the actual experience, but it might be just as effective to request prayer for "learning how to love my family better." After all, God knows all the details and some are better left to Him.

Repeatedly in this book we have focused on the soul of leadership. And once again, the inner part of the leader will influence these matters as well. A leader should not be selfish or greedy on the compensation issue. And the primary concern for the outgoing leader needs to be the concern about how a transition affects one's successor. And vulnerability will be no more than pious garbage dumping unless the action is properly motivated.

So we end this discussion with this point: A leader can be no better on the outside than what the inside allows. That is particularly true with regard to attitudes about compensation, transitions, and vulnerability.

16

Growth: How Much Is Enough?

ONE OF THE issues that a leader must ultimately address is the issue of organizational growth or, "how much is enough?" The issue is a broad one—nonprofits confront it on issues like number of programs and size of endowments; churches confront it on issues like number of staff, number of members, and size of facility and programs; businesses confront it on issues like size of plant, amount of product produced, and cost of services rendered. Eventually we all must decide where to draw the line.

Secular Culture and Its Influence on Modern Church-Growth Concepts

Before this issue is explored in the context of Scripture, it must be observed that much of our desire for growth, other than a desire for growth in an intangible way, is the result of a secular mind-set. Whether we like it or not, Charles Darwin has greatly influenced our thinking in this regard—even in Christian circles.

The Rise and Rule of Social Darwinism

Jeremy Rifkin in his book, *Algeny,* reviews the many ways Social Darwinism has come to influence our thinking. Rifkin argues, persuasively in my view, that Darwin, doing nothing more than reflecting the social and economic structure of his time, 19th-century England, proceeded to rephrase that social structure in the form of a scientific-sounding theory explaining man's relationship to nature. As Rifkin notes:

Darwin dressed up nature with an English personality, ascribed to nature English motivations and drives, and even provided nature with an English marketplace and the English form of government. Like others who preceded him in history, Darwin borrowed from the popular culture the appropriate metaphors and then transposed them to nature, projecting a new cosmology that was remarkably similar in detail to the day-to-day life he was accustomed to.[1]

And just what were these features of day-to-day life? The basic tenet of "Darwin's theory of the origin and development of species centered on the survival of the fittest."[2] Expressed as a "natural" principle, "in the struggle for survival, nature ensures that the strong will triumph and the weak will perish."[3] Translated into often bitter competition between Christian organizations, many work overtime to develop organizational strength so that they will be the most fit of the survivors. Indeed, the goal of many strategic planning initiatives is to do what needs to be done faster, better, and with less. John White puts the issue quite succinctly:

Expansion is unthinkingly accepted among Western Christians as something good and desirable in itself. And by expansion I do not mean the spread of the gospel, but the growth of particular institutions. Expanding organizations come into conflict over money, territory and workers. At times mature thinking prevails, and there is cooperation and collaboration. But equally often, conflict results in the kind of competitiveness I have already described, which is not the less fierce for being described in pious cliches as "a matter for prayer." So the operation gets bigger. If smaller groups get crowded out, maybe that proves that God has lost interest in them. They should have had more "faith." Just as in laissez faire capitalism so in the Christianizing industry . . . survival of the fittest must be the law of God himself. Obviously some Christian groups feel the pinch more than others. Some denominational missions have large reserves of capital. Wherever the pinch is felt most keenly, there the battle rages most fiercely. And a battle it is. Behind the firm handshakes and ecclesiastical jocularity, a struggle for economic survival often rages, nonetheless deadly for being covert.[4]

The modern thinking about many nonprofits, for example, suggests that not all will survive, except the strongest, the obvious inference being that the weak will perish. Many denominational church groups regularly assess which are their strong and weak churches and what should be done to keep strong churches strong and to help or shut down the weak. Not too many denominational leaders would express sadness at the loss of another denomination just as not many pastors would lament the fact that more people come to "my" church and less to "yours." There often is no shared commitment on the part of Christian organizations to see that each survives and thrives. Rather, the commitment is to see "my entity grow, at your expense if necessary," and to become as large as possible. If yours doesn't survive, maybe it didn't deserve to continue.

Many church leaders use as their motivation for growth and expansion the salvation of new converts. But as many church groups have learned, it doesn't follow that "new conversions" will always translate into new members. Church growth and efforts at evangelism are not necessarily directly related.

Another central feature of Darwin's theory of evolution was the ongoing improvement that was inherent in the process. This concurred with the "Victorian propensity to believe in progress."[5] As Rifkin observes, however, "the idea of 'no limit' to the process of improvement was not limited to Darwin." He quotes French aristocrat Marquis de Condorcet: "No bounds have been fixed to the improvement of human faculties—the perfectability of man is absolutely indefinite."[6] As Darwin saw it, survival of the fittest was the key point to this ongoing improvement or growth: "[There is]—one general law, leading to the advancement of all organic beings, namely, multiply, vary, let the strongest live and the weakest die."[7] Darwin observed that "too many organisms" were "competing for too few niches in nature." He went on to observe that "there are only two ways to promote an organism's survival; either compete for the existing niches or find new ones that have yet to be filled."[8]

One can readily notice the incredible similarities between how organizations, including Christian ones, reflect these Darwinian principles, including use of the latest marketing techniques. One could almost substitute the word organization for Darwin's word organism and the practical realities would be the same. His suggested way for survival would closely parallel classic business advice in marketing—find a need and fill it. Competition abounds, and to win, "more" is needed.

My involvement with Christian organizations suggests that Social Darwinism is alive and well. Such appears to be the case in terms of organizational operations, particularly the pursuit of customers, church members, and donors. Good customers, for example, are prime candidates for attention. Each organization wants more. And it doesn't matter how many one already has—one more will do. Well-known organizations go to great lengths to recruit new customers and new donors they believe would provide great benefit to them. Organizations throw great resources into the fray, including those prime "spiritual" variables such as venerated history and purity or superiority of mission. And why? Why do Christian organizations follow the best principles of Darwinism in their efforts to recruit customers or raise money? Is survival what life is ultimately about? Can this method be condoned by Scripture?

The irony of this "survival of the fittest" competition is that in terms of their religion, not many Christian organizations would identify themselves as supporters of Charles Darwin. But, in their operational practices, Darwin has become one of their best-followed prophets. Fortunately, Scripture does have something to say about all this. It appears that biblical thinking proceeds along two distinct lines. In terms of the intangibles of the kingdom, enough is never enough. But in terms of tangibles, be on your guard because "enough" might be too much. Let me elaborate.

A Biblical View versus Social Darwinism

My reading of Scripture does not suggest precise quantifiable limits that could be interpreted to mean any accumulation beyond a certain number of dollars, members, or customers is sin and will produce problems. Alternatively, the Bible does outline a number of principles which give guidance on the matter of possessions. Let's look at several.

God Desires to Determine the Growth and Decline of Organizations

God wants people, and presumably organizations, to accumulate or to de-accumulate only at His command so that hope and trust will always be in Him.

In Joshua 11 there was a huge army "as numerous as the sand on the seashore" being assembled to fend off the vastly outnumbered yet invading Israelites (v. 4). After telling the people that He would give them victory, God told them to make sure to "hamstring their [the enemy's] horses and burn their chariots" (v. 6). Why? Would not the collection of these marvelous instruments of war have done much to aid the Israelites in their next encounter? Yes, but God wanted the people unequivocally to have their dependence on and hope in Him alone. He knew that we humans tend to rely on our tangibles instead of Him. As Yoder has observed, "If . . . we forsake our goods to follow him, we are proclaiming our trust in a Father who knows our needs."[9]

Success Can Blind Us to God's Will

There comes a point in the accumulation of things where we trust in them and forget about God. Our eyes and ears are covered with the fat of luxury and convenience. Furthermore, even if we can still hear God's Word, we often ignore it because it interferes with our drive for "self-fulfillment."

A case in point is God's prediction that the Israelites would reject Him in part because they would come to rely on the bounty of the Promised Land: "I will take them into this rich and fertile land, as I promised their ancestors. There they will have all the food they want, and they will live comfortably. But they will turn away and worship other gods. They will reject Me and break My covenant" (Deut. 31:20, TEV). This point is made again in the Minor Prophets: "But when you entered the good land, you became full and satisfied, and then you grew proud and forgot Me" (Hosea 13:6, TEV). The concept seems clear: there comes a point when accumulation of things and experiencing "success" resulting from that accumulation turns peoples' hearts away from God.

God's Provision Is Always Adequate for Our Needs

No matter the conditions or circumstances, biblical history is filled with story after story of God's provision for the needs of people. During the Exodus, God moved the Egyptians to give extra supplies before the Israelites left on their long journey. When there was no water, water was provided. When people were in the desert, fresh meat was provided. And the ever-present "manna" was a needed source of food. Plus, clothing and sandals did not wear out during the journey. Coincidence or God's just-in-time supply?

Not only did God meet material needs. He was a source of answers for military conquests and campaigns so that victory, in the face of defeat, usually resulted. Often, if not usually, the Israelites were outnumbered and outflanked. But that didn't seem to matter as long as they went forward depending on God. Even when the people had the opportunity to add weapons of war, they were instructed not to. Why? Because God wanted people to depend solely on Him for their source of success and victory. It was the job of Moses to ensure this focus through his leadership. As a result, people were obedient to the Lord and God's provision was always enough.

Unlike Moses, we have reversed what appear to be fairly clear biblical priorities and mislabeled them. Why? First of all, modern Christian organizations tend to reward their leaders more for accumulating tangibles than for qualitative growth regarding intangibles. For example, I know of few leaders of Christian organizations who were asked to resign because of not enough time spent in prayer. To be sure, there have been those isolated cases where dismissal has resulted because of financial, or marital indiscretions. Alternatively, I know of a number of leaders who lost their jobs because they were not good enough accumulators—whether of customers, money, facilities, or endowment.

Is it not possible that God might want an organization to remain small and possess little in terms of facilities or financial resources? Certainly these comments are not intended to condone mismanagement or inattention to the best reengineering and marketing processes. From earlier discussions we saw where God had specifically instructed the Israelites not to accumulate and, further, not to take advantage of the latest technology to advance His purposes. Was He wrong and are we right? One might think so given the operating agenda for many Christian organizations.

Leaders of Christian organizations are alert to the ways the game is played. They proceed headily along the road to accumulation of things for their organizations. In the college world, for instance, enrollment had better increase, the endowment grow, and buildings be built. It's nice to know that qualitatively students are spending more time praying, that they're living out the commands of Scripture by attending to the needs of the elderly—but that won't lead to a raise or recognition elsewhere, let alone bring attention for the leadership of the "elite" Christian organizations. By having these kinds of tangible expectations for the leader, corporate boards, by default, implicitly approve operating principles that focus on accumulation.

In my many discussions with pastors of various denominations, they are quick to point out in confidence that their chances for promotion and recognition within their denomination depend on the opportunity to lead the right church. As a result, and without "praying" about it, decisions are made to avoid "serving" in smaller churches in order to optimize their chances for promotion within the denomination. All this is done with the effective use of spiritual-sounding language—"God hasn't led me" or "God has led me to the larger church." Indeed, God could have led that way, but many times our answers as to why we serve where we do amount to nothing more than spiritualized lying. Denominational officials play the game in reverse, giving key assignments to pastors who have played the game well in smaller churches. Obviously, one of the significant ways to get the attention of denominational officials is to have rapid church growth and a major, successful building program. Why? Because accumulation of tangibles gets rewarded.

Take almost any professional grouping of organizations and usually it will be the larger entities which supply the greatest number of speakers, seminar leaders, and board members. Thankfully, these are exceptions. Nevertheless, because we equate "big" to be better and "small" as less desirable than "bigness," there are hundreds of leaders who are damaging themselves, their marriages, and their families in order to do that extra something to get ahead.

While some boards and church leaders may be at fault for having misplaced priorities in these areas, the leader bent on integrity—whether an organizational president, pastor, or other leader—must accept responsibility for his or her own attitudes and actions. First, a leader has the responsibility to keep priorities and goals biblically based and Christ-centered, regardless of career impact. If one's leadership goal is to make a lot of money and head a prestigious Christian organization, then perhaps another agenda might be warranted. My commitment to Christ ought to say that I will follow Him anytime, anywhere He leads. If He leads to the small, out-of-the-way church, that's OK because He's God; He's promised to meet my needs, and I've promised to be obedient. If He takes me to the inner cities of a foreign country, that's OK, because He's promised to meet my needs, and I've promised to be obedient. If He leads me to be president of a small, less famous Christian organization, that's OK too. My sufficiency, after all, does not rest in the tangible assets of the organization I lead, but, rather, in Christ, and in Him alone.

It grieves my heart to hear leaders of Christian organizations talking about how they wouldn't want to go to a particular Christian organization "because of all the problems there." But that's the very point—God is enough! He is the miracle-working God who can take an impossible situation and make it work. We, however, have to give Him the chance to work, and perhaps He wants us to be a part of the solution.

One of the most disappointing things for me in the Christian circles I frequent is the way small organizations are written off as places where the "biggies" don't want to serve. In the smaller organization, however, there's just as great if not a greater opportunity for leadership skills to be used. Indeed, the problem-laden small organization may require greater leadership skill than the larger, "better-off" one.

Moses dealt with this important issue in several ways. For example, inheritance laws restricted the movement of tangibles between clans: "Tribal land must not be given to another tribe—it will remain the property of the tribe that received it. In the future any daughter who inherits land must marry someone from her own tribe. Israel's tribal land is never to be passed from one tribe to another" (Num. 36:7-9, CEV).

In other words, one clan's inheritance was not to grow at the expense of another. Wheeling and dealing for a larger share of the market was clearly not permitted by God.

In another way, Moses established an emphasis on bringing the first part of their tangible successes to God. We see this in Leviticus 23:9-10, CEV: "The Lord told Moses to say to the community of Israel: 'After you enter the land I am giving you, the first bundle of each crop must be given to Me. So bring it to a priest.' "

Clearly the people were not to get everything they could for themselves. This emphasis on the tithe and concern for the needy was yet another way of God saying that people didn't have to worry about doing these things because He was and remains more than adequate for meeting our needs.

Now, where does this lead us? First, organizations must address the "why" of the desire to get larger. If it is to satisfy gratification of ego, then growth should be rejected. If it is to help meet unmet needs, then it might be a candidate for organizational pursuit. Second, after prayerful discussion and consideration, if God is still directing more growth to achieve an even larger mission, by all means pursue it. Third, be careful in pursuing that expanded agenda to avoid divisive competition which destroys. Competition is healthy but competing and winning is not the bottom line. Building God's kingdom is. So whenever "God" is invoked as the reason for expansion, that must be an honest statement.

So how much is enough? In matters of character, enough is never enough. In terms of pursuing godliness, I never will reach that goal in this lifetime. But in matters of the tangible, I should avoid having so much that my confidence and satisfaction are based on what I've accumulated, not on God's sufficiency for meeting needs. These, hopefully, are comforting words for leaders.

17

Leaders and the Local Church

MANY CHRISTIANS WHO hold both formal and informal positions of leadership in organizations outside the local church see themselves as "just a layperson." They are not meaningfully involved within the church, despite their scriptural responsibility to do so. In his book, *Unleashing the Church,* Frank Tillapaugh observes: "The church's main problem is getting lay people involved in ministry."[1]

Whether or not one agrees with Tillapaugh's assessment, it is probably fair to observe that most churches are not overrun with active lay participation. We need to do better—much better. Indeed, the paradox is that without an active laity, the local church is doomed to struggle, if not fail. Unfortunately, many are content with that state of events, including laypersons and particularly those who lead outside the church. Before we further discuss this issue and what we might do about it, we need to define our terms.

The Laity

When I use the term laity, I am referring to individuals who do not hold a full-time paid position in the work of the local church. When I use the term church, I am not talking about a church building. While a church building may have legal and organizational standing, in the biblical sense a church building is simply one of the locations where the church meets. God doesn't dwell there.

I find of interest those many efforts made by well-intentioned people who suggest that the church building is like the temple of the Old Testament. But I am reminded of Solomon's observation: "No one can ever build a temple large enough for God—even the heavens are too small a place for Him to live in! All I can do is build a place where we can offer sacrifices to Him" (2 Chron. 2:6, CEV).

Recall for a moment Jesus' dialogue with the Samaritan woman (John 4:4-26, CEV). She was in essence arguing for a special worship location when she said: "My ancestors worshiped on this mount, but you Jews say Jerusalem is the only place to worship" (v. 20, CEV). Yet Jesus responded: "But a time is coming, and it is already here! Even now the true worshipers are being led by the Spirit to worship the Father according to the truth. These are the ones the Father is seeking to worship Him. God is Spirit, and those who worship God must be led by the Spirit to worship Him according to the truth" (vv. 23-24, CEV). And Paul reminds them: "All of you surely know that you are God's temple and that His Spirit lives in you?" (1 Cor. 3:16, CEV)

Well, then what is the church? According to Ephesians 1:22-23 (CEV), "God has put all things under the power of Christ, and for the good of the church He has made Him the head of everything. The church is Christ's body and is filled with Christ who completely fills everything." There we have it! Christ's body is the church. But what constitutes His body? Romans 12:4-5 (CEV) supplies the answer: "A body is made up of many parts, and each of them has its own use. That's how it is with us. There are many of us, but we each are part of the body of Christ, as well as part of one another." It appears, then, that all of us, leaders and followers, are part of the body of Christ if we have invited Him to be the Savior and Lord of our lives. We constitute His body. As Paul writes, "Together you are the body of Christ. Each one of you is part of His body" (1 Cor. 12:27, CEV).

As we study more carefully the biblical teaching on this subject we learn one more very important piece of truth: As part of the body of Christ, we each play a necessary or vital role. Some of the functions the body parts perform include teaching, giving, serving, and leading (see Rom. 12:4-8; 1 Cor. 12:1-18; Eph. 4:4-16; 1 Peter 4:10-11). In short, the church is composed of persons who have accepted Christ and who are fully prepared to exercise the spiritual gifts God has gifted them with.

Christ's body has no organizational membership requirements for admission or inclusion. We can't find much biblical support for a position that says "only members of the legally incorporated XYZ church can participate in our programs and activities." Indeed, persons who hold to this position may not only incompletely define the biblical church but may also replace biblical expectations of the body with a set of human requirements for involvement. While there are good organizational reasons to argue for membership in a local church, we cannot equate membership in a local church or denomination with membership in the body of Christ. Ironically, might this be one of the reasons a significant number of laypeople are not involved in the work of ministry? While we complain about lack of lay involvement, we tend to shut out their involvement at the same time. Again, we need to return to the biblical standard in this area.

Church Laity Are Essential to the Work

First, as we have just noted, without the involvement of laity, gifts and abilities needed for the body of Christ to function properly are simply not present. Indeed, there can be no healthy body without having all its parts involved and working properly.

All of us can point to mechanical examples of this principle. What amazes me is that we take such a relaxed attitude about lay noninvolvement in our churches. Lay noninvolvement ought to drive us to our knees. We should make every reasonable effort to encourage participation, whether or not church membership is required. None of us seems to be satisfied with a mechanical malfunction. Why are we content with a spiritual one? If only a few persons are using their gifts, what we end up with is an incomplete body—an exhausted body with only one foot, or one eye, or one arm. I would add that it appears that God has given at least one gift to each believer. If one did not have a gift, how would that person be a necessary part of the body?

Why More Laity Are Not Involved in Ministry

First, and surprising to many, is that some pastors don't want extensive numbers of laity involved in ministry. Surprised? Let me illustrate how this might be the case. For example, many pastors don't take the laity, including those who lead, very seriously and second, simply don't trust the laity to be involved in ministry. Again, note the words of Tillapaugh:

> I am convinced that many more laypeople will accomplish great tasks when they become convinced that we pastors are serious about allowing them to do ministry. . . . Unfortunately, church leaders . . . are often not accustomed to trusting people with ministry. . . . This style of ministry lessens their (pastoral) control.[2]

Many lay leaders, particularly those in leadership positions outside the church, are sometimes viewed as a personal threat to the pastor. Yet as Willimon and Wilson note, "The clergy must trust the layman to witness to [his] experience of the grace of God, not simply to serve on the finance committee. . . . We need to trust the laypeople to have the best interests of their church at heart."[3]

Pastors discourage participation another way—by creating a sense of distance between how much the pastor knows and how little the layperson knows. It's a kind of spiritual one-upsmanship. Again, note the words of Willimon and Wilson: "Too many of our clergy feel that laypeople do not really understand the Christian faith, even though it is the laity who give meaning and purpose to the pastoral ministry in the first place."[4] Yet they remind us that, "the clergy themselves are all secondary inventions of the church."[5]

They give us an extensive case study of John Wesley and his ministry in England to illustrate their concerns. "The Wesleyan revival in eighteenth-century England was in great part John Wesley's inspired attempt to reform the established Church of England through a reformation of the laity. . . . Wesley knew enough . . . to know the laity are the church. . . . He sought to use his lay preachers as a means of reinstating the parishes of the Church of England." While Wesley was classically educated at Oxford, "His true genius lay in his ability to speak to the laypeople in ways that could be understood and appropriated in everyday life." His argument for extensive use of the laity in ministry "was the Protestant doctrine of the 'priesthood of believers' — the belief that each Christian is . . . to be a priest to his or her own neighbor." First Peter 2:9-10 (CEV) addresses the whole church, not just the clergy when it states: "But you are God's chosen and special people. You are a group of royal priests and a holy nation. God has brought you out of darkness into His marvelous light. Now you must tell all the wonderful things that He has done. The Scriptures say, 'Once you were nobody. Now you are God's people. At one time no one had pity on you. Now God has treated you with kindness.' "

As Willimon and Wilson observe, however, before long, Wesley's church, the Methodist church, "had no room for lay guidance and input beyond the local church level." As to the way these differences continue, again, Willimon and Wilson note the following: "While the pressure to increase the educational requirements for clergy has many desirable consequences, it is also a means of our clergy's assuring themselves that the ministry is a 'profession'; similar to medicine or law." This elevated position or status is but another subtle way of saying to laypeople: "We'll let you be involved in selected areas of ministry, but only after we're sure you're qualified to do so." Ironically, Willimon and Wilson observe that it is usually the clergy, not the laity, which exerts pressure for increased educational requirements for ordination: "The gap between laity and clergy has widened with increased educational requirements for ordination. It should be noted that the pressure to increase the educational requirements of clergy has come from the ministers, not the laity."[6] In this way, we must be careful of how the laity might perceive the pastorate in our own churches and, in turn, be discouraged from lay ministry because of their perceived inadequacy or lack of knowledge.

How Pastors Can Encourage Lay Involvement

What are some of the ways laymen can be encouraged to participate in the ministry of the church?

Delegate Authority

The senior pastor of the church must be willing to release laypeople for ministry.

Tillapaugh, explains, "If he [the senior pastor] chooses not to share the leadership of the ministry in any significant way, he is responsible for that choice. . . . If the senior pastor is not willing to actually share the ministry, the church unleashed will remain a dream."[7]

Tillapaugh adds, "There is something woefully stifling to the ministry of the church when its people constantly get the message, 'I am the pastor.' "[8]

The specific types of responsibilities entrusted to the laity would most likely vary from denomination to denomination. But many functional, nontheological areas could be entrusted to laity without significant loss to the overall focus of the church.

Do Not Patronize the Laity

The pastoral staff must use terms which encourage lay involvement. For example, I am surprised at the many pastors who refer to themselves as the minister. In some denominations, every member is considered a minister while the pastoral role is reserved to professional clergy. I have seen that expanded to "every person, a ministry." While the pastoral staff does minister, so too might church members and attendees (who are Christians). With regard to this second example, I would suggest great care to avoid referring to the church as a building. Phrases such as "Be quiet, this is God's house" or "Come to our church" misrepresent and confuse. If as laypeople we fail to understand just what the church is, we will surely fail to help carry out its ministry.

Give the Laity a Vision of Their Responsibilities

The pastoral staff must present to the laity not only the vision of the church gathered but also the vision of the church scattered.

Again, I see this emphasis as particularly important for those laity who hold leadership assignments outside the church. When I use the term the "church gathered" I'm referring to those occasions when the members of the body of Christ come together as a group, large or small, for worship, admonition, rebuke, and exhortation — to name but a few of the church's purposes. I have in mind verses like Hebrews 10:24-25 (CEV): "We should keep on encouraging each other to be thoughtful and to do helpful things. Some people have gotten out of the habit of meeting for worship, but we must not do that We should keep on encouraging each other, especially since you know that the day of the Lord's coming is getting closer."

When I use the term "the church scattered" I have in mind the various "members" (I use this term loosely) going "into all the world" to do ministry, whether as leaders or followers, so that the world may see Christ and give glory to the Father in heaven (Matt. 5:16). On the other hand, it is difficult for some to think of lay responsibility beyond a church gathered. For example, in reflecting on one of their interviews with a given pastor, Robert Bellah and his coauthors of *Habits of the Heart* made this observation: "He (the pastor) was perhaps too quick to assume that Christian commitment meant taking some organizational or committee responsibility within the parish."[9]

Let me illustrate this further. If, as a layman, I think of ministry only as the church gathered, I soon observe that there are only a finite number of jobs needing to be done when the church is gathered. There are only so many choir slots, Sunday School teacher slots, board slots. When these positions are filled, they're filled. The larger the church gathered, the more acute the problem with the laity saying, "There's no place for me to exercise my gift."

However, when we think of the church scattered, an infinite number of opportunities exist for lay service and ministry. There are literally hundreds of thousands of circles, or what The Navigators call "spheres of influence," which laypeople regularly frequent and where pastoral staff would find entry extremely difficult. We must both encourage and release laypeople for ministry in this context.

Redefine the Concept of Ministry

The pastoral staff needs to think about diversified ministry—broadly defined, managed, and operated by the laity rather than to think of ministry in only the more narrow or traditional church-gathered ways.

In large part, a number of church-gathered programs are more the products of a church culture than of a reflection of New Testament practice, let alone biblical mandates. One would be hard-pressed to find a Sunday morning worship/Sunday School/Sunday evening/Wednesday night prayer meeting schedule supported by either New Testament practice or teaching. Yet, in some circles, these practices continue to move forward in our organized churches seemingly unchallenged because that's the way it's always been. My sense is that many pastors would be delighted to experiment with changes in these schedules but can't because of concern from the laity.

Given the church's mandate, it is imperative that lay leaders — indeed, all laity — become more actively involved in the local church. For those who hold leadership positions in organizations outside the church, this ought not be used as an excuse for noninvolvement in the local church.

It is on this last point that many in Christian leadership fail. I recently gathered togethered several of my colleagues, all fine Christians, from other parts of the world, who travel widely and frequently for their organizations. And I asked them this question: How do you stay involved with the local church? Sadly, each expressed regret at marginal involvement. Perhaps this is where team or shared assignments could be developed to allow more direct church involvement. Leaders who fail to nourish their souls will shortly starve because of spiritual malnutrition.

18

Chosen by God

WHEN I USE the term, "Chosen by God" what I mean is that every leader had better be sure the assignment is of God or that God is in it. The burdens are too great and the hours too long for it to be otherwise. It is important that those who have been given the responsibility for choosing the leader also share this sense of God's choice.

The fact that annually there are quick retirements after very short-term tenures indicate our fallibility in this regard.

For the leader, through the people of God, who is chosen by God, there are marks or guidelines for leadership.

Marks for a Chosen Leader

The account of God's installment of Joshua as the new leader of Israel is a rich source of information concerning what makes a chosen leader.

After the death of the Lord's servant Moses, the Lord spoke to Moses' helper, Joshua son of Nun. He said, "My servant Moses is dead. Get ready now, you and all the people of Israel, and cross the Jordan River into the land that I am giving them. As I told Moses, I have given you and all My people the entire land that you will be marching over. Your borders will reach from the desert in the south to the Lebanon Mountains in the north; from the great Euphrates River in the east, through the Hittite country, to the Mediterranean Sea in the west. Joshua, no one will be able to defeat you as long as you live. I will be with you as I was with Moses. I will always be with you; I will never abandon you. Be determined and confident, for you will be the leader of these people as they occupy this land which I promised their ancestors. Just be determined, be confident; and make sure that you obey the whole Law that My servant Moses gave you. Do not neglect any part of it and you will succeed wherever you go. Be sure that the book of the Law is always read in your worship. Study it day and night and make sure that you obey everything written in it. Then you will be prosperous and successful. Remember that I have commanded you to be determined and confident! Do not be afraid or discouraged, for I, the Lord your God, am with you wherever you go" (Josh. 1:1-9, TEV).

As the baton was passed from Moses to Joshua, God gave His newly chosen leader guidelines for successful leadership. I'd like to highlight several of them.

God Had Joshua's Attention

He was able to speak to him. I can look back on times in my leadership when God couldn't speak to me because I failed to place myself in a position where I could listen to Him. Thus, an important requisite for leadership is that we regularly put ourselves in a position to hear His voice. In other words, the lines of communication must be kept open through Bible reading, meditation, and prayer.

God Gave Joshua a Goal to Achieve

Many times in leadership roles we devise goals and then ask God to bless them. As leaders we must become more conscious of making sure His goals are our goals. God has given us such promises as:

I will instruct you and teach you in the way you should go; I will counsel you and watch over you (Ps. 32:8).

This is what the Lord says—your Redeemer, the Holy One of Israel: "I am the Lord your God, who teaches you what is best for you, who directs you in the way you should go" (Isa. 48:17).

What's more, He cautions us about following plans that are not His:

"Woe to the obstinate children," declares the Lord, "to those who carry out plans that are not Mine, forming an alliance, but not by My Spirit, heaping sin upon sin; who go down to Egypt without consulting Me; who look for help to Pharaoh's protection, to Egypt's shade for refuge" (30:1-2).

God's Plan for Joshua Required Action on Joshua's Part

The Lord told Joshua that he would be given every place where he set his foot. In short, the scope of his achievement would depend on the extent of his action.

Many times we do nothing, expecting God to do all the work. Of course, sometimes that is exactly the thing to do—nothing—and watch God give the victory. Other times, however, God wants us to be colaborers with Him to complete a task. Most leaders have known those times when little is expected from God and He honors our expectations! Other times, I believe, He's prepared to do far more than we expect. We need to pray like Jabez:

Jabez cried out to the God of Israel, "Oh, that You would bless me and enlarge my territory! Let Your hand be with me, and keep me from harm so that I will be free from pain." And God granted his request (1 Chron. 4:10).

God Promised Joshua Success Even Before Joshua Started

He also promised Joshua His abiding presence. Think of it! Even before Joshua began the task, he was assured victory.

Some may think it presumptuous to believe that God will always give victory over a foe, as was the case here. Perhaps. The problem many times is that the plan we're pursuing is not His but ours. And yes, God never promises the price will be cheap (cf. Heb. 11:35-40). However, if we hear His voice, if the plans are His, and if He has promised success, then we need to pray for enlarged boundaries.

Joshua Was to Be Completely Obedient to the Law of God

"Do not turn from it to the right or to the left," the Lord commanded (Josh. 1:7). Leaders constantly face the issue of incomplete obedience. The leader or the people being led sometimes want to be only partially biblical.

It is important that, in being biblical we must be biblical. In other words, we must not settle for pursuing biblical ends using unbiblical methods. This is one of the concerns, for example, addressed in Larry Richards' book, *The Screw-loose Letters*.[1] We can only imagine the results that incomplete obedience would have produced in the following biblical contexts: Noah builds a smaller ark? Joshua marches around Jericho three times? Gideon uses 30,000 troops?

Joshua Was to Always Be Preoccupied with the Word of God

As noted earlier, not enough Christian leaders are preoccupied with God's Word. And when boards reward leaders more on quantitative performance (more members, more customers, more buildings, more funds raised) than for qualitative performance, they may be contributing to the demise both of the leader and the organization.

Called by God

While other observations could be made, I want to reiterate the fact that qualitative spiritual development is indispensable to effective leadership. Elsewhere in this book we have identified some of the tasks of leadership. In various places each of those tasks are reflected in a biblical example. In addition to being aware of the tasks of leadership, leaders who are effective must be certain of the call of leadership.

It is a popular myth that those who hold leadership positions have eagerly aspired to those positions, are experiencing "life on easy street," and because of the "good life" provided, want to hang on to the position for as long as possible. While one can always point to an example or two in support of this myth, my conversations with leaders, coupled with my experience, would suggest a totally different picture: while persons in leadership are at peace with their current calling, they neither need it for purposes of ego nor desire it for reasons of security; in fact, most could eagerly identify another role responsibility in which they could function well and which they would probably prefer.

Simply put, most leaders are in the positions they hold only because they believe they have been chosen by God. A leader in a Christian organization who doesn't sense that certain call of God may end up being a very frustrated leader. Why is it important to have this sense of calling?

Detriments of Leadership

While there are, to be sure, certain benefits to given leadership positions, there are also a variety of detriments, including financial. Several examples of detriments might be helpful.

Every Constituent Stakes a Claim for Your Time

As the leader of the organization, the CEO serves all the people. And it's not uncommon, given the consumer orientation that has pervaded the marketplace, for the employee, or parishioner, or the board member to ask, "What's in this for me?" Who else is better qualified to address this concern than the leader?

The Leader's Family Priorities Are Constantly in Danger

The leader must fight carefully but persistently so that these family priorities are not placed in jeopardy. It is not unusual, even in Christian circles, to hear about such problems as marriages falling apart or children in open rebellion. Many leaders, therefore, are extremely time sensitive because time is perhaps the leader's most important asset and it must be carefully guarded.

Leaders Tend Not to Have Many Close Friends

This is due largely to their positions of responsibility, and because of the always pressing time constraints. Thus the job of a leader is many times a lonely position. To be sure, leaders have many friends but seldom are they close friends.

Leaders Are under Constant Stress

As a former CEO has put it, "The buck stops here." And there is a price to be paid for buck-passing. Every leader knows that power is necessary to achieve organizational goals. Few leaders relish its use, particularly when personnel matters must necessarily be dealt with or when budgets must be adjusted—both high-stress situations. While to be sure there are many positive sides to leadership, the other side is also part of the picture.

The point to be made here is not to stay out of positions of leadership. Rather, the point is that leadership is a fairly high-cost calling and persons are advised not to rush headlong into it unless, after counting the costs, they are persuaded that God has still called them into such a position. Perhaps the attitude should be one of a reluctant but willing servant.

In Oswald Sanders' book, *Spiritual Leadership*, he notes the following:

> True greatness, true leadership, is achieved not by reducing men to one's service but in giving oneself in selfless service to them. And that is never done without cost. It involves drinking a bitter cup and experiencing

a painful baptism of suffering. The true spiritual leader is concerned infinitely more with the service he can render God and his fellow men than with the benefits and pleasures he can extract from life. He aims to put more into life than he takes out of it.[2]

Here then is our answer—leaders must have a clear sense of being chosen by God for this leadership role.

If one has indeed been chosen by God, what limits if any does that selection suggest? If I am God's choice, does that mean I can serve for life? Surely the biblical examples just discussed might be interpreted by some to mean that.

However, I believe that the Scripture better supports the view that leaders ought to view their leadership assignment as stewardship of a temporary trust from the Lord rather than as something to be permanently clung to. The pattern in Scripture seems to be that as long as the leader obeyed the will of the Lord, God was prepared to use that person. As noted earlier, Saul lost his position of leadership because of his disobedience.

From everything we read about Moses, he too was diligent in his service for God: "There has never been a prophet in Israel like Moses; the Lord spoke with him face-to-face" (Deut. 34:10, TEV). Yet, in spite of Moses' outstanding record, in spite of the fact that he faithfully took care of the people while they wandered in the desert for forty years, God told him that he wasn't going to be able to go into the Promised Land:

Moses continued speaking to the people of Israel, and said, "I am now a hundred and twenty years old and am no longer able to be your leader. And besides this, the Lord has told me that I will not cross the Jordan" (31:1-2, TEV).

Just what did Moses do that disqualified him for leadership? God told Moses to speak to the rock so water would come forth; instead, Moses struck the rock (Num. 20). To the average reader, this hardly seems like an offense that warrants so harsh a sanction, especially since God had told Moses on an earlier occasion to strike a rock for needed water (Ex. 17:5-7). Yet this time because Moses did not obey the exact command, God saw it as breaking faith with Him and as not upholding His holiness.

Prerequisites for Chosen Leaders

Without question, this episode sets a very high standard for God-chosen leaders. From it, we learn the following:

God Sets High Standards

Leaders chosen by God have an incredibly high standard to meet, and that standard is set by God. The standard includes obedience and a concern for holy living.

God Does Not Guarantee Permanent Employment

Leaders chosen by God should not assume that they will always be leaders. Rather, a leader may remain in a position of leadership for a long period of time, but such longevity should result from the ongoing confirmation of God's Spirit, not from planned permanence from the beginning.

God Punishes Disobedience

Leaders chosen by God may not immediately experience the consequences of disobeying His standards. In Moses' case, his sin occurred years prior to the time when God punished him for his lack of accountability.

It's also important to note here that Moses' sin was not one that in all probability would have gotten him fired from a contemporary leadership position. He hadn't stolen money, didn't get drunk, nor did he abuse his family. Yet the standard that he violated was a standard important to God. It ultimately cost him his job, his retirement home, and his life — all in all, a pretty steep price for failing a leadership assignment.

God Wants Long-Term Commitment

Leaders chosen by God ought to think about longer-term commitments in the positions God has placed them.

Too many times, as has been noted elsewhere, leaders of Christian organizations play the leadership musical chair game. "I need to get to the bigger church so that I get noticed by headquarters." In Christian organizations it goes like this: "Well, I'll take the presidency here, stay a couple of years, and then see what opens up elsewhere." This could be translated to mean, "I really wish I were at a more famous, bigger place, and the first chance I get to make such a move, I'm gone." Perhaps the examples cited earlier suggest that this "promotion-by-moving" mentality needs to be reexamined.

Interestingly, those who observe Japanese business leaders note that one of the fundamental differences of Japanese companies, when compared with U.S. companies, is that the Japanese seem more committed to the long haul. In other words, American leaders have a tendency to opt for the quick bottom line. Their Japanese counterparts take the longer view. The leader who plans to be at the organization or the church for only five years and who is committed to bigger and better things may have a tendency to strive for the quick fix in order to get the impressive results that will make him or her more hirable at a bigger and better place. Interestingly, my observation of Christian organizations suggests that few "great" Christian organizations did not have at some point in their history a leader committed to remain there for a long period of time. While long tenure in a position is no guarantee of great achievement, there seems to be no great achievement without someone having made the commitment to long tenure.

"Chosen by God" is an important reminder for leaders. I am persuaded that Moses would not have been in a long-term leadership position if he were not absolutely convinced God had chosen him for this task. After all, being constantly separated from his family and wandering in the desert for forty years is not most leaders' idea of a "wonderful assignment." And he didn't want and hadn't sought the job. He stayed put because he was convinced God was in it. He had been chosen by God.

19

Spiritual Qualifications for Leaders

QUALIFICATIONS FOR POSITIONS of leadership within Christian organizations at first glance seem to be pretty straightforward. Usually applicants are expected to be persons of Christian commitment. Once that has been determined, then the inquiry moves into the more traditional areas such as educational qualifications, appropriate experience, and organizational fit. Local churches often expect that "leaders" be active "members" of the church organization as well.

Both the Old and New Testaments discuss at some length qualifications for holding positions of leadership, though there is a tendency for contemporary organizations to consider them many times in only a perfunctory way. After all, what does the Scripture know about contemporary management and leadership expectations? How can a book about religion speak to the many dilemmas which must be handled to survive the typical management jungle?

The Old Testament and Leadership

A sense of arbitrariness sometimes seems to characterize the leadership selections of the Old Testament. Obviously God can select whomever He desires to provide leadership; after all, He is God. We are but clay and He is the potter.

There is a sense, nevertheless, that a person's walk with

God is always seen as indispensable for a leadership assignment. For example, note the observation about Noah, God's choice to be the preserver of the human race from the Flood: "This is the story of Noah. He had three sons, Shem, Ham, and Japheth. Noah had no faults and was the only good man of his time. He lived in fellowship with God" (Gen. 6:9-10, TEV). We can perhaps assume that Noah's selection was based in part on his willingness to "walk with God." And then there's Abraham. We're not given the reason in Genesis 12 why God selected Abraham to be the one who would become the father of a great nation. But given the very positive relationship we witness between God and Abraham, we know that he either was a godly person when he was selected or at least became a very godly man after his selection.

There are numerous other examples which suggest that spiritual fitness and vitality are prime ingredients for leadership. Yet it is difficult to make the generalization that God always and only selected known godly people to carry out a leadership assignment. We don't know much about the initial spiritual condition of persons such as Gideon, Saul, or Aaron, yet God saw fit to use them in leadership roles. What additionally complicates our task is that particularly in the Old Testament, we also see some leadership assignments granted on the basis of family heritage. Following the family lines of Abraham, David, and the clan of Levi illustrates this. In the New Testament we even see a person selected for the important leadership role of "apostle" by drawing lots (Acts 1:24-26).

Paradoxically, there seem to be instances when God, in order to achieve a God-directed end, selected persons who were not necessarily known for their godliness to carry out His plans and purposes. This was particularly the case when God used an enemy of Israel to bring judgment on them. Examples here would include persons such as Nebuchadnezzar (see Jer. 27) and Cyrus, Darius, and Artaxerxes (see Ezra 1–5 and Neh. 1–2).

In short, the record of the Old Testament is filled with those chosen as leaders at God's own discretion. The message given by God to Jeremiah illustrates this point: "With My great power and outstretched arm I made the earth and its people and the animals that are on it, and *I give it to anyone I please*" (Jer. 27:5, emphasis mine). So, just what are some Old Testament qualifications for leadership?

God Looks for Leaders Who Have Hearts Perfect toward Him

As a general observation (and there are other examples to the contrary), the God of the Old Testament seems to be preoccupied with finding persons whose hearts are perfect toward Him.

His search in that direction appears to be continuous, though it does not always culminate with success. For the eyes of the Lord range throughout the earth to strengthen those whose hearts are fully committed to Him (2 Chron. 16:9).

God Looks for Leaders of Great Inner Spiritual Stature

Since God's prime requisite for His leaders is that their hearts must be close to His, His leaders must therefore also be people of great spirituality. God is not impressed with one's pedigree, formal education, or prior leadership experience. He goes way beyond all of that to the thoughts and intents of the heart. "Man looks at the outward appearance, but the Lord looks at the heart" (1 Sam. 16:7; see also 1 Chron. 28:9; Ps. 33:13-15). From these Scriptures and others, the most desired quality of character appears to be the inner self, dedicated and fully committed to the Lord. As a colleague has observed, "As leaders, our primary obligation is to become more Christlike. After all, one ministers and leads out of what one is."

The New Testament and Leadership

As with the Old Testament, the New Testament, particularly the Gospels, contains a variety of references as to how a leader ought to function in community. For instance, Jesus' clear teaching in Matthew (especially chaps. 5–7) is full of more spiritual meat and instruction than most of us can ever hope to master in a lifetime. The parables and other teachings of Christ throughout all of the Gospels likewise are storehouses of profound truth. The way Christ worked with people illustrates tremendous insight as to how we can be responsive to people and meet their needs. The methods He used to deal with government officials and those who claimed to be the proper religious authorities illustrate a variety of truths, including differences between political expediency and righteous action, and the proper roles and domains of a human political government in contrast with the kingdom of God.

As with the Old Testament, these teachings of Christ do not appear to be targeted or limited in any special way to leaders. As a matter of fact, Christ seemingly has words of caution for those either aspiring to be leaders or those already functioning as leaders, such as: Don't seek to be first; Prefer others; Don't lord your leadership over others. And we have previously noted His words in Matthew 23:10 (TEV): "Nor should you be called 'Leader' because your one and only leader is the Messiah."

Many times we are tempted to view the teachings of Christ as applying only to one's personal life, in isolation from one's organizational life. It's as if Christians in organizations read and understand the principles of Scripture but, in the practices of the organization, we simply don't see how these principles apply.

Why is it, for example, that persons who preach obedience to the commands of Christ Sunday after Sunday practice almost daily the exercise of secular power in other aspects of the church's organizational life, seeking always to be first and making sure that they hold absolute power within the church? Why is it that well-intentioned Christians who have degrees in theology and who hold positions of leadership preside over Christian organizations which, in some cases, follow practices and procedures that are clearly unbiblical? Why is it that at some of the better-known organizations (including churches, seminaries, and para-church enterprises) in North America, the leader is quietly referred to as "dictator"; where there is insistence on all of the perquisites of office of secular counterparts; and where the people know it is not in their best interest to "cross the boss"?

Rebecca Pippert gives an example of an international businessman who illustrates the concern I have in mind:

> I am on two boards. One is with a religious organization, and the other is with secular people. With the secular board members, I know that many are out for their own agenda. They manipulate and control and deceive. I know it, and so do they. But frankly, I've seen lots of the same controlling, manipulative, deceitful behavior on the religious board. The difference is not the behavior but in the fact that the secular board members often acknowledge their motives, whereas the believers don't. The believers not only deny them, but cover their motives with pious words. They talk spiritually, but they are playing the same game.[1]

It is for these reasons that our focus in leading must be on hearing and doing the Word of God. As James puts it quite clearly, "Obey God's message! Don't fool yourselves by just listening to it" (James 1:22, CEV).

Paul's Qualifications for the Leader

The lists of leadership expectations found in 1 Timothy 3 and Titus 1 are well worth reviewing. In these two important passages Paul generally discusses the qualifications for both elders/overseers and deacons. These roles tend to be similar yet different in the New Testament. Some, for example, suggest that the role of deacon slants in the direction of those responsibilities identified in Acts 6:2, while the role of elder slants in the direction of those responsibilities identified in verse 4. For purposes of this discussion, we will discuss primarily Paul's list from 1 Timothy 3. Further, since many similarities exist between the qualifications listed here for elders/overseers and deacons, we'll handle them together.

Above Reproach and Respectable (vv. 2, 8)

It appears to be Paul's sense that candidates for this position needed to be persons about whom people would not be able to find fault. And this clean record, so to speak, could not be one of recent standing. The record had to be clean over the long haul.

Does this requirement suggest that only perfect people from birth can hold these types of positions? Obviously not, as Paul himself (and Moses and others) failed to honor Christ in all that he did until later in life. What it does appear to mean is that the person considered for this type of leadership position ought to be one who is mature yet still growing in the faith, who understands both God's grace and His forgiveness, and who is seen by the people being led as having a reputation worthy of respect.

Perhaps one of the reasons for this requirement is to make sure that the leader never becomes the issue in leadership.

Husband of One Wife (vv. 2, 12)

Is this a statement directed at those who wanted to practice polygamy? Is it targeted to those previously married, divorced, and subsequently remarried? Paul was generally opposed to divorce (1 Cor. 7:11-12) and elsewhere he had written that "each man should have his own wife" (v. 2), a statement that illustrates his disdain for the polygamy that was regularly practiced in that culture. It seems to be clear, therefore, that Paul's concern was that church leaders are to have but one wife.

Temperate and Self-Controlled (v. 2)

These two appear to be related. Someone who is temperate is someone not given to wild extremes. This speaks to me about having an evenness to the way one lives and approaches life, not being subject to repeated highs and lows. Is Paul, therefore, suggesting that a person should be unemotional, never showing anger, never reflecting bitter disappointment and emotional upset over the loss of a loved one, never given to deep despair? Probably not. Alternatively, he couples the need to be temperate with self-control. Obviously one does this (and perhaps can only do this) through the strength of Christ Himself (Gal. 2:20).

Paul in numerous places talks about the importance of self-control in the Christian walk. For example, in Galatians 5 he lists it as part of the fruit of the Spirit: "God's Spirit makes us loving, happy, peaceful, patient, kind, good, faithful, gentle, and self-controlled" (vv. 22-23, CEV).

What Paul seems to be saying is that one of the character qualities of a believer is self-control. And this is particularly true for leaders. Accordingly, as a leader, I am called upon to exercise restraint and to be temperate, to demonstrate an evenness in all of life, and to be under control in how I approach my leadership responsibilities. Can my conduct reflect frequent outbursts of rage? Probably not.

Hospitable (v. 2)

The dictionary defines this term as "giving, disposed to give welcome and entertainment to strangers or guests." Both Paul and Peter encouraged this. Paul exhorted us to: "Share with God's people who are in need. Practice hospitality" (Rom. 12:13). Peter said it this way: "Offer hospitality to one another without grumbling" (1 Peter 4:9).

Able to Teach/Teachable (v. 2)

An effective leader must reflect both a teachable spirit in how matters are handled and be able to teach well. One who possesses a teachable spirit will be a better learner.

Paul also intended for these church leaders to be good teachers of the Word of God. Perhaps he had this in mind when he said to Timothy: "Do your best to present yourself to God as one approved, a workman who . . . correctly handles the word of truth" (2 Tim. 2:15). Interestingly, the literature on leadership underscores the fact that one leads by and through what one teaches. Alternatively, people also teach by and how they lead. Good leaders teach and great teachers lead.

Not Given to Much Wine (vv. 3, 8)

While other Scriptures, particularly Old Testament ones, speak to the issue of abstinence, this is not one of them. While Paul does not insist on abstinence as a requirement for leadership, he is careful to identify only wine, not beer (Prov. 31:4) or other fermented drink (Lev. 10:9) as permissible. Further, he notes that even in one's use of wine, one must exercise restraint and self-control, including its nonuse if to do so would cause other followers of the Lord to fall (Rom. 14:21).

Not Violent but Gentle, Not Quarrelsome (v. 3)

Again, part of the fruit of the Spirit is peace and gentleness. Elsewhere in the epistles Paul cautions against divisiveness, complaining, and arguing; for example, "The Lord's servant must not quarrel; instead he must be kind to everyone" (2 Tim. 2:24). The writer of the Proverbs tells us that a gentle answer turns away wrath (Prov. 15:1). Peter tells us that in giving others an answer about our faith we are to do so with gentleness and respect (1 Peter 3:15-16). Effective leaders are called upon and expected to be gentle and peaceable.

Following this list of qualities of character that are expected of leaders, Paul turns next to two other potential areas of concern—family and money.

Proper Management of Family and Obedient Children (vv. 4, 12)

Candidates for positions of leadership are typically asked questions having to do with prior experience in organizational leadership situations, but how often are they questioned about their families? Paul states this expectation fairly strongly: "He must manage his own family well." However, he doesn't provide, here at least, evidences of a well-managed family.

Proper management of one's family might raise other questions. For example, does this include how I handle money and the other economic necessities of life?

Not a Lover of Money, but Pursuing Honest Gain (vv. 3, 8)

Elsewhere Paul cautions us that the love of money is a root of all kinds of evil. So it is not surprising that he gives us this caution here. We know that contentment (see also Heb. 13:5) with what God has provided ought to mark the way we live and further, that people who have the desire to get rich may ultimately end up in ruin and destruction.

Not a Recent Convert (v. 6)

It was Paul's observation that candidates for positions of spiritual leadership should not be recent converts. While he doesn't state what lapse of time should take place, he does suggest that it should be long enough so that selection as a leader would not make the person conceited. Paul himself moved fairly quickly from being a person who persecuted Christ to one who became His loyal and faithful servant.

Often we are tempted to conclude that longtime Christians are those who are the most mature in the faith. My observations suggest that such is not necessarily the case. I have seen Christians who claim they have been growing Christians for thirty years when in fact they have repeated the same year of growth for thirty years. This group, perhaps, was the kind the writer of Hebrews had in mind in Hebrews 5:11-14 when he wrote about those still needing spiritual "pablum" who should have been dining on more mature fare. I have seen other much younger Christians who have demonstrated incredible growth over only a very few years. So evidences of Christian growth, not just the passage of time, might be what Paul is getting at.

Wives Worthy of Respect (v. 11)

In the same way that the husband-leader is to meet certain leadership expectations, so too should his wife (or presumably her husband?). Paul says it this way: "In the same way, their wives are to be women worthy of respect, not malicious talkers but temperate and trustworthy in everything." Presumably, if the husband is committed to and loves his wife as he ought, and manages his family well, this expectation would be a natural result of the process.

So much for self-declared leadership. The biblical texts do provide lists and specific qualifications for leadership. The problem for many Christian organizations is that there is too much distance between their hiring procedures for leadership and these types of spiritual qualifications. Often things are added while others are ignored.

The task for Christian leaders is to integrate these spiritual qualifications with other functional ones and to do so in that order. What good is it to have the best degrees and experience if the condition of the heart, or the spiritual qualifications, are not right? Here is where the soul of leadership is critical to the Christian organization and where the ultimate organizational realities will be either given birth or will suffocate and die.

20

The Spiritual Gift
of Leadership

WE NEXT WANT to look at just who is qualified to serve in a leadership role. Must the leader possess the spiritual gift of leadership? Does God distribute His gifts on the basis of sex or along some other line? Is leadership a spiritual gift? If so, does this mean that my formal educational preparation for leadership is irrelevant? And what about my experience in previous places of employment—is that too irrelevant to spiritual leadership? While we will not address all of these questions in this chapter, we do want to spend time on the difficult issue of spiritual giftedness as it relates to leadership.

Confusion about Spiritual Giftedness

The matter of discussing spiritual gifts (I have in mind passages such as Rom. 12:6-8; 1 Cor. 12:7-10, 28; Eph. 4:7-8, 11-13; and 1 Peter 4:10-11) in ministry has not been without controversy. Persons far more knowledgeable than I have indicated their reluctance to deal with the matter. Tillapaugh's comment is illustrative:

> The topic of gifts is too complex and controversial to be dealt with in the scope of this book. In fact, I recently heard a pastor I respect very much say that he would never try to help people discover their spiritual gifts. A

great deal of confusion exists on the topic of spiritual gifts and I feel no compulsion to add to it.[1]

The respected writer on Christian leadership, Kenneth Gangel, adds a caution of his own as he writes on this subject: "No one is more aware than I that we venture at this point into a very controversial aspect . . . doctrine."[2] The matter appears to be complicated and confusing for several reasons. I want to note only three here.

Must a Leader Must Have the Gift of Leadership?

People argue that those who don't have the spiritual gift of leadership ought not be leaders. The assumption is that only a limited number of people have the spiritual gift of leadership. Therefore a key determination before a leader is appointed is whether or not such an aspirant is spiritually gifted to be a leader. As the argument goes, if one does not have the spiritual gift of leading, then one ought not be in a leadership position. It is my opinion that some of the confusion on this point can be eliminated if we start with a different assumption, and further, distinguish between a leader and an officeholder. That assumption is: God bestows on every believer gifts that can influence others for the cause of the kingdom. One can be a leader and yet not hold an office or formal leadership role.

For example, I believe that all Christians to some extent have a bit of a leader in them. Note the words of John Stott, quoted by Gangel: "God has a leadership role of some degree and kind for each of us."[3] I share Stott's position on this point. There are few Christians anywhere who don't exercise some degree of influence in a godly direction over someone else to achieve some kind of God-honoring objective or to take some kind of God-honoring action, whether it be the church, home, or an organization. And as McKenna has noted: "*Every* Christian is called to be a follower of Christ and a leader of others" (emphasis added).[4]

However, it doesn't follow that everyone who exercises leadership in some informal way is necessarily interested in or qualified to hold a leadership office in the context of an organization. A person can be a leader within a given sphere of influence and yet can be totally disinterested in holding a formal position of leadership elsewhere. As we have seen, the Scripture has some clear teaching as to the qualifications for the more formal officeholder. I find it to be of more than just passing interest that possessing the spiritual gift of leadership (Rom. 12:8) is not one of the requirements stated by Paul in his lists setting forth qualifications for deacons and elders (1 Tim. 3:1-13; Titus 1:6-9). Do we not consider pastors or elders to be leaders? Do we err in our expectation that pastors be leaders? Perhaps the answer has something to do with our definitions of leadership and, further, our assumptions about just who leaders are.

As we observed, not everyone who "manages or administrates an office" is a leader. The occupant may be a superb administrator or manager but that alone may not make that person a leader.

How Does One Receive the Gift of Leadership?

Confusion exists about how one receives or obtains the spiritual gift of "leadership." For instance, does the Spirit of God make nonleaders into leaders? If so, is this a progressive or a one-time, one-event occurrence? Is one born with the ability to lead or are leaders made? While I am not so presumptuous as to try to answer all of these questions, others have provided some useful commentary.

Seminary professor, Robert Clinton argues that in the context of leadership development, "the most important development during the middle sub-phase involves discovering spiritual gifts and using them confidently."[5] He then sets forth in sequence the eight phases of the "giftedness discovery process." He further defines spiritual gifts as "those special capacities given by the Holy Spirit to every believer and energized by the Holy Spirit in the believer's ministry."[6] He notes that "a spiritual gift is a unique capacity for channeling the Holy Spirit's power into a ministry."[7]

In his book *Ablaze for God*,[8] Duewel has a useful chapter (chap. 28) on this subject. His starting point appears to be the recognition that whatever ability we have must be viewed as God-given and is to be used for God's glory: "Every natural ability God gives us is a trust which we are responsible to use."[9] Duewel suggests that there are at least three types or groups of spiritual gifts listed in Scripture. First, he notes the supernatural spiritual gifts, or the gifts which are "completely dependent upon God's miracle power. . . ." In this group are gifts having to do with matters such as prophecy, healings, the ability to speak in unknown languages, and the like. Leadership and administration do not appear to be included in this group.

The second group of gifts are those "abilities with which we were born or which we have developed."[10] These gifts Duewel refers to as natural gifts. All of us have seen in our children and in others the expression of these God-given natural gifts. Some people take a God-given gift and do nothing to develop or enhance it. Others take great lengths to do so. Whether or not the possessor of the gift recognizes the "natural gift" as a gift from a loving Heavenly Father, it is a God-given gift just the same. For the Christian, these kinds of gifts can be specially used of God: "God can add a special supernatural touch which supplements the natural gift with the divine, guides and empowers the natural skill with the supernatural supervision, and maximizes and multiplies the effectiveness by the enabling and anointing of the Spirit."[11]

The third group of spiritual gifts Duewel identifies are what he calls practical gifts such as "serving, administrating, encouraging, faith, giving, helps, knowledge. . . ." My sense is that Duewel would include in this third group many of those practical vocational gifts that are listed in Old Testament references such as Exodus 35:30-35 and 36:1-2, 8.

Arthur Miller and colleagues writing in *The Truth about You,*[12] while certainly allowing for the expression of supernatural spiritual gifts, reflect Duewel's "natural gifts" approach to this matter of giftedness. At some risk of oversimplification, and relying on texts such as Psalm 139:13-14, their argument is that careful study of these and other verses will yield the conclusion that part of the process of shaping and knitting together in the womb includes God's giving to people individual patterns (biological, personality, interests, etc.) which influence future directions. These patterns are present at birth and will naturally work themselves out in the process of living life. As Miller observes: "People could . . . only become . . . who they were designed to be."[13] "People begin with a specific design that remains consistent through life and the design cannot be changed. This is not to say that there cannot be alterations in a person's life, since there are areas in people which need development or modification. . . . As astounding as this discovery was to us, there was no doubt as to the validity of this truth, after experiencing absolute consistency in case after case (more than 3,000 cases)."[14]

All of us have seen children demonstrate at an early age all kinds of different interests and abilities. Sometimes we see these same personality traits evident in either the mother or the father. Sometimes we see interests that are nowhere close to interests or aptitudes of the parents. The child who enjoys selling lemonade at age four not surprisingly is enjoying selling real estate, cars, bonds, ideas, at age thirty-five. The child who is preoccupied with numbers at age six not surprisingly ends up in a profession that requires considerable use of the manipulation of numbers and figures.

Each person, Miller argues, has been given groups of "motivated abilities" which can be developed through experience and enhanced through education. Miller argues that five key ingredients are in everyone's motivational pattern. First, the pattern has one primary motivational thrust. Second, "there is a recurring way of operating with others."

Third, "there is a group of abilities present." Fourth, "there is recurring subject matter." Fifth, "there are recurring circumstances." One task of normal growth and development, then, is to ascertain, through study of my history, just what my motivational patterns are. With regard to vocational employment, then, my task is to find those positions which fit my pattern of God-given motivated abilities.[15]

Interestingly, these motivated ability patterns are given to people by the time of birth, which by implication means that both Christians and non-Christians receive them. These abilities can be further developed and enhanced by experiences and education. For the person who comes to know Christ personally, these abilities will be used to further His kingdom and to build up the body of Christ instead of being directed at the pursuit of only selfish interests.

Bruce Jones gives us a very solid discussion of this subject in his book *Ministerial Leadership in a Managerial World*. He sees that "spiritual gifts and natural talents are both a part of a biblical theology of management."[16] "Spiritual gifts, like natural talents, can be developed to varying degrees of effectiveness. And, finally, effectiveness for a Christian requires that our motive be for the glory of God and that our ministry be performed in the power of the Spirit."[17] Jones also provides a useful discussion of the offices of overseer, pastor, and elder[18] and offers additional insight on the "gift of leadership," quoting Peter Wagner as observing that "the gift of leadership for the minister is an essential prerequisite in church growth."[19]

I would recommend further study of these and other authors who have written on this important subject. Their efforts appear to be biblical, logical, and fit many observations we all have noted about Christian leaders and Christian leadership.

Only a Few Have the Gift of Leadership?

Our own experiences have produced additional confusion about the spiritual gift of leadership. All of us, for example, have observed Christians who have claimed the spiritual gift of leadership struggle in a formal leadership role. We have seen pastors who have acted as dictators "in the name of Jesus." We have seen people with "nice" personalities and a "happy" smile perform in dysfunctional ways in a formal leadership role. (I thank the Lord that there are many examples of positive leadership as well!) We have also seen people with secular, non-Christian mind-sets function well in leadership roles within the secular organization. Paradoxically, I have talked with many people who are part of Christian organizations who wish their organization were run in a way similar to some secular organization so that the employees would be treated with greater dignity and worth. All of us are aware of Christian organizational "nightmares" with regard to how personnel are cared for. Many Christian books dealing with leadership often cite with approval the work of some secular writers on this subject. And seeing the "successful" leadership of non-Christians raises questions about the nature of leadership as a "spiritual gift."

Sorting Out Spiritual Gifts

Where does all this take us with regard to the spiritual gift of leadership? I understand that the Spirit doesn't operate by man's categorizations or lists and will do His work as He sees fit whenever and wherever He chooses. And so you, the reader, will need to study this further and draw your own conclusions. Nevertheless, here is how I approach this difficult subject. I make these comments with appropriate caution.

Natural Gifts

I start with the "natural gift" approach, noting that God, as an act of creation, shapes people in the womb according to certain intentional patterns and abilities. Each person is born as a gifted person, with gifts and abilities which can be redeemed for God's glory when the possessor commits himself or herself to Christ and becomes a Christ-one or Christian. But whether the person establishes a personal relationship to Christ or not, the element of giftedness (but not spiritual giftedness) still remains.

It follows, therefore, that whenever the possessor of these God-given abilities comes to accept Christ personally, these gifts are then given over to the Lord for His purposes, for His use and glory. Paul's teaching in Romans 12:1-2 is helpful to me here. This giving over to Christ of my body, which presumably includes God-given abilities, Paul calls an act of spiritual worship. The gifted musician who becomes a Christian gives to Christ the gifts and abilities of music as part of his or her spiritual worship. Many effective leaders of secular organizations who come to know Christ bring their leadership abilities to Christian organizations as part of their spiritual worship.

All of us have witnessed the good teacher who is empowered by the Holy Spirit as spiritual truths are being imparted. Further, as Christians, those exercising these types of gifts certainly must do so depending on the leadership of the Holy Spirit for strength. The work that is done is carried forth in the mighty name of Jesus.

Practical Gifts

"Practical gifts," such as administrating, encouraging, giving, and showing mercy, illustrate the fact that all Christians are gifted by God to meet a given need within the body of Christ. As the person who names the name of Christ exercises these practical gifts empowered by the Holy Spirit, the gifts become spiritual gifts. Peter's words are instructive:

> Each one should use whatever gift he has received to serve others, faithfully administering God's grace in its various forms. If anyone speaks, he should do it as one speaking the very words of God. If anyone serves, he should do it with the strength God provides, so that in all things God may be praised through Jesus Christ. To

Him be the glory and the power for ever and ever
(1 Peter 4:10-11).

Supernatural Spiritual Gifts

It appears that the Scripture teaches that certain spiritual gifts exist which are fully supernatural, wholly miraculous, though I would not include leadership among them. Of course I recognize and note that the Scripture also adds specific limitations on the use and purposes of these gifts. Further, however we define spiritual giftedness, we must observe that the purpose and results of spiritual gifts are for the benefit of the body of Christ, for the common good.

Paul's words in Ephesians 4 explaining the "why" of giftedness are particularly helpful: "So that the body of Christ may be built up until we all reach unity in the faith and in the knowledge of the Son of God and become mature, attaining to the whole measure of the fullness of Christ" (vv. 12-13).

The Spiritual Gift of Leadership

Is there the spiritual gift of leadership? Romans 12:6-8 clearly allows for that gift: "We have different gifts . . . if it is leadership, let him govern diligently." But at the same time the text doesn't appear to clearly distinguish how one comes into possession of the gift of leadership. It could be a supernatural gift in the way that we have previously used the term.

For example, I'm reminded of Saul, the future leader of Israel, as we see him in 1 Samuel 10:10: "The Spirit of God came upon him in power, and he joined in their prophesying." It might be a gift such as that given to Gideon, where it appears that a nonleader experienced God's blessing in an unusual way and became an effective leader. It might be the gift of leadership such as we see with Daniel, an effective leader throughout his lifetime. Paul honed his intellectual and debating skills and then was captured by the Lord for a significant leadership role.

In brief, whether through supernatural endowment, whether God-given at birth, whether developed through broad and diverse experience, for the Christian, leadership at all levels, both informal and formal, needs to be viewed as a trust given by a loving Heavenly Father to be used for His purposes.

The Formal Office of Leadership

When we are considering people for positions of formal leadership, perhaps it's more helpful not to look solely at the source of the gift of leadership (because God is the source of all good gifts) but rather at how the gift might be or is being exercised, toward what ends would those efforts be directed, and perhaps most importantly, what is the spiritual character of the person being considered for leadership. As McKenna notes: "We learn that Christian leaders are different in 'being' as well as 'doing.' Our incarnational 'being' is to embody the Spirit of Christ; our incarnational 'doing' is to empower His people."[20]

Addressing these kinds of questions is particularly important for one being considered for a leadership role. Given the ends aspired to in leadership as well as the purposes for leadership, my hope would be that all who name the name of Christ would aspire to be a follower of Christ, to be indwelt and empowered by His Spirit, and to be a leader and a follower of others. As we pursue the work of the kingdom, "every Christian is called to be a follower of Christ and a leader of others."

21

Spiritual Commitment in Leadership

THERE IS LEGITIMATE concern on the part of many in society that commitment is a word for an older and past generation. Commitment suggests a lack of freedom to make current choices. And if there is one value which governs contemporary society, it is the value that I can't jeopardize my ongoing freedom to make choices. As a result, we have adopted a contractual way of living which has infected much of what we do.

Contractual Obligation or Loving Commitment?

Classic "contract law" suggests, for example, that for a contract to be valid, the parties must each benefit and must each suffer a detriment or cost. For example, in the commercial world, if I want to purchase a car, I sign a contract which has benefits for both me and the car dealer. My benefit is that I now have a new vehicle. The detriment or cost to me is that I part with hard-earned cash. On the part of the dealer, the benefit is that she now has more money. The detriment or cost is that she now has one less car to own or control.

As was noted earlier, this concept from the commercial world has, in many ways, been carried over to the noneconomic areas of life. In terms of marriage, for example, the vows "until death do us part" have become subordinate to this contract view of commitment. "Vows" tend to be interpreted primarily as benefit from the marriage contract. When I cease to get the benefits I think I'm entitled to, I set about to break or otherwise modify the contract. "What's in it for me" tends to become the value of significance.

Robert Bellah and his coauthors of the secular best-seller *Habits of the Heart* make these observations about the ascendancy of this contract view over against that of the perceived value of commitment:

> The question "Is this right or wrong?" becomes "Is this going to work for me now?" By its own logic, a purely contractual ethic leaves every commitment unstable. Parties to a contract remain free to choose, and thus free to remake or break every commitment, if only they are willing to pay the price for doing so. Perhaps a contract model . . . cannot carry the weight of sustained and enduring commitments.[1]

It can easily be seen that this contract mentality has multifold ramifications in many areas of life, whether job-related, the view of the family and family responsibilities, my view of the role of government and the citizen's responsibility, my view of whether or not I "owe" society or "am owed" by society, or indeed with regard to my relationship to God.

In many cases, this contractual view of life has defined the idea of commitment and, to the great regret of many, this secular version of commitment has permeated Christian thinking. Take the church, for example. The church itself has tended to insist on a revision of the New Testament idea of being a member and integral part of the body of Christ. The church has instituted, and equated in many cases, the idea of "membership" in the local organized church with being part of the body of Christ. Indeed, membership requirements or commitments bear some reflection to the idea of the contract we have previously discussed. Just as with a club membership, church members contract to attend faithfully, give funds, and adhere to group expectations and guidelines. In some circles, the church membership's policies and procedures acquire a spiritual quality and seemingly take the place of actual scriptural guidelines.

All of these comments are preliminary to the subject of this chapter—the leader as a committed person. Are people basically uncommitted? What do we mean by commitment? What is meant by complete commitment? What are evidences of commitment? It's to the delineation of these and related matters that we now turn.

All Leaders Are Committed to Something or Someone

As I see the matter, the issue is not whether I am a committed person. Rather, the matter appears to be better stated this way: To whom and/or to what am I committed? All leaders are committed persons. Interestingly, this seems to be an a priori assumption of the Scripture as well. Seldom does the Scripture discuss committed or uncommitted people. It assumes, it seems to me, that people will be committed. With that assumption, it then presents options for commitment along with a corresponding appeal for commitments which are God-honoring. Several examples might be useful.

In Paul's letter to the Romans, he notes the tension between being dead to sin and being alive in Christ. He makes several observations, but one of particular note for our purposes is found in 6:16 where he asks his readers, almost rhetorically, the following question:

> Don't you know that when you offer yourselves to someone to obey him as slaves, you are slaves to the one whom you obey—whether you are slaves to sin, which leads to death, or to obedience, which leads to righteousness?

Among other things, Paul seems to be saying that the issue isn't really one of whether or not one is committed or obedient. Rather, the issue remains the object of that obedience or commitment. And Paul presents us with only two choices at this point. We can choose to be slaves to sin, which leads to death, or we can choose to be obedient slaves to the teachings of Christ. It's almost as if he's saying, "That's it. These are your only choices when it comes to commitment. You can choose either sin or Christ. There's no middle ground." By extension, then, Paul does not allow for the seemingly middle ground of uncommitment. Rather, he encourages commitment to one choice or the other. Obviously, he argues that the right choice ought to be commitment to Christ.

Again, two choices are presented. One can choose commitment to God, or one can choose to be committed to not serving God. We turn back to the New Testament for our second example.

In his second epistle Peter writes among other reasons to warn the people about false prophets and teachers. This is particularly the focus in chapter 2. After a variety of observations about false teachers, he makes this observation about humankind in general in verse 19 (TEV): "They promise them freedom while they themselves are slaves of destructive habits—for we are slaves of anything that has conquered us." Whereas in the other passages two choices and related consequences are presented, Peter seems to be suggesting a further but similar point of departure: You can observe the object of commitment by viewing who or what has mastered (or controls) a person. Again, the issue is not whether or not one is living as a committed person. Rather, the concern seems to be to whom or to what am I committed. And, notes Peter, one can make that determination by observing the object or person of mastery.

The story is told of a man walking along one of the streets of Chicago wearing a sandwich board. As one approached this walking "advertisement" one would read these words: "I'm a fool for Christ." Obviously this brought chuckles and laughs of derision from onlookers. And then the viewer would read the back side of the sign as the man passed by: "Whose fool are you?" Stunned silence. That's the point of these verses on commitment. All of us, as committed persons, are somebody's fool. Whose fool are we?

What Are the Costs to Commitment to Christ?

Having a clear answer to the issue of commitment (yes, I am committed!) does not alone resolve the issue, for I must go yet a step further. Assuming I choose to be committed to Christ, what does that involve? As I view the matter, commitment to Christ is an act of the will which is based on my knowledge of Christ and my understanding of the costs involved. While, to be sure, there are costs associated with a choice not to be committed to serving Christ, our Lord made it very clear that there likewise are costs to being committed to serving Him. Let's look at several.

In Luke 9:23-24 (TEV), Jesus makes sure His disciples are aware that this work of serving Him is potentially life-threatening.

And He said to them all, "If you want to come with Me, you must forget yourself, take up your cross every day, and follow Me. For if you want to save your own life, you will lose it, but if you lose your life for My sake, you will save it."

In verses 57-62 of that same chapter, Jesus again makes it clear that serving Him is a matter of greater urgency than having a regular place to sleep, of greater import than making funeral arrangements, and of more pressing concern than family good-byes. Jesus then wraps up His teaching by noting that the one committed to service in the kingdom doesn't look back to the former things: "Jesus said to him, "Anyone who starts to plow and then keeps looking back is of no use for the Kingdom of God" (v. 62, TEV). Jesus' point is obviously clear—there is a cost to serving Him. Commitment is costly!

Christ Desires and Deserves Total Commitment

This matter of Christian commitment is no part-time, easy task for the faint of heart. Christ desires all that I have and am. He instructs as follows in Mark 12:30-31 (TEV):

> "Love the Lord your God with all your heart, with all your soul, with all your mind, and with all your strength." The second most important commandment is this: "Love your neighbor as you love yourself." There is no other commandment more important than these two.

This expectation suggests complete commitment. I ought not have much left over for me if I'm successful at loving Him. Christ tells me how much I am to love Him and also which of my many conflicting priorities ought to be first. He then moves to specific expectations He has for my physical body:

> Sin must no longer rule in your mortal bodies, so that you obey the desires of your natural self. Nor must you surrender any part of yourselves to sin to be used for wicked purposes. Instead, give yourselves to God, as those who have been brought from death to life, and surrender your whole being to Him to be used for righteous purposes (Rom. 6:13, TEV).

This kind of commitment, a commitment which acknowledges Christ, not me or another, as supreme, differs dramatically from the type of contractual commitment we discussed at the beginning of this chapter. In "therapeutic contracts" the focus for commitment is always on the self—what's in this for me? Will this help me or otherwise make me look good? Am I getting what I want? Obviously, the kind of commitment Christ demands of me goes substantially in another direction. As a result, that kind of commitment ought to make a major difference in the way I lead and follow.

Ways to Evaluate My Commitment to Christ

It's one thing to talk about my commitment to Christ. It's quite another to test or have that commitment tested. How can I do a commitment "checkup" as I honestly attempt with His help to serve as a leader? Let me suggest some evidences of intensive commitment to Christ.

I will live contrary to the ways of the world. Let me approach this from two different vantage points. I want to begin with Romans 12:2 (TEV):

> Do not conform yourselves to the standards of this world, but let God transform you inwardly by a complete change of your mind. Then you will be able to know the will of God—what is good and is pleasing to Him and is perfect.

While more could be stated on this subject, it should be sufficient to observe that as one committed to Christ, and as a leader, I should be relentless in my pursuit of a changed and renewed mind which is contrary to and not conformed to the patterns of the world.

I will be prepared to experience and/or suffer persecution. Jesus said it this way: "Remember what I told you: 'Slaves are not greater than their master.' If people persecuted Me, they will persecute you too; if they obeyed My teaching, they will obey yours too" (John 15:20, TEV). Paul made this observation: "Everyone who wants to live a godly life in union with Christ Jesus will be persecuted" (2 Tim. 3:12, TEV).

Persecution doesn't appear to be a popular subject, at least among American Christians. Yet it appears to be an evidence of Christian commitment. Elsewhere around the world, committed Christians suffer daily for their faith in Christ. During a trip to Egypt, we visited many Christian leaders who know the reality of these verses. The paradox here is that we sometimes attempt to avoid the very persecution which for many believers serves to make their Christian faith strong and vital. Perhaps we ought to pray for more persecution. At the very least we ought to be involved in intercessory prayer for the strength and perseverance of Christian brothers and sisters around the world who daily do experience persecution.

I will place little value on material things. Jesus was not opposed to talking about money. Indeed, He talked about money more than any other topic. Note this observation by Ron Blue in his book *Master Your Money:*

> Sixteen out of thirty-eight of Christ's parables deal with money; more is said in the New Testament about money than heaven and hell combined; five times more is said about money than prayer; and while there are 500 plus verses on both prayer and faith, there are over 2,000 verses dealing with money and possessions.[3]

Yet as much as He discussed money or material things, Jesus never saw them as important, but as matters of little consequence and certainly as no cause for worry. For example, Jesus told His disciples not to worry about food, clothing, or the body: "Don't keep worrying about having something to eat or drink" (Luke 12:29, CEV). And He concluded His instruction by making this radical observation: "Sell what you have and give the money to the poor. Make yourselves moneybags that never wear out. Make sure your treasure is safe in heaven, where thieves cannot steal it and moths cannot destroy it. Your heart will always be where your treasure is" (vv. 33-34, CEV).

I will gladly and willingly surrender my personal rights. In a day and in a society which place a high premium on personal rights, this is a tough one. Some are quick to note, for example, that even Paul was not hesitant to invoke his rights of Roman citizenship. Nevertheless, and however difficult, personal rights for the Christian leader cannot hold center stage in the theater of life.

I will be involved in the lives of others. Significant involvement in the lives of others is a tough thing for many, particularly for "busy" leaders. Yet Jesus clearly envisioned that such would be the rule, not the exception. He observed that the world's evidence that people were His disciples would be the love Christians have one for another. He said it this way in John 13:34-35 (CEV): "But I am giving you a new command. You must love each other, just as I have loved you. If you love each other, everyone will know that you are My disciples."

I will not be ashamed of Christ and His words. I want to note Christ's seemingly clear teaching on this matter in Mark 8:38 (TEV):

> If you are ashamed of Me and of My teaching in this godless and wicked day, the then Son of Man will be ashamed of you when He comes in the glory of His Father with the holy angels.

In Egypt, Christians carry registration cards with the clear notation of "Christian" in plain view. And this identification may be cause for harassment from many sources, especially if one has converted to Christianity. Alternatively, in North America, many churches have limited their application of this verse to the "altar call." Persons in attendance "at church" hear the pastoral reminder that if they are unwilling to get up in front of their Christian friends attending church with them, they violate this verse, which the pastor then quotes. While indeed this may not be a misapplication of the verse, it seems that our Lord is more concerned that His name and words be upheld by people who are committed to Him in front of people who are sinful and adulterous. This does not sound very much like the congregation in the local church. Inasmuch as Christ's teaching on this point also appears in the same Luke passage that discusses the need for one to "deny himself," the maintenance of this kind of unashamed testimony of one's love for Christ in front of a watching pagan world appears to be clear evidence of commitment to Christ.

Summary

Commitment is an ongoing dynamic concept. The focus for the disciples was on Christian growth, not inertia. The process of "giving as much of myself as I know to as much as Christ as I know," is a dynamic exercise. And the experience has got to be firsthand, not lived through others.

Again, as my wife Marylou, has stated the matter, "Many leaders live off of stale bread. Interestingly, even a malnourished leader can further the kingdom. . . ." But their are dangers, faultlines.

And because of the commitment to God I desire, my relationship to Him must be continuous and dynamic. Otherwise, I will quickly lose the focus of leadership.

22

Leadership and Obedience

SMALL PUT, OBEDIENCE is not a "politically correct" expression. Leader-types take great comfort in verses such as Hebrews 13:17 (TEV): "Obey your leaders and follow their orders. They watch over your souls without resting, since they must give to God an account of their service. If you obey them, they will do their work gladly; if not, they will do it with sadness, and that would be of no help to you." To follower-types, however, the word has a pejorative ring to it. To them, obedience suggests images of a severe taskmaster with subjects cowering before him. When the adjective "blind" is added as a qualifier to obedience, the negative images become even more heightened. The word "obedience" suggests an order giver and an order obeyer. It suggests a higher authority. And in our enlightened age where we are driven by such concepts as participative government and management, we don't take kindly to orders, only suggestions and guidelines. To obey, therefore, is hard enough. To obey without question or "blindly" brings forth all of our remaining cultural resentments and resistance.

The Definition of Obedience

The dictionary defines obedience along these same lines: "act or practice of obeying; dutiful or submissive compliance; a sphere of authority, or a body of persons, etc., subject to some particular authority, especially ecclesiastical." In a society that strives for an egalitarian approach to many things, obedience is not an easy concept to discuss, let alone practice. The typical Sunday School discussion comment that "wives are to obey their husbands" does little to ease our uncertainties or anxieties.

When I think about the concept of obedience, a couple of Scriptures come to mind immediately. One is the verse from Hebrews mentioned earlier in this chapter. The other is: "Children, it is your Christian duty to obey your parents, for this is the right thing to do" (Eph. 6:1, TEV). The latter verse stands out more prominently in my mind because of its seeming frequent use during my childhood days.

If we're honest, we leaders tend to practice the idea of selective obedience. For instance, when we think it is in our best interest to have others practice obedience, then we think obedience is a great concept. For example, parents believe it is positive for their children to obey. Business people expect that the terms of a contract, whether for the sale/ purchase of a home or car, or a rental agreement, will be adhered to. Judges can reasonably expect that the terms of a court order will be obeyed. Physicians expect patients to obey their medical instructions. The motorist is always expected to obey the rules of the road, including speed limits. And the military commander can expect that orders will be followed and obeyed.

On balance, then, most of us would probably agree that to obey is a good thing. Indeed, it is difficult to see how a society would function properly without some commitment on the part of its citizenry to the practice of obedience. Yet to those who desire diligence in both their walk with Christ and in their leadership, obedience is still a difficult concept.

Why the Leader Should Learn Obedience

For the leader, Scripture has much to say about obedience. While we may readily see the importance of obedience in the areas just listed, we somehow lose sight of the fact that as children of the Heavenly King, we are to reflect obedience in our lifestyle. We need to both think and practice obedient Christian living.

Jesus identifies this point very clearly in the Gospels, particularly as recorded in the Gospel of John where He says, "If you love Me, you will obey My commandments. . . . Those who accept My commandments and obey them are the ones who love Me. My Father will love those who love Me; I too will love them and reveal Myself to them" (14:15, 21, TEV). These verses suggest directly or by implication the following ideas: He measures my love for Him more by how I act than by what I say; walking in obedience to His commands counts for more than does mere spiritualized rhetoric; and I am how I act, not what I believe.

It is on this latter point that many Christians struggle, because many times we have substituted our "talk" in place of an obedient "walk." We have impressed ourselves so much with our theologically correct language that we have overlooked God's preoccupation with our obedience to His commands and instructions.

I want to carefully note at this point that I am not arguing against precision in the use of theological language. What I am arguing for, rather, is that right talk which isn't likewise coupled to right action doesn't appear to count for much in our Lord's evaluation. The statement that we are to "preach the Word always, and if necessary, use words" says volumes on this point.

Christ Learned Obedience

It is important to note that Christ learned obedience. Let's look, for example, at Hebrews 5:7-9:

During the days of Jesus' life on earth, He offered up prayers and petitions with loud cries and tears to the One who could save Him from death, and He was heard because of His reverent submission. Although He was a son, *He learned obedience from what He suffered* and, once made perfect, He became the source of eternal salvation for all who obey Him (emphasis mine).

The text indicates that Jesus Christ learned obedience as a son through suffering and was made perfect. As a result, He has become the source of eternal life "for all who obey Him." Most of us would prefer to be in charge and "demand obedience" to our expectations. It is harder still to learn and practice obedience to another's expectation or command. Yet learn we must if we are to faithfully follow and lead.

Christ Practiced Obedience

Not only did our Lord learn obedience, He practiced obedience. While a number of Scriptures come to mind which make this point, one of my favorites is Philippians 2:5-11, a passage we have previously considered. We must note that while this text was addressed to "all the saints" at Philippi, Paul makes special note that "all the saints" includes the deacons and overseers (1:1).

So he could have just as readily begun verse 5 this way: "Now listen up, all you saints, including you leader-type deacons and overseers. Your attitude should be the same as Christ's." Paul doesn't use "cop-out" words such as "similar" or "like" when describing Christ's attitude. Rather, he makes it clear that our attitudes should be "the same" as that of Jesus Christ. That's an exceedingly high standard. And in a "my rights"-driven society, that's an exceedingly tough standard. Yet it's the biblical standard.

Then Paul so movingly and beautifully tells us once again this story of Christ. Even though He was God, He did not see equality with God to be something He, Christ, should strive for. Rather, Christ humbled Himself and "walked the path of obedience all the way to death—His death on the cross" (2:8, TEV). What a powerful example and model for the leader who struggles with submission and obedience.

The Biblical Case for Obedience

Both the Old and New Testaments make a compelling case that obedience to the commands of Scripture is an essential part of biblical living. Indeed, in some ways, one could argue that the Scriptures are preoccupied with the concept of obedience.

Some have argued, rightly in my opinion, that the major decision for the Christian is whether or not to be faithfully obedient to the commands of the Scripture.

I emphasize this concern about obedience for several reasons. Many times in my selective obedience pertaining to "nonspiritual" matters, I tend to carry over a similar attitude with regard to spiritual ones. Simply put, this makes me a terrible follower of the living Christ. Further, if I selectively follow only those commands of the Scripture that I want to, and declare all the rest to be optional or unnecessary, I will not be the leader He wants me to be. So disobedience adversely impacts both my ability to lead and my capacity to follow. There are many illustrations of this in the Bible.

Samuel and Saul (1 Sam. 15:1-23)

In this passage the writer makes it painfully clear that religious exercises are not a substitute for obedience to a clear command of God. Even though Saul was right in wanting to have a sacrifice offered to the Lord before going into battle, he had previously been instructed that he was not the one to offer the sacrifice. Yet Saul went ahead and offered the sacrifice anyway—and it cost him the kingdom.

> Samuel said, "Which does the Lord prefer: obedience or offerings and sacrifices? It is better to obey Him than to sacrifice the best sheep to Him. Rebellion against Him is as bad as witchcraft, and arrogance is as sinful as idolatry. Because you rejected the Lord's command, He has rejected you as king" (vv. 22-23, TEV).

Saul's failure to obey the Word of the Lord had a devastating impact on his ability to lead. Because he was not a good follower, it cost him the opportunity to lead.

Moses and the Children of Israel (Deut. 5:1, 29; 6:1-3; 8:1)

In these passages, Moses is reviewing for the Children of Israel the things they need to know about their relationship with God as they anticipate their new lives in the Promised Land. While the specific commands Moses sets forth are intended solely for the Israelites, we see very clearly God's preoccupation with the need for the people to be obedient to His commands.

God and Israel (Isa. 29:13-14; Amos 4:4; 5:21-23)

These passages are again directed to God's chosen people. In Isaiah God calls His people up short for claiming to belong to Him while continuing to practice disobedience. He specifically cites His concern for their worship and the fact that it amounts to "mere words learned by rote" (Isa. 29:13, TLB).

The specific concern according to the Amos references is that the people apparently thought that if they followed certain religious practices (if, for example, they offered regular sacrifices to God, practiced consistent tithing, and had a first-rate music program), they would honor the Lord. But here, the Scripture makes it clear that the pursuit of these otherwise seemingly appropriate activities by themselves, when God wanted pure hearts coupled with obedience to other commands, was both inadequate and unacceptable.

The Temptation of Jesus (Matt. 4:1-4)

In this passage, Jesus, obviously hungry after just finishing a forty-day fast, is approached by Satan who offers a suggestion as to how He might get food (turning stones into bread). Jesus answers with a strong no and then reaffirms the critical role that obedience plays in providing "real" sustenance for living: "No one can live only on food. People need every word that God has spoken" (v. 4, CEV). Jesus makes it very clear that obedience to the Word of God is critically important to life itself. Indeed, it's more important than physical food.

The Beatitudes (Matt. 5:3-20)

In this portion of the Sermon on the Mount Jesus makes clear that He wants more than just talk about the commands of Scripture. It is those who obey or practice these commands who are great in the kingdom of heaven. Our Lord wants more than just outward displays of righteousness, which the Pharisees apparently were good at. Followers of Christ are to practice inward righteousness — something we humans can't see but which is highly visible to God.

Judging Others (Matt. 7:21-22)

Jesus again warns His listeners to beware of those religious types who talk about God but don't practice His commands. Again, note His words: "Not everyone who calls Me their Lord will get into the kingdom of heaven. Only the ones who obey My Father in heaven will get in" (v. 21, CEV).

These verses and dozens more elsewhere in Scripture make it clear to the leader that disobedience to the Scripture is never an option. Whether responding to the board or to the various other constituencies of an organization, the place to start is not "thus saith the people" or "thus saith the board" but "thus saith the Lord." And my sense of this "thus saith the Lord" perspective is that such ought not run counter to the revealed "Word of God." As a leader, once I submit myself to being obedient to the Father in heaven, it follows that I must be a person who both hears and does the Word.

Obedience in Organizations

I make the "thus saith the Lord" qualification for several reasons. First, where people who name the name of Christ come together in a corporate arrangement to do work for pay under conditions and terms imposed by external authority or by the organization itself, everyone involved in the association has submitted themselves to a higher (spiritual) authority and implicitly has agreed to be a "direction taker." The ultimate source of direction as to how we deal with one another in Christian organizations, then, becomes the Scripture.

An operative expectation must be communicated at every level in a Christian organization, which goes something like this: "We try to run this organization based on biblical principles. When you see us doing something that appears to run counter to the clear teaching of Scripture, you have the responsibility and obligation to point that out to us so we can correct the error." How better to communicate to all in the organization the answer to the question of ultimate obedience. All of us are called to be obedient first of all to Him.

And this leads to a second reflection about a commitment to a "thus saith the Lord" perspective within the organization: Such a perspective will not be pursued in isolation of or to the exclusion of insights from other believers involved in the association. Too many times, leaders claim by practice that they alone have the "private line" to God and He leaves everyone else out in the cold. Indeed, to even raise questions about the leader's private revelation is taken by these types of leaders to show disrespect and insubordination.

My experience is quite to the contrary. Indeed, I have found that when some action is clearly of the Lord it will usually be confirmed in the hearts of others by the same Holy Spirit who confirms it in mine. Assuming the presence of spiritual maturity on the part of persons in the workforce, it would be frightening to take a radical course of action that didn't have the confirmation, support, or even acquiescence of other brothers and sisters within the organization.

Does that mean that no action is taken by the leader until

everyone agrees with the choice recommended? Obviously not. What it does mean is that usually there will be general support, however that support level is ascertained, for an action taken or anticipated. Notice I didn't say "agreement with." Rarely does everyone agree with every action taken in an organization.

Are there times when the leader must decide to take action which doesn't have the support of others in the organization? Probably, assuming the action anticipated is not counter to the clear teaching of Scripture. But I would see this happening only on limited occasions. This approach forces all to listen for the "thus saith the Lord."

In brief then, the biblical standard of obedience clearly communicates to all that for both the "order taker" and the "order giver," there is a higher standard that all must be alert to. And that standard is the reality and necessity for all who name the name of Christ, including leaders who follow and followers who lead. Both need to profess and practice obedience to the clear teachings of Scripture. There are simply no options for the leader to be disobedient to this standard.

Further, adherence to this standard, when taken seriously, provides a kind of protection to all others involved in the organization, regardless of rank or function. For when I as a leader publicly declare my allegiance to Christ and my willingness to be obedient to the teachings of Scripture, I am in essence saying that I will let the Scripture govern how I act toward others in the organization. By implication and for example, I give up my right to act arbitrarily and capriciously within the organization. But how do I come to know the standards which I must commit myself to? Stated another way, how can I be obedient to His commands which impact how I operate in the organization if I don't know what those commands are? Indeed, if ignorance is bliss, would I not be better off not knowing biblical commands so I don't have to obey them?

The answer, of course, depends on the extent to which I

want to take my commitment to Christ seriously. It seems implausible that I would, on the one hand, talk about wanting to be a faithful and obedient follower of Christ and on the other, to argue that if I don't really know the kinds of biblical expectations the Scripture has for me as a leader, then I don't need to be obedient to them.

Learning and Practicing Obedience

We observed earlier that Jesus learned and practiced obedience. So too must we. Yet obedience demands an object or a principle or a commandment. I can't be obedient to something I don't know about. It is for these reasons that leaders who name the name of Christ must engage in the never-ending process of Bible study — getting to know God better.

A process that has been helpful to me as I have tried to study the Scriptures is to ask three questions about the passages I study. First, according to the passage studied, what is God's desire for the Christian? Second, compared with the biblical expectations stated in the passage, what is my life like? This leads logically to the third question: In order to bring my life into conformity with the Scripture, what has to change? This process of getting to know what God desires of me and then making appropriate changes to make my life conform to His stated desire is for me what growth in Christ involves.

Several years ago I was interviewing a prospective staff member for a position. As is my practice, I asked him to talk to me about his growing commitment to Christ. His answer, and I have previously referenced this, was both simple and profound: giving as much of myself as I know to as much of Christ as I know. And once I have invited Christ into my life, as I continue to get to know myself better and as I continue to get to know Him better, I continue to give Him more of me. That dynamic process is essential for effective leadership.

Complete Obedience

At all costs we must avoid the pitfalls of incomplete or partial obedience. The record of the Scriptures illustrates time after time the results both of obedience and disobedience. The point, it seems, is clear. Where God has clearly communicated His standard or expectation, He wants complete obedience. Negative consequences are certain for anything less.

Obedience to our Lord is often difficult. Yet it is essential to following and leading. Indeed, it is at the heart and soul of leadership.

23

The Leader's Need to Pray

IN HIS PROVOCATIVE article, "Tyranny of the Urgent," Charles Hummel quotes P.T. Forsyth as follows: "The worst sin is prayerlessness." Notes Hummel, "We usually think of murder, adultery, or theft as among the worst. But the root of all sin is self-sufficiency — independence from God. When we fail to wait prayerfully for God's guidance and strength we are saying, with our actions if not our lips, that we do not need Him."[1] While we might quarrel with Forsyth's characterization of prayerlessness as the "worst sin," none of us should quarrel with the leader's essential need to be a person of prayer.

Christian leaders of the past have often stated the importance of prayer for the Christian who leads. "Andrew Murray asked, 'What is the reason why many thousands of Christian workers in the world have not a greater influence? Nothing save this — the prayerlessness of their service. . . . It is nothing but the sin of prayerlessness which is the cause of the lack of a powerful spiritual life.' 'Great praying,' wrote E.M. Bounds, 'is the sign and seal of God's great leaders. [A leader] must be preeminently a man of prayer. His heart must graduate in the school of prayer. . . . No learning can make up for the failure to pray.' "[2]

Duewel says it this way: "The foundation on which all ministry and leadership is built is your prayer life. Your leadership is never greater than your prayers. Successful leadership requires much more than prayer, but no leadership can ever be ultimately successful apart from much prayer. . . . Other things being equal a praying leader with a praying people will be blessed of God."[3] "Prayer is the basis for whatever ministry one has. . . . Many Christian leaders' prayer lives are inadequate for the work they are attempting to do."[4] "The apostles . . . decided to give themselves to two things: 'We . . . will give our attention to prayer and the ministry of the word' " (Acts 6:4). Notes Duewel, "You need audience before God before you attempt audience with your people. Stand in God's presence before you stand before them. You must prevail before God before you can prevail before them. Not till you have worshiped with the seraphim are you ready to worship with your people. Only when you come from the presence of God can you lead them into the presence of God."[5]

Prayer Defined

Before we proceed further we need to define what we mean by prayer. Leith Samuel has defined prayer this way: "Prayer is not an attempt to change God's mind. Real prayer is communion with God: By it we express our trust in Him, seek to know His mind on the decisions of life, submit to His will, resist in His name the efforts of the devil to frustrate God's loving purposes in human lives." Another has noted this about prayer: "In our communication with God, there must be time for both listening and speaking. God primarily speaks to us through the Scriptures. We speak to God through prayer."[6]

Biehl and Hagelganz also give us some helpful insights on prayer: "In straightforward terms, prayer is simply talking with God—and the simpler the talking, the better. In other words, *prayer is conversation with God*" (emphasis mine).[7] The emphasis is on both conversation (what and how we communicate) and on the Triune God (the Person we communicate with). These writers see prayer as consisting of more than words; it is also the "deep expression of the soul."

Biehl and Hagelganz also see prayer as listening, "as God talks with you."[8] As such, they suggest that meditation can be an important part of prayer. They suggest further that prayer is telling God, "So let it be," noting that the word amen is "really a scriptural word of affirmation in the belief that God has heard our prayer."[9]

The rest of this chapter focuses on the importance of prayer in leadership. We will begin by looking at reasons why prayer is not pursued more diligently. Then we will briefly review what prayer involves, noting particularly the role of prayer in the life of Jesus. We'll also briefly review the practice of prayer as seen elsewhere in the Scripture. We'll close by suggesting how we as leaders might be more involved with personal prayer. It is important that I note from the start that I write these paragraphs from the perspective of one who has much to learn about prayer and about praying. These words, then, reflect what I am learning about prayer as the Lord continues to teach me.

Why Leaders Don't Pray

Prayer As Duty or Discipline

Many times prayer is presented as primarily a spiritual discipline or duty, as spiritual drudgery, a kind of spiritual "have to." As Regent College professor, James Houston observes: "Many people have the impression that prayer is simply another thing we do, alongside all the other activities we pack into our lives. This way of thinking, which sees prayer as an interest or a duty, may prompt us to read about prayer in exactly the same way that we learn from 'how-to' books about cross-country skiing or stamp collecting."[10]

Prayer As Low Priority

There are so many other spiritual things to do, such as meditating, fasting, and reading the Scripture. There are so many family needs to be met. And then there are the many vocational demands on my daily activities. All of us tend to be busy—most of the time doing good things. And prayer simply becomes one more boat floating on the already crowded sea of busyness, constantly pushed farther and farther away from the harbor of the important things in life.

Prayerlessness As Self-Centeredness

In some parts of the world there is an unhealthy emphasis on becoming self-fulfilled and achieving one's potential. This leads to a preoccupation with oneself at great expense to a proper understanding of the individual in community. Self-interest clearly dominates over any sense of common interest. Houston observes that "such a faith drives us all to become Robinson Crusoes, each in our personal desert-island paradise, living according to our own fantasies. . . . Prayerlessness is simply part of a larger picture of modern life, of being alone in a crowd."[11]

Sadly, this independence from others carries over into an independence from God. Self-sufficiency and dependency on Christ are mutually exclusive concepts. While the pursuit of "my potential" may be a worthy goal, its attempted fulfillment outside of my total dependency on Christ will drive me away from an active life of prayer.

Prayer As a Mirror

Perhaps one of the reasons we don't spend more time in prayer is that when we honestly pray we cannot be involved with charades. Seeing ourselves as God sees us can sometimes frighten us to our very depths. Again, as Houston has noted:

Knowing ourselves is usually uncomfortable. That is why so many people live inside masks to prevent others discovering the uncomfortable truths they have found out about themselves. Knowing yourself is not flattering. We often evade what we do not like inside by condemning other people for exactly the same weaknesses. This is where prayer cuts across all our pretensions. Prayer is the mirror of the soul, and in it we see ourselves most clearly.[12]

Communicating with the all-knowing God precludes our indulgence with pretense. He sees all that we do and knows our motive for doing it. Coming to Him in prayer requires brutal honesty and openness. And it's our difficulty in so doing that sometimes keeps us from the transforming power of prayer. As we see from James 1:22-25, the Word of God can function as a mirror for us, as long as we honestly respond by doing what we hear and see. Yet many of us either refuse to look into the mirror or we carry away a less than honest picture of what we see. We hate mirrors because they reflect us as we are. And many times we despise what we see. This often leads to continued prayerlessness.

Prayer As Relationship

If there is one overriding observation I would make about prayer, it is this: prayer flows out of our relationship with the Father, Son, and Holy Spirit. This puts the matter of praying clearly on the side of "want to" or privilege rather than on the side of "have to" or duty. Nothing has transformed my idea of prayer more than this.

To help explain what I mean here, I first want to focus on the relationship which exists between the Father and the Son. For it is in the context of their relationship that we come to understand better Christ's teaching on prayer. Second, we will look at the relationship between the Son and His followers.

Between the Son and the Father

Christ saw Himself as totally dependent on the Father. Throughout the Book of John, Jesus discusses this relationship:

Jesus told the people: "I tell you for certain that the Son cannot do anything on His own. He can do only what He sees the Father doing, and He does exactly what He sees the Father do" (5:19, CEV).

I cannot do anything on My own. The Father sent Me, and He is the one who told Me how to judge. I judge with fairness, because I obey Him, and I don't just try to please Myself (v. 30, CEV).

These verses and many others suggest that Christ was totally intent on doing the will of His Father rather than His own. This is probably nowhere better illustrated than in Christ's prayer in Gethsemane, right before He went to the cross. On three separate occasions He pleaded with His Father to be released from drinking the Father's cup. Yet on each occurrence, He clearly submitted His own request to that of the Father's will.

Between the Son and His Followers

In a similar way that Christ and His Father had an intense relationship, Christ desires that same relationship with those who follow Him—with us! We see this desire in several ways, first in terms of a general expectation for believers.

When asked by a legal expert which was the greatest commandment in the Law, Jesus answered: " 'Love the Lord your God with all your heart, with all your soul, and with all your mind.' This is the greatest and the most important commandment" (Matt. 22:37-38, TEV). Whatever else this verse teaches, it teaches Christ's desire for relationship with us. Further, not only does He desire relationship with us, He tells us that apart from Him we will not experience any fruitfulness in our lives:

Remain united to Me, and I will remain united to you. A branch cannot bear fruit by itself; it can do so only if it remains in the vine. In the same way you cannot bear fruit unless you remain in Me. I am the vine, and you are the branches. Those who remain in Me, and I in them, will bear much fruit; for you can do nothing without Me (John 15:4-5, CEV).

Prayer As Fellowship

It follows, then, that if we see prayer as relationship, we also will see prayer as fellowship. We have a tendency in the North American church to see fellowship as a social time among fellow believers, something associated with eating and refreshment. While I believe these may be important parts of Christian fellowship, there is definitely more to it than that. At a recent Sunday School class, our study group was asked to identify key ways that we fellowship with people. Here are several of the key elements we discussed:

● Regular two-way communication, involving talking and listening;
● Expressed and genuine interest in another person or persons;
● Presence; that is, being physically with others — if possible — rather than settling only for letters and phone calls;
● Sharing common meals; and
● Sharing joys and burdens.

While fellowship may have other components, these are some of the ways we "fellowship" at the human or horizontal level.

The Scriptures also present a vertical dimension to fellowship. A good illustration of this is found in 1 John 1:3 (CEV): "We are telling you what we have seen and heard, so that you may share in this life with us. And we share in it with the Father and with His Son Jesus Christ." Indeed, this verse illustrates both dimensions of fellowship, the horizontal (with people) and the vertical (with the Lord).

In a similar way, then, that we desire fellowship with each

other, we pursue fellowship with the Father. He certainly desires this of us. We pursue fellowship in order to sustain our "lives in Christ." And prayer is one of the ways we communicate with and accordingly fellowship with the Father.

Jesus' Teaching about Prayer

My intent here is not to provide an inclusive list of the Lord's teachings on prayer, but I do want to explore several key passages, particularly Matthew 6.

According to Matthew's account, Jesus had just finished teaching about how people should love their enemies: "But I tell you to love your enemies and pray for anyone who mistreats you" (5:44, CEV). Jesus then turns to instruction on how people were to pursue acts of righteousness, dealing first with the matter of giving to the needy, then praying, and finally fasting. His general concern seems to be that we not "show off" our acts of righteousness.

On the subject of prayer, He appears to have several concerns. First, He specifically cautions against praying in public, to be seen by people. One commentator suggests this represents Christ's concern that we guard against "ostentatiousness" in prayer.[13] Rather, He seems to encourage private prayer ("go into your room, close the door") without embellishment.

Second, Jesus cautions against people "babbling like pagans" in their praying. This same commentator[14] remarks that Christ's concern was for unnecessary "formality" in prayer, noting that the Greek translates "vain repetitions" as to "speak words without thought or meaning."

A third concern Christ had about people's prayers was their "lack of trust in their Heavenly Father who knew all their needs."[15] This was another reason, apparently, why there was no need to babble or to use words meaninglessly.

One implication of these preliminary observations about prayer is that our attitude in coming to prayer is critically important. I need to make sure my heart is "clean." As I pray I need to acknowledge the Father as the giver of every good gift. As I pray I must be careful not to use words that I might think will manipulate God into responding favorably to my requests. To do so serves no good purpose because He knows my needs even before I pray.

Now, let's examine a bit more closely Christ's instructions on prayer as found in the Sermon on the Mount, highlighting seven specific guidelines.

We Are to Pray to "Our Father" (Matt. 6:9)

While He may be my Father, He is not mine alone. Prayers need to be directed to our Father. Jesus taught elsewhere that the Father is the One who gives us the answer to our requests: "When that day comes, you will not ask Me for anything. I am telling you the truth: The Father will give you whatever you ask of Him in My name" (John 16:23, TEV). And when we pray to Him we must recognize His holiness ("hallowed be Your name").

We Are to Pray for Our Father's Will to Be Done (Matt. 6:10)

We need to acknowledge the primacy of God's kingdom and ask that His will be done in our lives, "on earth as it is in heaven." In brief, whatever we ask must be consistent with His kingdom and His will for us. Too often, we pursue the reverse emphasis, asking that our desires be superimposed on His kingdom. Jesus' teaching illustrates the way He lived His own life: "My Father, if it is possible, take this cup of suffering from Me! Yet not what I want, but what You want" (26:39, TEV). We need always to align our requests with His will for us.

We Are to Ask Our Father to Take Care of Our Daily Needs (6:11)

We start our petitions by asking for our daily bread. This instruction clearly allows us to make requests of the Father, here, for our needs of the day. Jesus reemphasizes this "daily" focus later on when He tells His hearers: "So do not worry about tomorrow; it will have enough worries of its own. There is no need to add to the troubles each day brings" (v. 34, TEV).

We Are to Ask Our Father for Forgiveness (6:12)

We are to request our Father to forgive us our debts or sins as we have forgiven others who have sinned against us. The nature of this request has to do with the spiritual needs rather than physical ones. It has to do not only with the cleanliness of my own heart but also of those I'm involved with in community. This request notes the importance of making sure that I and those I work with serve the Father with clean consciences—such is the Father's will. Later in this same passage Christ underscores the focus on community so strongly that He notes individual forgiveness from the Father is impossible if we choose not to forgive others who have sinned against us and who have requested our forgiveness (vv. 14-15). The Father wants to make sure we have clean hearts and forgiveness from others before we request forgiveness for ourselves from Him.

We Are to Ask Our Father for Protection (6:13)

We should ask the Father to protect and deliver us from the temptations of the evil one. Jesus reminds us that the battles of life involve more than our physical needs (daily bread) or more than making sure we live in proper relationship with others in community. He reminds us that we're involved in a battle for our souls with other spiritual powers. I'm reminded of Paul's words in Ephesians 6:12 (TEV): "For we are not fighting against human beings but against the wicked spiritual forces in the heavenly world, the rulers, authorities, and cosmic powers of this dark age."

Someone has described discipleship as consisting of three primary relationships: (1) dependency on God; (2) interdependency on people; and (3) independency from culture. This matter of prayer falls clearly on this dependency on

God. If we view prayer as relationship; if we view prayer as presence; and if we view prayers as fellowship, then we will not view prayer as limited to only location. In other words, knowing of God's promise of His presence with us, prayer will be an ongoing exercise of conversation and listening. It will not be relegated to something I do only in church or only at the beginning of a meeting or a meal. It's very natural, then, for prayer to be ongoing and continual.

This is not to say that Christians ought not engage in the discipline of sustained, focused prayer, whether in a closet or in concert with others. Nor is it to say that public prayers in church or at meals are inappropriate. Indeed, I have been led in worship by powerful prayers from the heart, prayed by others.

As leaders, people also need to think of prayer in a way as almost like breathing and as a natural part of a healthy relationship with the Heavenly Father. All leaders have had the experience of being so overwhelmed with the weight of leadership, that help in prayer from the Holy Spirit has been absolutely essential. In this context, prayer as relationship, communion between our souls and the heart of God, makes all of the sense in the world. And, it needs to be the foundation and bedrock on which effective leadership is built.

24

Spiritual Restoration, Revival, and Leadership

JUST WHAT IS spiritual restoration and is it connected in any way to a leader's personal renewal? How do leaders "bring" revival, if they do? These are the questions we'll attempt to answer in this chapter.

From a variety of perspectives I see a close relationship between personal renewal and spiritual restoration. While we can do much to prepare the way for both, personal renewal and revival (throughout the balance of this discussion I will use the terms spiritual restoration and revival interchangeably) ultimately are the results of the Spirit of God at work in us, producing the kind of fruit He desires. I remain convinced, however, that personal renewal can do much to make revival possible.

For example, all of us tend to get captured by the routine of the ordinary. We like our lives to remain the same. Major changes in our lives, however, produce a context where positive change can occur: "It is not unusual to find that the major changes in life — marriage, a move to a new city, a change of jobs — break the pattern of our lives and reveal to us quite suddenly how much we had been imprisoned by the comfortable web we had woven around ourselves. . . . We don't know that we've been imprisoned until after we've broken out."[1]

It is at times like these that we are ripe for spiritual restoration and revival.

Our Need for Spiritual Restoration and Revival

I know of few leaders in Christian organizations who are not in need of revival. I know of few Christian organizations (by this I mean the people within them) who would not benefit from revival. All who know Christ should desire to live the way Christ desires them to live. While many of us initially concur with this observation, we may ultimately have some reservations about getting too serious about revival, because we're not sure what God will ask us to do. Spiritual restoration can be quite risky.

Nonetheless, the Scriptures reflect a strong interest in revival or spiritual restoration. Nowhere can I find a passage of Scripture where God is indifferent to a person's spiritual condition. Rather, we see a God who is actively at work drawing people to Himself both for fellowship and service. His priorities for us seem to be first godliness and then work which results in His receiving glory. He wants new life and growth, constantly pruning to produce it. If necessary, He can bring dry bones back to life (Ezek. 37) to achieve His purposes. He wants both holy living and unity to be reflected among His followers. He wants holy living because it reflects His character; He wants unity in order to demonstrate on earth what is true in heaven (John 17:23; Rom. 15:5-6; Ps. 133; Phil. 2:1-2).

Second, our Lord knows that we will not be able to achieve His agenda, either corporately or individually, without our being part of the living Christ. As Jesus Himself said, "But you cannot do anything apart from Me" (John 15:5, CEV).

Third, God wants people of godly character. He is preoccupied with the unseen things while we tend to focus only on those things which can be seen by others. What's more, we are never completely successful in covering up those unseen things. Each of us has a storage bin in his or her heart; God knows its contents and its overflow will eventually become known to others. As the Scripture says, "A good person brings good out of the treasure of good things in his heart; a bad person brings bad out of his treasure of bad things. For the mouth speaks what the heart is full of" (Luke 6:45, TEV). As our Creator, the Lord is a discerner and judge of "the desires and thoughts of our hearts" (Heb. 4:12, CEV).

Fourth, and as we have seen, He wants obedient leaders and followers who will be faithful models and messengers of the need for spiritual restoration. In this regard I think of Jonah and merely note several key elements of his story. God wanted Jonah to be (1) an obedient servant, (2) who was willing to share a message of good news, (3) to a hostile audience. Further, (4) Jonah's failure to deliver the message had negative consequences for not only the intended audience but for the reluctant messenger as well. While Jonah's sin was initially disobedience to a clear command of God, he most likely did not see it as sin in the same way he saw the evil of the Assyrians, the people he was sent to confront. Why? Because he did what we often do . . . categorize sin.

Christian Sin Lists

One of the difficulties in pursuing spiritual restoration is our failure to objectively and then subjectively deal with the issue of sin. Sin is not a popular sermon topic and when it is discussed, often, only really "bad" sins are usually involved.

One curse of contemporary Christianity is that we have developed acceptable and unacceptable sin lists. Socially acceptable sins include pride, divisiveness, gossip, and the like, while socially unacceptable sins include alcohol abuse and drug addiction. Often our lists of "sins" represent a rapidly decreasing ledger of do's and don'ts. Why is it that some people feel more comfortable "pushing the limits" about all the things they can do and still be a Christian rather than pursuing those actions that "honor Him the most"? I say this knowing I myself have sometimes been guilty of just such a mind-set.

Another problem with sin lists is that they cause us to focus on the list rather than on the holiness of God. The writer of Hebrews notes that it is the spiritually mature who have learned to discern between good and evil (5:14). Yet given their nature, lists don't require much spiritual discernment. Unfortunately, and as Elisabeth Elliot observes, "thus saith the board" sometimes acquires a higher Christian cultural value than "thus saith the Lord." Might it be that our spiritual legalism, and its usual companion sin lists, have driven us away from godliness because we have exchanged compliance with a list for godly holiness?

John White and Ken Blue[2] give us their list of sinful tendencies, habits we tend not to call sin. It's a fairly inclusive list: laziness, gluttony, alcoholic overindulgence, greed, unbelief, prayerlessness, unkindness, gossip, materialism, vanity, pride, neglect of spouse and family, wrong ambitions, a host of harmful habits, critical spirits, grumbling spirits, grouchiness, lack of Christian openness, manipulative tendencies, petty deceit, white lies, black lies, spite, con artistry, selfishness, irresponsibility, fantasy lives, sexual sins. They remark:

We are not merely naive about sin; we are blind to it. And as churches we have become so because we are worldly. And in our blindness we do not see sin around or within our ranks as it really is. We are too naive about human sinfulness, both inside and outside the church. We tend not to see sin that takes place under our noses, and when we see it, we react with shock and dismay. We do not expect to find sin because we do not know our own hearts.[3]

Gordon MacDonald also makes several interesting comments about our efforts to rank sin as serious and nonserious:

It is a human tendency, however, to want to spotlight certain misbehaviors that seem worse than others. We do this because they are particularly repugnant to us in our generation or because we perceive that they have greater consequences than others. And when people are exposed or confess guilt in these categories, we refer to them as fallen. But the truth is that we are all fallen people, whether or not we have been guilty of a major misbehavior.[4]

While I would choose the word sin for his use of the word misbehavior, I believe MacDonald's point is valid. When we talk about the need for spiritual restoration and revival it is imperative that we see sin from God's perspective, not just from our own. If we view sin only from our perspective, we will rationalize and justify our shortcomings as not terribly significant (particularly when we compare our sin to others' sin) and as permissible for a variety of reasons. But if we see sin, any kind of sin, as causing a serious breach in our fellowship with the Father, we will go to any length to seek our restoration with Him.

God wants relationship with us. He will do whatever is necessary to restore that relationship. The fact that we don't pursue intense relationship with Him is a serious indictment of our spiritual condition.

We must begin every day with this searching inquiry of ourselves, asking God's Holy Spirit to identify sin in our lives. And this daily search is ultimately a matter of the heart. Then we have to deal with that sin, first vertically along the lines set forth in 1 John 1:9, and then horizontally, if that sin has affected others.

In the process of identifying sin, all of us will realize our tremendous need for God's forgiveness, mercy, and grace, as well as the significance of verses such as Lamentations 3:22-23: "Because of the Lord's great love we are not consumed, for His compassions never fail. They are new every morning; great is Your faithfulness." Thus we will have cause to celebrate His great love, His compassion, His forgiveness, and His faithfulness.

Guidelines to Spiritual Restoration

As a leader Ezra possessed the critical qualities needed for spiritual restoration or revival. What are these qualities?

Ezra Was Faithful, Obedient, and Devoted to God

Somehow we have a tendency to overlook these qualities. After all, we all are committed people to some extent. And we work hard at our devotion to God while trying to be obedient. Many times all of that purposeful devotion stays private and seldom finds corporate expression. While we have discussed at length the appropriateness of and the leader's need for spiritual inner qualities, in the context of an organization the ultimate expression of those inner qualities must become visible to the people.

If you are a leader in a Christian organization, whether pastor, president, or executive director, you must become more concerned about your godly character (as God sees and knows you) than about your reputation with your people. Notes Henri Nouwen: "The question is not: how many people take you seriously? How much are you going to accomplish? Can you show some results? But: are you in love with Jesus?"[5]

I am learning anew that the quality of my work will be heavily determined by the godly character of my inner commitments. I must pursue my love for God as my paramount calling. The comments of Ezekiel 22:30 (TEV) reflect perhaps a pending contemporary tragedy: "I looked for someone who could build a wall, who could stand in the places where the walls have crumbled and defend the land when My anger is about to destroy it, but I could find no one."

Ezra Acknowledged Their Sin and Dealt with It

For spiritual renewal or revival to occur, sin has to be acknowledged and dealt with. Again, here is where we have to be brutally honest with God, with ourselves, and with each other. We see in Ezra 9:1-2 a concern for the sin of leaders.

Certain leaders came forward and expressed concern to

Ezra that the previous commands forbidding intermarriage with the neighboring pagan countries had been violated, and that the leaders and officials had led the way in this unfaithfulness. Once the issue of the leaders' sin was "on the table," how did Ezra deal with it? In Ezra's response we see a third step in the process of spiritual restoration.

Ezra Was Visibly Mournful for Their Sin

Ezra involved himself in a response, not of outrage, but of public humility and sorrow before the Lord. He abased himself before the Lord: "I sat there appalled until the evening sacrifice" (9:4). His response also involved fasting (10:6).

There are several reasons why I believe Ezra's action was appropriate for a leader. I want to suggest only one. As a leader, if I first humble myself before God before I act, quietly reflecting on my own life and character and the nature of a subsequent response, this has a way of guarding my intent and my motive. It assures me of both cleanness of heart (private) and cleanness of action (public). As someone has suggested, all of us must be alert to the reality that many of our assumptions about others are aroused by our knowledge of ourselves.

Ezra Prayed before the Lord

Next Ezra prayed before the Lord. "When the time came for the evening sacrifice, I got up from where I had been grieving, and still wearing my torn clothes, I knelt in prayer and stretched out my hands to the Lord my God" (9:5, TEV).

In his prayer, he included himself as he expressed concern for "*our* sins" (v. 6, emphasis mine). He not only identified with the people, but he allowed for the fact that he too in some way might have sinned before the Lord. Notice too that his prayer was public.

Ezra's Humility and Prayers Motivated the People to Action

This is not a situation where Ezra had to badger the people. Rather, while Ezra was praying, the people who had gathered "wept bitterly" (10:1). They told Ezra that they had been unfaithful to the Lord and would support him in any corrective action he wanted to take: "Now we must make a solemn promise to our God that we will send these women and their children away. We will do what you and the others who honor God's commands advise us to do. We will do what God's Law demands. It is your responsibility to act. We are behind you, so go ahead and get it done" (vv. 3-4, TEV).

Ezra's actions and the people's response suggest the need for public prayer to seek forgiveness from sin which prevents fellowship with the Lord. His actions also suggest that prayer ought to be offered in a spirit of humility and self-abasement. Ezra's prayer was not a prayer for the pagan world but rather for the fallen people of God.

Ezra Dealt Thoroughly and Uncompromisingly with Their Sin

The action taken to deal with sin followed a process, involved careful investigation, and was specific. We see from the text that the specific sin forbidden was intermarriage (9:10-12). The process followed was to be based on the Law (10:3) and was to include careful investigation (v. 16).

Interestingly, the Scripture has identified processes for dealing with both individual and corporate sin (Matt. 18 and 1 Cor. 5 respectively), yet not many churches follow these practices. Why? Because many churches feel uncomfortable dealing with sin in a "my rights"-oriented society. Dealing with both individual and corporate sin is a critical element of spiritual restoration.

Brokenness and "Spiritual" Restoration

Thus far, we have talked about tears, certain kinds of spiritual activity, and fasting, steps which if genuinely pursued out of a proper motivation to deal with sin, could lead to spiritual restoration.

We ought not fool ourselves, however, into believing that tears alone or religious activities such as fasting will of themselves automatically lead to spiritual restoration. There are many examples in the Scriptures of these kinds of activities failing to impress God: Isaiah 58:3, 6; Hosea 6:6; Joel 2:13; Amos 5:21-23; and Malachi 2:13-16.

Genuine brokenness which produces repentance, however, can be an important part of spiritual restoration and revival. Furthermore, some argue that we ought to see brokenness as a gift. James Houston, in a presentation at Regent College, observed that "we can volunteer for brokenness, and sometimes God gives us the gift of brokenness. And in that brokenness we begin anew." Sometimes we look at our spiritual walk as something we can manipulate for results, including being broken, anytime we choose to do so. We tell ourselves that we'll take care of that "sin" tomorrow. So we pack off God into our little box until we're ready to do Him the favor of doing what He wants us to do. We assume that we can push this button, pull that lever, play this song, and pray that prayer, and presto—people become broken.

Certainly, we can open or close ourselves to God's work in our lives through belief or unbelief. To be sure, we can confess our sin. But it is God who grants forgiveness. It is His work, not ours alone. We need to accept what He does for us and in us—whether through tears and brokenness or something else—as His gift to us. We can't "buy" brokenness and we can't bring spiritual restoration only with tears. We can, and should, pray for spiritual restoration, but only the Spirit of God can make it happen.

Summary

We have seen in this chapter that the Lord has an intense desire for His people to be "hot" in their walk with Him. His strong dislike for spiritual indifference is evident in Revelation 3:15 (TEV): "I know what you have done; I know that you are neither cold nor hot. How I wish you were either one or the other!" We have also looked at the need for personal renewal in leadership. And while there are many considerations, I remain persuaded that there is a strong connection between my experiencing personal spiritual renewal and my willingness to honor the concept of the Sabbath we have discussed in this book.

It is not a coincidence, to my mind at least, that Joseph was given a position of even more effective service after he was pulled out of the mainstream, so to speak, and learned to know God through the circumstances of imprisonment. And we can only imagine that the desert experience of Moses, which immediately followed his experience with the leadership elite of Egypt, did much to prepare him for future leadership.

In my discussions with many Christian leaders, I have learned that some of the biggest lessons, the ones which literally transformed them both spiritually and then in their leadership, occurred because they were taken off of the "fast track" and put into a place where "listening to God" could become reality, not just a pious wish. We've seen lives, marriages, and leadership styles transformed as a result.

Marylou and I were, ourselves, the beneficiaries of this kind of experience during a time when I was a visiting scholar in residence at Regent College (Vancouver, British Columbia), while on sabbatical. We sought physical and spiritual renewal, and were, in addition, given brokenness and spiritual restoration. Thankfully, God gave us these gifts in the midst of incredible natural beauty, in the midst of tears, and in the midst of listening to God in ways which were new to us. We had to practice what I have talked about in this chapter. But it was an experience we would not have traded for any price.

There is then, a clear relationship between my "listening" to and my "knowing" God. My desire, as a leader in process, and as a follower of Christ, is to know Him better. And this happens best in the soul of leadership.

Conclusion

LEADING AND FOLLOWING, as we used the terms, are incredibly important to the future prospects of any organization. As this book has attempted to show, however, leading and following, required of all who participate in an organization, are functions not easily carried out.

We began this book by reviewing and discussing the ideas of leadership and its related concepts, including those of power and authority. As we noted, leaders can't lead without having authority and leaders can't possess authority without having power. As Stott has noted:

A certain authority attaches to all leaders, and leadership would be impossible without it. . . . Leaders have power, but power is safe only in the hands of those who humble themselves to serve.[1]

The issue, then, in leading, is not "power versus authority" but rather how power and authority have been acquired, how they are being handled within the organization, and, further, the ends to which they are applied.

For the Christian leader who leads and follows—and one must do both to be effective—both the process of leading and the "ends" of leading are extremely important. Leaders must be neither masters nor bosses. Stott has observed:

Among the followers of Jesus, therefore, leadership is not a synonym for lordship. Our calling is to be servants not bosses, slaves not masters. . . . The emphasis of Jesus was not on the authority of the ruler-leader but on the humility of a servant-leader.[2]

And as John White has noted:

The true leader serves. Serves people. Serves their best interest, and in so doing will not always be popular, may not always impress. But because true leaders are motivated by loving concern rather than a desire for personal glory, they are willing to pay the price.[3]

Many times, and in some organizations, an emphasis on servant leadership produces no action, or stagnation, in the leader-follower (or constituent) relationship. As a result, the organization ceases to exist — or if it continues to exist, serves no useful purpose. Alternatively, what we have tried to say in this book (and I must emphasize this point) is that an effective leader, even though a servant of the people, nevertheless helps keep the people moving on a given course or direction. The shepherd, for example, doesn't serve the sheep well if the flock is permitted to move randomly in all directions at will.

Further, we have also tried to emphasize that effective organizational leadership, within the context of an organization's purpose or mission, must have a healthy preoccupation with the people of the organization. As Gardner has noted, "We believe, with Immanuel Kant, that individuals should be treated as ends in themselves, not as means to the leader's ends."[4] Indeed, people in the organization are critically important to the organization's goals.

Leadership involves knowing the past, working in the present, and planning for the future. And the leader must retain a primary concern and focus for the people being led. As I have attempted to show, this goal is best carried out when centered on biblical principles.

In Rosabeth Moss Kanter's book, *The Change Masters*, she provides yet another reason for a leadership focus on the people within an organization. Organizations need new ideas to survive, and "the source of new ideas is people."[5] As she notes, there are too many organization problems and too few ideas resident within the organization to address them unless leadership "frees up" human potential toward that end.

She then provides this startling reminder:

> The true "tragedy" for most declining American companies struggling to keep afloat . . . is not how far from the potential for transformation but how close they might come and not know it.[6]

Thus, we have come full circle. Christian leaders have long known of their biblical responsibility to be committed to the people they lead. What we need to continually remind ourselves is that failure to adhere to these biblical priorities also deprives the organization of its opportunity to achieve its potential.

Organizations need leaders — a certain kind of leader — after all. We don't need the kind of leaders John White describes: "petrified little people who dream of power."[7] Rather, we need godly men and women who are wholeheartedly committed to serving both God and the people within the organizations they lead. These leaders may not be in great abundance, but they have always been there and are appearing in a growing number or organizations.

These kinds of leaders "are meant to be facilitators not despots . . . (and) they must use their authority in the way Jesus did."[8]

As White has noted:

> There has always been a true elite of God's leaders. They are the meek who inherit the earth (Matthew 5:5). They weep and pray in secret, and defy earth and hell in public. They tremble when faced with danger, but die in their tracks sooner than turn back. They are

like a shepherd defending his sheep or a mother protecting her young. They sacrifice without grumbling, give without calculating, suffer without groaning. To those in their charge they say, "We live well if you do well." Their price is above riches. They are the salt of the earth.[9]

But this is not the end of the matter. Christian leaders must also concentrate on the inner dimension of leadership, what I have called in this book, the soul of leadership. It is in this area where the hidden battles of leadership are fought and where effectiveness in leadership is ultimately determined.

I remain persuaded that the inner side of leadership is critically important for those who name the name of Christ, whether leading in the context of a Christian organization or in a secular one. If "being" precedes "doing" and I am convinced that is the case, then wherever God calls me to serve, I need to display in both my personal and my organizational actions what He calls me to be as a Christian. Paul's instructions in Galatians 6:10 help me understand this better: "Therefore, as we have opportunity, let us do good to all people, especially to those who belong to the family of believers."

The quality of my leadership will be largely determined by the attention I pay to this inner side of leadership. In this domain I must honestly and regularly grapple with such questions as: How is my walk with the Lord? How is my relationship with my covenant partner in marriage? What about my children? What is the quality of my devotional life? My prayer life?

Interestingly, many if not all of these areas are seldom seen by the public. People may see my family in church; they may hear me or my wife speak at a meeting; they may see our children in isolated roles. Yet it is the family who knows best what the "leader" is really like. Of course God knows as well. To be sure, the inner qualities of character are ultimately seen in some form by a watching world as it observes the leader as a leader. But if the right kinds of qualities are missing, the wrong kinds of things will happen in leadership. So, before I lead, I must be a follower of Christ. I must know Him and His resurrection power and then let Him, through the Holy Spirit, empower me and transform the inner side of my leadership. Where He leads, I must follow.

That Paul was concerned about this inner dimension is amply illustrated in many of his New Testament writings. One of my favorites is Ephesians 3:16-21 (TEV):

I ask God from the wealth of His glory to give you power through His Spirit to be strong in your inner selves, and I pray that Christ will make His home in your hearts through faith. I pray that you may have your roots and foundation in love, so that you, together with all God's people may have the power to understand how broad and long, how high and deep, is Christ's love. Yes, may you come to know His love— although it can never be fully known—and so be completely filled with the very nature of God. To Him who by means of His power working in us is able to do so much more than we can ever ask for, or even think of: to God be the glory in the church and in Christ Jesus for all time, forever and ever! Amen.

Among other things, Paul was concerned about the Holy Spirit's empowerment of his readers' inner beings; he was concerned that they would have understanding in order to grasp the incredible dimensions of Christ's love. These truths in themselves, put into practice, would be enough to transform an organization and its leadership. But then Paul provides the incredible thought that Christ, through His power that is at work in us, within our inner being, is able to do "so much more than we can ever ask for or even think of." What encouragement for those who desire faithfulness in their service for Christ. Presumably this includes leaders.

While reading books on leadership can help in leading, while taking coursework can add a depth of understanding about leadership, we must continually be taught by and learn from the One who tells us to follow—Jesus, the Master Leader. As leaders, we need to hear afresh His call to follow Him: "Come to Me, all you who are weary and burdened, and I will give you rest. Take My yoke upon you and learn from Me, for I am gentle and humble in heart, and you will find rest for your souls. For My yoke is easy and My burden is light" (Matt. 11:28-30). These are not the words of a commander or boss. These are the gracious words of One who gave His life for us, of One who learned obedience, of One who did the bidding of His Father and became a servant. This is leading at its very best.

Henri Nouwen, in his books *The Wounded Healer* and *In the Name of Jesus*,[10] perceptively comments on the importance of this dimension of leadership. He notes, for instance, that our preoccupation with busyness tends to hide our real need, to know Jesus better. Sometimes we pretend that our busyness is job-related. But many times honesty compels us to admit that busyness may only be a mask to cover up our need to address our innermost thoughts. Nouwen recounts the story of a colleague who with despair was recounting "his hectic daily schedule—religious services, classroom teaching, luncheon and dinner engagements, and organizational meetings." According to Nouwen, this colleague observed the following about his own busyness: "I guess I am busy in order to avoid a painful self-confrontation."[11] Might it be that our busyness in leadership is sometimes only a disguised attempt to avoid knowing who we really are as leaders?

Nouwen further observes that our capacity to focus on our inner side actually gives us freedom to lead. (The reverse, unfortunately, is probably also true.) Knowing who we are on the inside helps us empower others. Says Nouwen: "When we have found the anchor places for our lives in our own center, we can be free to let others enter the space created for them."[12] He even goes so far as to make the intriguing observation that one of the roles for future leaders is to be "articulators of inner events." Yet he notes that many leaders are unprepared for this important leadership role: "It is a painful fact indeed to realize how poorly prepared most Christian leaders prove to be when they are invited to be spiritual leaders in the true sense. Most of them are used to thinking in terms of large-scale organization, getting people together in churches, schools and hospitals, and running the show as a circus director. They have become unfamiliar with, and even somewhat afraid of, the deep and significant movements of the Spirit."[13]

We learn yet a further principle of inner leading from Nouwen, and it is this: Centering on the inner dimensions of leadership and being preoccupied with Christ permits us to be persons of hope. Because of our relationship with Christ, we not only have an inner hope, but we also have hope in the future and in other people.

A Christian leader is not a leader because he announces a new idea and tries to convince others of its worth; a person is a leader because he faces the world with eyes full of expectation, with the expertise to take away the veil that covers . . . hidden potential.[14]

A Christian leader is a man of hope whose strength in the final analysis is based neither on self-confidence derived from his personality, nor on specific expectations for the future, but on a promise given to him. . . . Leadership . . . is not called Christian because it is permeated with optimism against all the odds of life, but because it is grounded in the historic Christ-event.[15]

Finally, Nouwen observes that the most important element and need for leaders and leadership is for us to be people of God, who are deeply in love with the Saviour: "If there is any focus that the Christian leader of the future will need, it is the discipline of dwelling in the presence of the One who keeps asking us, 'Do you love Me?' 'Do you love Me?' 'Do you love Me?' '[16] Nouwen writes:

> It is not enough for the priests and ministers (executives, teachers, etc.) of the future to be moral people, well-trained, eager to help their fellow humans, and able to respond creatively to the burning issues of their time. All of that is very valuable and important, but it is not the heart of Christian leadership. The central question is, are the leaders of the future truly men and women of God, people with an ardent desire to dwell in God's presence, to listen to God's voice, to look at God's beauty, to touch God's incarnate Word and to taste fully God's infinite goodness!"[17]

To paraphase J.I. Packer, once we as leaders understand that our primary business in leading is to follow Him, that we are here "to know God," then our other problems and agenda in leadership "fall into place of their own accord."[18] We follow Him "so that every word spoken, every advice given, and every strategy developed can come from a heart that knows God intimately."[19]

To be sure, leaders lead and followers follow. There are also leaders who follow and followers who lead. In the same way there are power-hungry leaders who think leading is "bossing" and impressing people with "my" power, rather than helping them through empowerment. The call of this book is for leaders who will lead from inside their souls. We know that indeed this is a paradox: "The paradox of Christian leadership is that the way out is the way in."[20]

In my travels throughout North America and in other parts of the world, I have seen many wonderful examples of people who have discovered the soul of leadership. They, like Moses, represent men and women, young and old, and can be found in denominations of all types. And there are many situations where I have witnessed leadership and followership of the type we have discussed in this book. I want to share one such situation as I close.

As I entered a maximum security prison just outside of Buenos Aires, Argentina, we were asked to leave all of our personal belongings with security. Then we were ushered through several sets of doors to meet an associate of the prison warden. We learned that because of the influence of Christians, prison management had been able to reduce the guards in this 3,000 prisoner operation from 300 to 30. And that the cell blocks had become transformed.

Then we met the Christian leaders. They told us of the long-term prayer which had taken place for this prison before the government officials, in desperation, and because of the failure of government programs, had asked for a Christian presence to provide an alternative. The effort resulted in about one-third of the rotating prison population professing Christ.

And did we ever see leadership and organization! There were daily performance reports on all: who had committed their lives to Christ; who were leading and attending Bible studies; and who were studying which Bible lessons and who were praying for whom. We learned that while prisoners slept, Christians maintained a round-the-clock vigil, two reading the Scriptures, two in prayer, and two stopping by each sleeping prisoner and praying. Fasting was a regular practice. And we learned that as these Christians completed their prison sentences, they were leaving prison and starting new churches all over Argentina.

In brief, all of the tasks of leadership were being practiced. Spiritual gifts were being used; planning was being done; the Holy Spirit was visibly present; and qualities of character were being modeled and taught. But first and foremost, these leaders realized, that apart from understanding the importance of the soul in leadership, they would not move forward. I've seen this realization in leaders from all around the world, in churches, organizations, and in homes.

As I write these words, I'm visiting with future leaders in Washington, D.C. These young people, all in their twenties, are actively working in careers or involved in graduate school. And they're learning what it means to be effective leaders. As I stood overlooking the beautiful Chesapeake Bay, one young man, Tucker, said it this way: "I'm involved in the most important quest of my life; I'm learning to listen to and then respond to the voice of God." And another one, David, put it this way: "The most fundamental issue in life is not driven by the search for vocation. Rather, it is in knowing God and finding total fulfillment in Him. And that makes all other matters secondary."

That's ultimately what rediscovering the soul of leadership is all about:

"But seek first His kingdom and His righteousness, and all these things will be given to you as well" (Matt. 6:33).

Notes

Introduction
1. William Hybels, *Who You Are When No One's Looking* (Downers Grove, Ill.: Intervarsity, 1987).
2. Stephen R. Covey, *First Things First* (New York: Simon and Schuster, 1994).
3. Frances Hesselbein, quoted in *Chief Executive*, January/February, 1995, 38.
4. "Keeping Faith in His Time," *US News and World Report*, October 9, 1995, 72.

Chapter One
1. John Kotter, *The Leadership Factor* (New York: The Free Press, 1988), 124.
2. Robert Kelley, *The Wall Street Journal*, April 8, 1988.
3. John W. Gardner, *The Moral Aspect of Leadership* (Washington, D.C.: Independent Sector, 1987), 9.
4. Robert Kelley, "In Praise of Followers," *Harvard Business Review* (November–December 1988), 146.
5. Rosabeth Moss Kanter, *The Change Masters* (New York: Simon and Schuster, 1983), 363–64.

Chapter Two
1. John W. Gardner, *The Tasks of Leadership* (Washington, D.C.: Independent Sector, 1986), 5.
2. Ibid., 7.
3. Ibid.
4. Ibid., 9.
5. Ibid.
6. Ibid., 10.
7. Ibid., 13.
8. Ibid.
9. Ibid., 15.
10. Ibid., 18.
11. Ibid., 19.
12. Ibid.
13. Ibid.

14. Ibid., 20.
15. Ibid., 22.
16. John W. Gardner, *Self-Renewal* (New York: Harper and Row, 1963, 1964), 58.
17. John W. Gardner, *The Nature of Leadership* (Washington, D.C.: Independent Sector, 1986), 15.
18. Ibid., 16.

Chapter Three

1. Fremont E. Kast and James E. Rosenzweig, *Organization and Management* (New York: McGraw-Hill, 1974), 333.
2. Ibid., 334.
3. John W. Gardner, *Leadership and Power* (Washington, D.C.: Independent Sector, 1986), 3.
4. Ibid., 19.
5. Ibid., 21.
6. Ibid., 19.
7. Cheryl Forbes, *The Religion of Power* (Grand Rapids: Zondervan Publishing House, 1983), 87.
8. Ibid., 151.
9. Ibid., 87.
10. Charles Colson, *Who Speaks for God?* (Westchester, Ill.: Crossway Books, 1985), 40.
11. Ibid., 41.
12. Richard T. Pascale and Anthony Athos, *The Art of Japanese Management* (New York: Warner Books, 1981), 246.
13. John W. Gardner, *The Heart of the Matter* (Washington, D.C.: Independent Sector, 1986), 11.
14. Ibid., 18.
15. Louis B. Barnes, "Managing the Paradox of Organizational Trust," *Harvard Business Review* (March–April, 1981), 108.
16. Pascale and Athos, 126.
17. Ibid., 129.
18. Barnes, 110.
19. Ibid., 112.
20. Gardner, 19.
21. Ibid.

Chapter Four

1. J. Oswald Sanders, "Lessons I've Learned," *Discipleship Journal,* Issue Fifteen, 14.
2. Denise Webb, "The Power of Positive Eating," *Your Body Health,* Winter, 1993, 40–42.
3. Gordon MacDonald, *Ordering Your Private World* (Nashville: Oliver Nelson, 1984, 1985), 103.

4. J. Oswald Sanders, *Spiritual Leadership* (Chicago: Moody Press, 1967, 1980), 148.
5. Ibid., 151–52.
6. Stephen R. Covey, *First Things First* (New York: Simon and Schuster, 1994), 49.

Chapter Five
1. Ted W. Engstrom and Edward R. Dayton, *The Christian Executive* (Waco: Word Books, 1979), 93.
2. Ibid., 95.
3. Ibid., 98.
4. Ibid.
5. Ibid., 96.

Chapter Six
1. John Stott, *Involvement: Social and Sexual Relationships in the Modern World*, Vol. II (Old Tappan, N.J.: Fleming H. Revell Company, 1984, 1985), 216. See also Jeffrey W. Comment, "Conducting Business with the Opposite Sex," *Mission in the Market Place* (Kansas City: MITM Publishing, 1995), 67–75.
2. Cheryl Forbes, *The Religion of Power* (Grand Rapids: Zondervan Publishing House, 1983), 73.
3. Stott, 215.
4. Forbes, 79.
5. Richard T. Pascale and Anthony Athos, *The Art of Japanese Management* (New York: Warner Books, 1981), 218.
6. Forbes, 75.
7. Ibid.
8. Marylou Habecker, "Sometimes You Need to Get Away From It All," *The United Brethren*, January 1991, 13–15.

Chapter Seven
1. Lawrence M. Miller, *American Spirit: Visions of a New Corporate Culture* (New York: William Morrow and Company, Inc., 1984), 15.
2. John Stott, *Involvement: Social and Sexual Relationships in the Modern World*, Vol. II (Old Tappan, N.J.: Fleming H. Revell Company, 1984, 1985), 249.

Chapter Eight
1. John Gardner, *Self-Renewal* (San Francisco: Harper & Row, 1964), 9–11.
2. John Kotter, *The Leadership Factor* (New York: The Free Press, 1988), 28.

3. Ibid., 29–30.
4. Marylou Habecker, "Sometimes You Need to Get Away from It All," *The United Brethren*, January, 1991, 13–15.
5. Manfred F.R. Kets de Vries, *Prisoners of Leadership* (New York: John Wiley & Sons, 1989), iv.
6. Wesley L. Duewel, *Ablaze for God* (Grand Rapids: Francis Asbury Press, 1989), 231.

Chapter Nine
1. Gary Inrig, *A Call to Excellence* (Wheaton, Ill.: Victor Books, 1985), 11.
2. Thomas J. Peters and Robert H. Waterman, Jr., *In Search of Excellence* (New York, Warner Books, 1982).
3. Ibid., 26.
4. John W. Gardner, *Excellence* (New York: Harper & Brothers, 1961).
5. John W. Gardner, *Self-Renewal* (New York: Harper & Row, 1963, 1964).
6. Gardner, *Excellence*, 127–28.
7. Ibid., 86.
8. Ibid., 131, 133.
9. Inrig, 36.
10. Anthony Campolo, *The Success Fantasy* (Wheaton, Ill.: Victor Books, 1980).
11. Robert T. Sandin, *The Search for Excellence* (Macon, Ga.: Mercer University Press, 1982).
12. Ibid., 4.
13. Inrig.
14. Jon Johnston, *Christian Excellence* (Grand Rapids: Baker Book House, 1985).
15. Inrig, 25.
16. Ibid., 27.
17. Ibid., 28.
18. Ibid., 31.
19. Ibid., 32.
20. Johnston, 30.
21. Ibid., 33.
22. Gardner, Self-Renewal, 58.

Chapter Ten
1. Eugene B. Habecker, *The Other Side of Leadership* (Wheaton, Ill.: Victor Books, 1987), 60–72.
2. *The Chronicle of Higher Education*, May 28, 1986, 20.
3. See Frank Goble, *Excellence in Leadership* (Caroline House Publishers, 1972), 6 and Stanley O. Ikenberry, "1990: A President's Perspective," *Planning*, vol. 14, no. 3 (1986), 2.

4. Donal E. Walker, "Administrators v. Faculty," *Change,* March/April, 1986, 9.

5. Robert K. Mossie, Jr., "Prophets to Profits," *Best of Business Quarterly,* vol. 8, no. 1, Spring, 1986, 15.

6. John W. Gardner, *The Nature of Leadership* (Washington, D.C.: Independent Sector, 1986), 25–26.

7. Gardner, 6.

8. Ibid., 7.

9. Ibid., 8.

10. Daniel Katz and Robert L. Kahn, *The Social Psychology of Organizations,* 2d. ed. (New York: John Wiley and Sons, 1978), 527.

11. Ibid.

12. Ibid., 528.

13. Ibid., 532.

14. Ibid.

15. Ibid.

16. Ibid., 536.

17. Ibid., 540–547.

18. Ibid., 545.

19. Ibid., 546.

20. Ibid., 569.

21. Ibid.

22. Ibid., 571.

Chapter Eleven

1. John W. Gardner, *The Moral Aspect of Leadership* (Washington, D.C.: Independent Sector, 1987), 9.

2. "Followership," *Christian Leadership Letter,* September, 1986, 1.

3. Elihu Katz and Paul Lazarsfeld, *Personal Influence* (Glencoe, Ill.: The Free Press, 1955).

4. Ibid., 137.

5. John W. Gardner, *The Heart of the Matter* (Washington, D.C.: Independent Sector, 1986), 5.

6. Ibid., 6.

7. Ibid.

8. Ibid.

9. Ibid., 8–9.

10. Ibid., 10.

11. Ibid., 12.

12. John H. Yoder, *He Came Preaching Peace* (Scottsdale, Penn.: Herald Press, 1985), 20, 46, 91, 130.

13. "Followership," 1.

14. Ibid., 2.

15. Ibid.

16. Ibid.

17. Ibid.

18. Ibid., 3.

19. Ibid.
20. Ibid.
21. Gardner, 15.
22. Ibid.
23. Ibid.
24. Ibid.

Chapter Twelve
1. Fred Smith, *Learning to Lead* (Waco, Texas: Word Books, 1986), 104.
2. David Augsburger, *Caring Enough to Confront* (Ventura, Calif.: Regal Books, 1973).

Chapter Thirteen
1. John White, *Excellence in Leadership* (Downers Grove, Ill.: Inter-Varsity Press, 1986), 47–48.
2. Several readers will most likely desire additional information on planning, especially on strategic planning. One of the best books on this subject, and one which has guided the strategic planning efforts of the American Bible Society is C. Davis Fodd, *Team-Based Strategic Planning* (New York: AMACOM, 1994).

Chapter Fifteen
1. Richard T. Pascale and Anthony G. Athos, *The Art of Japanese Management* (New York: Warner Books, 1981), 273.
2. John W. Gardner, *The Heart of the Matter* (Washington, D.C.: Independent Sector, 1986), 23.
3. John W. Gardner, *The Moral Aspect of Leadership* (Washington, D.C.: Independent Sector, 1987), 4.
4. Ibid.
5. Michael Youssef, *The Leadership Style of Jesus* (Wheaton, Ill.: Victor Books, 1986), 163.
6. Ibid.
7. James L. Fisher, *Power of the Presidency* (New York: MacMillan Publishing Company, 1984), 45.
8. Ibid., 46.
9. Pascale and Athos, 217.
10. James Carr, "Familiarity Breeds Contempt," *Pace*, December, 1986, 19.
11. Charette B. Kvernstoen, "The Secrets of Friendship," *Partnership*, January/February, 1987, 19.

Chapter Sixteen
1. Jeremy Rifkin, *Algeny* (New York: The Viking Press, 1983), 72–73.
2. Ibid., 74.

3. Ibid., 79.
4. John White, *The Golden Cow* (Downers Grove, Ill.: InterVarsity Press, 1979), 112–13.
5. Rifkin, 83.
6. Ibid., 82.
7. Ibid.
8. Ibid., 91.
9. John H. Yoder, *He Came Preaching Peace* (Scottsdale, Penn.: Herald Press, 1985), 52.

Chapter Seventeen
1. Frank Tillapaugh, *Unleashing the Church* (Ventura, Calif.: Regal Books, 1982), 124.
2. Ibid., 77.
3. William Willimon and Robert Wilson, *Rekindling the Flame* (Nashville: Abingdon Press, 1987), 104.
4. Ibid.
5. Ibid., 112.
6. Ibid., 98–101.
7. Tillapaugh, 103.
8. Ibid.
9. Robert Bellah, *Habits of the Heart* (San Francisco: Harper & Row Publishers, 1985), 241.

Chapter Eighteen
1. "The true and safe leader is likely to be the one who has no desire to lead but is forced into a position of leadership by the inward pressure of the spirit and the external pressure of the situation." Comments on "The Ideal Leader" by A.W. Tozer as quoted in *Alliance Life*, November 29, 1995, 9.
2. J. Oswald Sanders, *Spiritual Leadership* (Chicago: Moody Press, 1980), 15.

Chapter Nineteen
1. Rebecca M. Pippert, *Hope Has Its Reasons* (San Francisco: Harper & Row, 1989), 5.

Chapter Twenty
1. Frank Tillapaugh, *Unleashing Your Potential* (Ventura, Calif.: Regal Books, 1988), 191.
2. Kenneth Gangel, *Feeding and Leading* (Wheaton, Ill.: Victor Books, 1989), 124.
3. Ibid., 31.

4. David L. McKenna, *Power to Follow, Grace to Lead* (Dallas: Word Books, 1989), 25.

5. J. Robert Clinton, *The Making of a Leader* (Colorado Springs: NavPress, 1988), 91.

6. Ibid., 255.

7. Ibid., 91

8. Wesley L. Duewel, *Ablaze for God* (Grand Rapids: Francis Asbury Press, 1989).

9. Ibid., 194.

10. Ibid., 195.

11. Ibid.

12. Arthur F. Miller and Ralph T. Mattson, *The Truth about You* (Old Tappan, N.J.: Fleming H. Revell, 1977).

13. Ibid., 16.

14. Ibid., 17.

15. Ibid., 41–42.

16. Bruce W. Jones, *Ministerial Leadership in a Managerial World* (Wheaton, Ill.: Tyndale House Publishers, 1988), 55. See in particular chapter 3 entitled "How Do We Use the Gifts?"

17. Ibid., 57.

18. Ibid., 58–62.

19. Ibid., 62–67.

20. McKenna, *Power to Follow, Grace to Lead,* 16.

Chapter Twenty-One

1. Robert Bellah et al., *Habits of the Heart* (San Francisco: Harper & Row Publishers, 1985), 129–30.

2. Ron Blue, *Master Your Money* (Nashville: Thomas Nelson Publishers, 1986), 19.

Chapter Twenty-Three

1. Quoted in "Tyranny of the Urgent" in *Growing Strong in God's Family* (Colorado Springs: NavPress, 1987), 21–22.

2. Quoted in Wesley L. Duewel, *Ablaze for God* (Grand Rapids: Francis Asbury Press, 1989), 211, 213.

3. Ibid., 170.

4. Ibid., 182, 184.

5. Ibid., 211–12.

6. Quoted in *Growing Strong in God's Family,* 30, 32.

7. Bobb Biehl and James W. Hagelganz, *Praying* (Sisters, Ore.: Questar Publishers, Inc., 1989), 12.

8. Ibid., 15.

9. Ibid., 18.1

10. James Houston, *The Transforming Friendship* (Batavia, Ill.: Lion Publishing, 1989), 25.

11. Ibid., 14.

12. Ibid., 19.
13. *The Abingdon Bible Commentary* (Nashville: Abingdon-Cokesbury Press, 1929), 965.
14. Ibid.
15. Ibid.

Chapter Twenty-Four

1. John Gardner, *Self-Renewal* (San Francisco: Harper & Row, 1964), 11.
2. John White and Ken Blue, *Healing the Wounded* (Downers Grove, Ill.: InterVarsity Press, 1985), 165–79. Another writer has taken "sin lists" one step further by noting "moral lapses have happened so frequently, that it is easy to believe some evangelical public-relations-type person must have developed the 'evangelical moral lapse damage control plan. . . .' 1. Cancel your upcoming performances. 2. Admit what everyone knows, deny everything else. 3. Attack those who have 'judged' you. 4. Go to counseling. 5. Become 'accountable' to a group of well-respected people. 6. Lay low for a while. 7. Start your career again. 8. Use the 'pain' and 'humiliation' of your uncovered sin as a basis for your bold new 'refreshingly honest' album (or book). Quoted in "Guest Commentary," *The CCM Update*, Vol. 9, No. 44, Nov. 6, 1995, 2, 7.
3. Ibid., 167, 169, 200.
4. Gordon MacDonald, *Rebuilding Your Broken World* (Nashville: Oliver Nelson, 1988), 52.
5. Henri Nouwen, *In the Name of Jesus* (New York: The Crossroad Publishing Company, 1989), 24.

Conclusion

1. John Stott, *Involvement: Social and Sexual Relationships in the Modern World,* Vol. II (Old Tappan, N.J.: Fleming H. Revell Company, 1984, 1985), 259.
2. Ibid., 258–59.
3. John White, *Excellence in Leadership* (Downers Grove, Ill.: InterVarsity Press, 1986), 88.
4. John W. Gardner, *The Moral Aspect of Leadership* (Washington, D.C.: Independent Sector, 1987), 9.
5. Rosabeth Moss Kanter, *The Change Masters* (New York: Simon & Schuster, 1983), 363.
6. Ibid., 356–57.
7. White, 88–89.
8. Ibid., 41.
9. Ibid., 89. See also, Donald V. Siebert, *The Ethical Executive* (New York: Simon & Schuster, 1984).
10. Henri Nouwen, *The Wounded Healer* (Garden City, N.Y.: Image Books, 1979) and *In The Name of Jesus* (New York: The Crossroad Publishing Company, 1989).
11. Nouwen, *The Wounded Healer*, 90.

12. Ibid., 91.
13. Ibid., 37–38.
14. Ibid., 75.
15. Ibid., 76.
16. Nouwen, *In the Name of Jesus*, 28.
17. Ibid., 29–30.
18. J.I. Packer, *Knowing God* (Downers Grove, Ill.: InterVarsity Press, 1973), 29.
19. Nouwen, *In The Name Of Jesus*, 30.
20. Nouwen, *The Wounded Healer*, 77.